TWO KINDS OF TRUTH

LIU BINYAN

TWO KINDS OF TRUTH

STORIES AND REPORTAGE FROM CHINA

Edited by Perry Link

Indiana University Press

BLOOMINGTON AND INDIANAPOLIS

This book is a publication of

Indiana University Press
601 North Morton Street
Bloomington, IN 47404-3797 USA

http://iupress.indiana.edu

Telephone orders   800-842-6796
Fax orders   812-855-7931
Orders by e-mail   iuporder@indiana.edu

Portions of this book were first published as *People or Monsters? And Other Stories and Reportage from China after Mao* © 1983 Indiana University Press

The paper used in this publication meets the minimum requirements of American National Standard for Information Sciences—Permanence of Paper for Printed Library Materials, ANSI Z39.48-1984.

Manufactured in the United States of America

Library of Congress Cataloging-in-Publication Data

Liu, Binyan, date
  Two kinds of truth : stories and reportage from China / Liu Binyan ; edited by Perry Link.
      p. cm.
  Includes bibliographical references.
  ISBN 0-253-34778-5 (cloth : alk. paper) — ISBN 0-253-21861-6 (pbk. : alk. paper)
  1. Liu, Binyan, 1925-2005—Translations into English. I. Link, E. Perry (Eugene Perry), date II. Title.
  PL2879.P5A27 2006
  895.1'35—dc22

                                        2006003547

1 2 3 4 5   11 10 09 08 07 06

For Zhu Hong,
Lifetime companion, rock of support

Contents

Editor's Note

The present volume is a revised and expanded version of Liu Binyan's *People or Monsters? And Other Stories and Reportage from
China after Mao* (Indiana University Press, 1983). In 1981, when
I began to work on that book, I had never met Liu Binyan. The
year before, my requests in China to meet him had met with stock
answers such as "He is traveling," or "Your request is not too con-
venient." I wrote to him, but my letter seems not to have been delivered. Liu had become for me the high priest of post-Mao "scar
literature," a gray eminence who, although unreachable, best ex-
emplified the exciting literary protest in those years.

I needed to be careful in preparing a book of his writings for
English publication in the United States. Those were days in which
such an event could cause—or at least become the pretext for—a
writer to be branded "bourgeois liberal" and to suffer accordingly.
Hence in my author's note to the published book I wrote, "Liu
Binyan was not consulted about this book and bears no responsibility for its conception or the selection of pieces."

Since then much has changed. I have met Liu Binyan and we
became good friends. He was expelled from the Communist Party
in 1987 (or "re-expelled," since this also happened in 1957). He
left China in 1988, and after he denounced the Beijing massacre
of June 1989, Party leaders never allowed him to go back. He

spent his later years not far from me in New Jersey. I was able to consult him in detail about the present version of the book, and this time there was nothing to be lost in saying so.

I know of no one outside China, among either Chinese or Western "China-watchers," who has followed social and political conditions inside China over the last two decades as assiduously as Liu Binyan did. He was indefatigable: he read every scrap of reporting he could find, interviewed travelers, and even broadcast his home fax number on Radio Free Asia so that listeners in China could send him their perceptions directly. Most important, though, was his ability to interpret the broad flow of information he received. His mind combined a powerful analytic ability with a rich bank of memory and knowledge of life at many levels of Chinese society. He knew how to put the pieces together, and how not to be fooled.

His exile from China was painful to him, but, in broader perspective, what China lost by the separation was greater than what he lost. How much could this magnificent ancient country, in trying to conceive and to build a modern version of itself, have benefited from the knowledge, analytical power, and idealism that Liu Binyan offered? Where could the Chinese people have found someone more devoted to their well-being, and to the building of a just and decent modern society? When the top leaders of the Communist Party in the early 1990s issued their blacklist barring Liu and fifty-two others from returning to China, they were obsessed with protecting their own grip on power. By the same act they were also wasting one of China's finest resources.

This book includes two pieces of reportage and two review essays that did not appear in the earlier edition. It also includes, in lieu of an introduction, an extended interview with Liu Binyan.

The dedication to Zhu Hong, Liu's wife, was the result of consultation among family and friends shortly after Liu died on December 5, 2005. By chance, it was only a few days before Liu's death that editors at Indiana University Press asked me whether there would be a dedication for this book. On my last visit with Liu, as he lay in a hospital bed, I gently raised the question. I believe he understood it, but was too weak to answer. Later I consulted with Liu Xiaoyan, Binyan's daughter, with whom he was particularly close, as well as with some of Liu's friends. Everyone felt the dedication to Zhu Hong was the right choice.

I am grateful to Human Rights in China for a grant in support of publication of this volume, to *The New York Review of Books* for permission to reprint "An Unnatural Disaster" and "A Great Leap Backward?" and to my friends and colleagues who contributed translations.

Perry Link
Princeton, New Jersey
January 2006

TWO KINDS OF TRUTH

An Interview with Liu Binyan
Perry Link, September 2004

Q: How did you get interested in writing?

A: I liked art and fiction when I was young. When I was about eleven or twelve, I thought I wanted to be a fiction writer when I grew up, but I had no materials to work with. In those days, in China, nobody did. To Westerners in the twenty-first century, the daily life of China in the 1930s might be unimaginable in a literal sense. China may be famous for its "four great inventions"—one of which was paper, another printing—but that doesn't mean there were a lot of books around. Quite the contrary.

My home, for example, wasn't too bad by standards of the time: my father was a Chinese-Russian interpreter for the Central Manchurian Railway, and we had what you might call a "middle class" home in Harbin in the 1930s. But what books did we have? We owned a collection of Sun Yat-sen's essays and the *Liaozhai zhiyi* stories,[1] but that was about it. The only other printed things I remember seeing around the house as a boy were an almanac and a poster of the kitchen god. That was it. In that context, to aspire to be a writer was a huge leap of imagination. I also really liked music, and at one point thought I would like to be a Peking Opera singer—but again didn't have much chance actually to hear music.

I was lucky in the parents I had. They gave me a lot of freedom. They let me read whatever I could find, and the more I read the more curious I became. I was curious about everything.

Q: And the attachment to reading and writing has been with you ever since?

A: Yes, but as I read I got more and more interested in political questions—like Japan's attacks on China, and Hitler's invasion of Czechoslovakia. Intense political interests began to overshadow my earlier interests in literature—although the passion for reading was the same. I started worrying about the World War, and then about the world in general. I got interested in the Soviet Union and communism. I joined a reading group—what the communists called a "peripheral organization"—and started reading Marxism-Leninism. We read literary theory, too, and read some Russian writers. Turgenev was a major author for our group—bigger than Dostoevsky. But my interests in the looming world crisis determined my choices in life.

Q: What did you do?

A: I joined the Communist Party underground. In 1943 I went to Tianjin, hoping to go from there to Yan'an. But the Party told me there was plenty of work to do right there in Tianjin and that I should stay there, so I did.

Q: "Liberation" in 1949 must have felt good to you.

A: For a while everybody felt good. Those were heady times. People were volunteering, donating things, supporting the new government, and looking to the future with optimism. And yet, looking back, I can see that those were exactly the years when my dissent was born. That may seem odd—since the early 1950s were easy years, and safe years compared to what I had just been through and would go through later. But to me there was something worrisome about the public mood. The unity of thought was disturbing. The people at the top announced what to think, word was passed from top to bottom, and everybody agreed. People weren't forced; most agreed willingly. But I was somehow bothered that there weren't any different opinions. My job was reporter and editor for *China Youth News,* the main newspaper for young people, but I found the work fairly unappealing. There was a lot of recording of the words of the leaders and mechanical passing of them down to the readers.

I was still interested in the Soviet Union, and thought the Soviets were doing better than China in allowing a variety of views. Their newspaper *Pravda* [*Truth*] tolerated at least a small amount of critical opinion. They also had a magazine called *The Crocodile* that specialized in satiric cartoons, and another satire magazine called *Hot Peppers.* I admired the Russian writer Valentin Ovechkin, whose literary reportage exposed problems in society. So why, I thought, did China have to be so unified, so straight—so boring? The Chinese Communists had done even better than Stalin at homogenizing everyone's views. Why, I wondered, was this? How could it come about?

Q: What would be your own answer to that question?

A: I'm afraid it has something to do with the nature of the Chinese people. They generally submit to authority, seek an appearance of public unity, and are embarrassed by breaks in decorum. In 1957, when word came from the government that "rightists" should be criticized, most people didn't know—didn't even ask —what a "rightist" was supposed to be. They just joined everybody else in the "correct" criticism of rightists. Ironically, if they *had* looked into the question of what a rightist was, they would have found that we rightists had been voicing many of their own complaints, and that actually they agreed with us. But they didn't ask.

I can also answer your question using myself as an example. When I heard in 1957 that I had been named a rightist, I felt inside that something was wrong. There must be a mistake, I thought. But on the surface I accommodated the pressures and went with the flow. A person does this not just because of threats from the authorities. There is also the sense of a great ocean of public opinion. All of those workers, peasants, and soldiers—and their organized movements—surround a person. To surrender to the multitude offers a person a sense of security. To oppose it one has to stand all alone—or at least it feels that way. The pressures can be overwhelming.

Q: But some people—like you—do resist. How do you explain that?

A: The reasons no doubt differ from person to person. In my own case, I think, several factors were at work. Harbin, where I grew up, had more of a free-speaking atmosphere than other places. The people of China's Northeast, as you may know, are mostly migrants from Shandong and often think of themselves as refugees, of a sort, from the traditional rigidities of the Chinese heartland. Harbin in my youth also had some Russian—that is, European—influence that contributed to the freer atmosphere. In addition my own parents, as I have said, gave me unusual freedom. I read whatever I could lay my hands on, and they let me. Another important seed of my rebelliousness was the shock of having to drop out of school. When the Japanese invaded my father lost his job. My parents couldn't afford tuition for me, and I had to leave after the ninth grade. I deeply resented this. It is a major reason why I was drawn to the Communist Party underground. I felt the revolution was not only going to help China as a whole but would liberate me personally. I joined the revolution as a rebel, not as a follower.

Q: So all of this helps to explain why you dared to write "On the Bridge Construction Site"[2] in 1956?

A: I think so. That piece was based on a true story I encountered in Lanzhou, Gansu Province, but it illustrated an important nationwide problem. It showed why a clear-thinking practical manager was better than a narrow, obedient bureaucrat. I had been inspired, too, by events in the Soviet Union, where literary policy had relaxed since Stalin died in 1953. I sent "Bridge Site" to Qin Zhaoyang, the editor of *People's Literature*. He published it and went out of his way to praise it. The story was the first example since Mao's 1942 "Talks at Yan'an"[3] of "criticism" being aimed at friends. (Mao had said that criticism was only for the enemy.)[4] Overnight I found myself famous. I was surprised. Then, pretty soon, we heard about Khrushchev's "secret speech" denouncing Stalin and I was even more encouraged. My next piece, "The Internal News at This Newspaper," was fiction, not reportage, but it discussed very real and obvious problems of the fetters on expression in the Chinese media. It had a big influence in literary circles. It also had a major impact on journalists, who championed it as a sort of manifesto for freedom of the press. I'm afraid I made a lot of "rightists."

Q: What do you mean by that?

A: I mean that a lot of young people grabbed the story's point and ran with it, and as a result were labeled "rightists" a year later. This wounded many of them for life, and they never regained their willingness to speak out.

Q: And of course you yourself were made a "rightist."

A: Not just a rightist but an "extreme rightist." I was made an example in the media, and then banished to the countryside for four years. My time in the countryside taught me a lot about China, but was very hard on my wife and family. My wife, Zhu Hong, was an editor at *China Children's News;* she had plenty of talent but was not a Party member, so couldn't go to certain meetings or see certain reports, and never got promoted. When I was sent away she had to care for our two children and two of my sister's children as well. She did this on her own salary, staying up nights to mend socks for everybody, and so on. I had free time but couldn't help, and my salary had been cut to a pittance. I felt terribly guilty toward Zhu Hong. I was afraid, too, that my political taint had become a burden to my family. More than half of the 1957 "rightists" got divorces—mostly trying to protect their children from political taint (even though it didn't help, because the taint survived divorce). When people asked Zhu Hong why she didn't "draw a clear line" between herself and me, she had to answer them. But she never even mentioned divorce to me.

In late 1961 all the rightists at *China Youth News,* where I was working, had their "rightist caps removed"—all except me, anyway. Getting one's cap removed didn't mean freedom from taint. You were still a "former rightist," which was something like being a former child molester in the U.S.—people always suspected and despised you. In subsequent campaigns, former rightists were always among the first to be targeted as possible troublemakers.

"Un-capping" was much less a relief than "rehabilitation" [*ping-fan*], which implied that the original charges had been wrong and that a person was due an apology.

When I turned out to be the only rightist at *China Youth News* that didn't even get "un-capped," the psychological pressure that I felt increased severalfold, and I felt even guiltier toward my family. The leaders did let me come back and work at the newspaper in 1962, but only to do technical tasks—nothing remotely political. In 1959 there had been another campaign against "rightist tendencies," and in 1962 almost all of its victims were being "re-screened" and even "rehabilitated." At the same time a number of people high in the Party felt that the 1957 rightists should be treated the same way, and many places began to move in that direction. But Mao stopped this in its tracks. He issued a statement that "there can be no question of re-screening or rehabilitating" 1957 rightists. I think he did this because he knew there had been so many wrong accusations in 1957 that to handle the problems of a comprehensive re-evaluation would just be too much, and the whole Anti-Rightist Movement, which he himself had initiated, might be repudiated.

Q: So your hat stayed on.

A: Yes, until March of 1966, when it suddenly came off.

Q: Really? I never knew that.

A: Yes, for me and some others. We were thrilled. But in real terms it was only a very modest change. The "rightist" labels came off but we still walked around as "uncapped rightists," and that was still pretty bad. For a while, though, it felt like a whole new life had begun.

Q: A spiritual emancipation, at least.

A: It didn't last. Just a few months later, in August, the Cultural Revolution descended. The "rebel faction" at *China Youth News* "seized power," reversed the decisions, and declared me an "unreformed rightist." Then came charges that I was a "traitor" and a "Soviet spy." I belonged to the "cow ghosts and snake spirits" and was confined in "cow sheds" for a few years.

Q: How many?

A: From summer 1966 until spring of 1972. At first I was confined right at the newspaper office. In 1969 I was sent to "cadre school" in Henan, where the inmates did labor and lived in some pretty poor conditions. Yang Jiang has written about this life in "Six Chapters in a Cadre School,"[5] but her treatment is too rosy. In 1969 Zhu Hong was sent to the same cadre school, where we could glimpse each other, but were forbidden to talk. She brought our son, Dahong, with her. Our daughter, Xiaoyan, stayed behind in Beijing, and was alone for a year even though she was only fifteen. She couldn't get a job assignment because she was the daughter of a rightist, a spy, etc., so she ended up volunteering for farm labor. She wrote us long, politically correct letters. She studied English, but after three years the only English sentence she could write was "Long Live Chairman Mao."

Q: What were your own feelings about Chairman Mao through all of this? Did you start to have doubts?

A: In 1957 the "rightist" label shocked me but did not make me doubt Mao. Even though I thought the charge was a mistake, I peered inside myself to see if there was some problem Mao could see that I had missed. When things went wild during the Cultural Revolution, I still generally assumed that Lin Biao or the Gang of Four was causing the trouble—not Mao. The Lin Biao incident[6] in 1971 led many people, especially young people "sent down" to the countryside, to start doubting Mao. If Lin Biao was a traitor, and had also been Mao's "closest comrade in arms," then, they began to ask, how clean could Mao be? But my own serious doubts about Mao came only in 1975.

Q: 1975? Why then?

A: In 1975 Mao decided to let Deng Xiaoping come back for another stint in the central leadership. Deng immediately set to work trying to end the Cultural Revolution and begin to repair the damage. Word also spread through the grapevine that Mao was distancing himself from his wife, Jiang Qing, the leader of the radical Gang of Four. We political outcasts thought China had some hope again. But then, very abruptly, Mao seemed to reverse himself and launched yet another crackdown on Deng Xiaoping.[7] For me that was it. I began to doubt Mao then. People like me started turning our hopes toward what might happen after Mao died. Some who had access to books turned to the *Comprehensive Mirror for Self-Government,* Sima Guang's eleventh-century classic that contains plenty of examples of what happens when dynasties fall.

Q: A few years later, in 1979, you wrote "People or Monsters?" You became pretty bold pretty quickly.

A: People say I was "bold," but it didn't really feel that way to me at the time. The story of Wang Shouxin [the center of corruption in "People or Monsters?"] had already been reported in the newspapers. Wang had already been convicted. I was not breaking the story, but did feel that the published reports hadn't dug deep enough. In spring of 1979 the top leaders were discussing "practice as the test for truth." This slogan was code for de-Maoification; it meant that blind adherence to Maoist theory was no longer necessary and that the truth of actual conditions is what should count. There were some general conditions in Chinese society that the Wang Shouxin story made clear, and I thought we writers should dig deeper into them.

Q: For example?

A: Well, for example, what did it mean that all ten of the guilty parties in the Wang case were Communist Party members? And why, after the case was over, were there still people defending Wang and the way her group had behaved? There was something deeper, more systemic about the corruption, and it had to do with the Party—and these factors had been ignored.

Q: But still—why was it you who saw these things and asked these questions? Didn't anyone else notice?

A: Oh, sure, many people noticed. Local writers in Harbin were much closer to the facts than I was. But I had, in an odd sense, the advantage of being a sort of outsider. My work as a reporter had been suddenly cut off in 1957, so when I returned to look at Harbin in 1979 it was as if from a time capsule. The corruption and cynicism that I saw shocked me. Problems jumped out at me because I still had the standards of the mid-1950s in mind. To local writers in Harbin, all the economic devastation and social decay since the 1950s had become so pervasive that it seemed almost normal, sort of like bad weather. That doesn't mean people liked what they saw. I knew a young writer in Harbin who couldn't write anything because he was too depressed.

Q: And it was exactly the "normality" of the corruption problem that gave "People or Monsters?" such broad national impact, right?

A: Yes. The impact was obvious from the readers' letters that poured in from all across the country. Official reaction indirectly told the same story. I was attacked by Party leaders not only in Heilongjiang, where the "People or Monsters?" story happened, but in many other places—Liaoning, Shandong, Shaanxi, Hubei, Shanghai, and elsewhere—where similar things had been going on.

Q: How did provincial leaders object? What did they say?

A: In Heilongjiang the Party leaders wanted people to believe that after Wang Shouxin was tried and executed the whole problem of corruption was finished and over with—it was a thing of the past, a creation of the Gang of Four, and now that the Gang was gone, corruption was gone, too. They complained that "People or Monsters?" implied that corruption was pandemic and still a problem. On that point they were right, of course. That was exactly what I wanted to say, as well as the reason why readers liked the piece so much.

Q: So "People or Monsters?" put the question of systemic corruption squarely into the public domain, where the Party could not pretend that it wasn't there.

A: Yes. At the Tenth Plenum of the Twelfth Party Congress—in late summer, 1983—there was a lot of talk about "rectifying the Party," and that plenum actually passed a resolution about it. In Party jargon "rectification" meant, in fact, rooting out corruption, but you couldn't use the word "corruption" [*fubai*]. It was taboo. That word was supposed to apply only to the death of the Guomindang regime in the 1940s. It couldn't apply to the Communist Party. For the Communist period you had to refer to "use of power for private purposes," "improper tendencies," or "excessive eating and drinking." You could summon "the glorious tradition of our Party to overcome all obstacles," but you couldn't mention the word "corruption," let alone refer to the structural problems it created.

Q: Structural problems? Like what?

A: There were two major facts in the structure of corruption that no one at the Tenth Plenum dared to mention. One was the role of "backstage supporters." Whenever corruption cases were exposed, everything was blamed entirely on the person who got caught. No matter how serious the offense—even if the person was executed—no one probed deeper into the web of how higher-ups had chosen and protected that person, had exacted fealty in return for protection, and so on. These corruption webs were omnipresent in China, had been around for a long time, and there is no way that higher-ups were not involved. The second problem was revenge and fear of revenge. Everyone knew that if you crossed the wrong people in China they would come after you with a vengeance—and this deterred most people from even complaining about corruption. But the Party reports at the Tenth Plenum wouldn't go near these two problems; the top Party leaders didn't dare to try—and didn't even want—a cleanup of corruption that went that far. The "rectification" effort was not really sincere, in my view.

Q: But better than nothing?

A: No, actually. Somehow it actually made things worse. In 1983 it led to the campaign to "Eradicate Spiritual Pollution," which was an attack on the reformers. There is an odd pattern in Chinese Communist Party history in which efforts to "rectify" the Party always seem to precipitate crackdowns on the rectifiers—the liberals. This happened at Yan'an in 1942, when the Party's first rectification campaign turned into an arrest and denunciation of Wang Shiwei, the literary dissident. It happened on a larger scale in 1956–57, when invitations to help the Party correct itself turned into the Anti-Rightist Campaign. And here, in 1983, the same pattern appeared. I don't know what makes this pattern happen; someone should study the question.

Q: So you're not sure why the top leaders launched the campaign to Eradicate Spiritual Pollution?

A: The deep reasons for it are hard to explain, but the surface reason, anyway, was pretty clear. 1983 was the hundredth anniversary of the death of Karl Marx, and the Party set up a big meeting to observe the occasion. Zhou Yang delivered a speech, which Wang Ruoshui, editor of People's Daily, and Wang Yuanhua, a literary scholar from Shanghai, had helped to draft. The speech pointed to a major problem of "alienation" in Chinese society.

Q: And that got them into trouble . . .

A: Did it ever! It became the pretext for an all-out assault on intellectuals that lasted several years. The leftists claimed that Marx was being misquoted, that alienation was impossible under socialism, and that Zhou Yang and Wang Ruoshui were badly misleading the people.

Q: Misleading them?

A: In real life, the term *yihua* [alienation] was so strange that most people had no idea what it meant. You had to explain it to them. Once you did, though, they recognized it immediately. "Of course! Of course there's *yihua!*" But meanwhile the campaign to Eradicate Spiritual Pollution steamrollered forward, eliminating all external signs of "pollution": lipstick, curly hairdos, bell-bottom jeans, and the like. And the chilling effects went much deeper than that.

Q: Did you see any of those effects personally?

A: Oh yes, I was witness to perhaps the biggest chill of all. I saw the purge of Hu Jiwei and Wang Ruoshui at the *People's Daily.* In the early 1980s the newspaper office was a stronghold of the reformers; Hu Jiwei was chief editor and Wang Ruoshui was deputy chief. One day in late October of 1983—it was a Sunday—the conservative heavyweights Hu Qiaomu, who had been Mao Zedong's secretary in Yan'an, and Deng Liqun, another Maoist ideologue, announced a meeting for all Party members at the *People's Daily.* They came in person to the newspaper office to preside. They denounced the paper's "liberal tendencies"; all the good things that we had accomplished were, in their view, bad things.

Wang Ruoshui was publicly humiliated. They didn't even give him a chair to sit in. As he took verbal abuse in turn from both Hu and Deng, he looked like the accused at a trial. But I admired him because he refused to resign; he obliged them to fire him. Hu Jiwei resigned, which was more face-saving, but there was a cost: once you resign, you cannot be reinstated.

Q: It must have devastated the staff.

A: That's what I expected, too, but I was surprised to see how many of my colleagues at the meeting clapped in support of Hu Qiaomu and Deng Liqun. How in the world, I wondered, could they clap? It was a real eye-opener. I saw how willingly some people—even my good colleagues at *People's Daily*—could bend with the wind when a power holder came along. And that made me wonder whether my perception of *People's Daily* as a stronghold of reform had been right in the first place. Maybe these benders-with-the-wind had only been pretending to agree with the reformist spirit, too. Maybe it was only a matter of two different kinds of wind. In retrospect, though, I should have realized that some people at the *People's Daily* had been opposed to reform all along. There had already been incidents where people at the paper had sided with my opponents in cases that I had been investigating. I hadn't paid enough attention to these details.

Q: You were too idealistic.

A: And even afterwards, I kept on feeling optimistic. I had a gut feeling that the repression couldn't last, that it would only be a passing thing. I did feel sorry for my friend Wang Ruoshui, though. He had had a long string of bad luck.

Q: Oh? What do you mean?

A: In 1979, some young editors and activists from Democracy Wall came to the *People's Daily* offices, noticed Wang Ruoshui in the hallway, and asked if they could have a chat with him. Wang said yes, had the chat, and then it turned out that one of the youngsters had been an undercover agent for State Security. That same afternoon a report on Wang went into the secret police system. After that he became a marked man; nobody's "good word" could save him now. Even his wife slandered him, saying that he had opposed both Mao Zedong and Deng Xiaoping, and claimed that he had had extramarital affairs. She divorced him, then induced their daughter to rifle through her father's drawers in search of more incriminating evidence. It had been a long, awful story even before he was fired.

Q: It sounds like 1983 was the low point of the 1980s—until 1989, anyway.

A: 1985 was even worse, in my view.

Q: Oh? I thought 1985 was a good year, especially for writers. Wasn't that the year of the "creative freedom" slogan, and the year when the Writers' Association was allowed for the first time to elect its own leaders? Ba Jin and you won that election, right? From the outside, anyway, 1985 looked pretty good.

A: Yes, and that part of the story is true. Until the Writers' Association meeting, which spanned the last days of 1984 and the first of 1985, Deng Liqun and the conservatives had handpicked all of the Association's officers. But that year Hu Yaobang turned the whole system around by announcing free elections and unveiling the "creative freedom" slogan. I think he probably had a go-ahead from Deng Xiaoping before he did these things.

Q: But then what was so bad about 1985?

A: It was a turning point, the beginning of the end of serious political reform in China. Wang Zhen, the hard-line military leader who had made speeches about "cleaning the ranks" during the spiritual pollution campaign, was furious about the results of the Writers' Association election. He and the other conservatives began to turn the tide against the reformers in 1985. Hu Yaobang was forced to retreat step by step, and two years later had to resign.

Q: But when Hu died in April 1989, his death sparked the famous Tiananmen Movement, so he obviously still had a popular following. What do you think of the 1989 Tiananmen Movement—looking back now after more than 15 years?

A: Too much media attention, both then and now, has gone to some fairly superficial aspects of that movement: the students in the Square, on television before the world, with their banners and slogans about democracy, and the Goddess of Democracy in the background. People don't perceive the longer-term trends toward more openness that lay deeper in society among the ordinary Chinese people.

Q: Tell us more about those deeper trends.

A: By the late 1980s the attitude of the Chinese people toward political authority was very different from what it had been in the 1950s. Just compare how I was viewed after my two expulsions from the Communist Party—first in 1957 and again in 1987. In 1957 I became a pariah overnight. Nobody but a few close relatives would have anything to do with me. I think I had two visitors in twenty-two years. But in 1987 things were entirely different. People lined up at my doorway to express their support. They didn't care that my apartment was probably bugged, and they knew that plainclothes police were watching outside, taking down names—but it didn't matter! They came anyway. They brought me presents—medicine, food, money, *baojianqiu*.[8] People sometimes dared to stand up in political meetings to defend me. Some told me that when they heard officials reading out lists of my offenses, they actually thought, at first, that I was being praised.

The point here isn't me. The point is the sea change in the Chinese people's attitudes. In the 1950s Mao was amazingly successful at turning all the Chinese people into his blind followers. He was a genius at that. But after he led China into a number of blind alleys the people began to wake up. By April 5, 1976, resistance had grown to a point where millions of protesters—when Mao was still alive!—headed for Tiananmen Square to denounce the Cultural Revolution. A few years later, in 1978–79, we saw a Democracy Wall movement. By the late 1970s farmers were demanding to till their own land. Most of the people in these movements were not intellectuals. They were from the lower levels of society—mostly young workers and farmers who were only modestly educated. China's resistance movements had very different origins from those of the Soviet Union and Eastern Europe, where intellectuals were the leaders and had very little contact with workers or farmers. In China the breakthroughs came from the lower classes, and in 1989 those classes were ready to keep on marching.

Q: Who opposed them? The official class?

A: Not really. The rank and file of the Communist Party had also changed over the years, and by the 1980s was also looking for more flexibility and freedom. The Party's two original pillars of strength—by which I mean its almost religious unity of thought and its ironclad organizational control—both crumbled during the Cultural Revolution. When the post-Mao leaders spoke of "reform," people were really ready for it. Reform in China faced much less resistance than, by comparison, it did in the Soviet Union after Stalin. The conservatives in China tried several times during the 1980s to bring back Maoism—and launched a few campaigns against "liberalism"—but never could make it work. With each attempt the liberals somehow ended up stronger than they had been before. The last time this happened was after 1987, when Hu Yaobang was sacked. The man who replaced him, Zhao Ziyang, turned out to be just as strong a proponent of reform as Hu. Political reform under Zhao actually sped up.

The overall point here is that powerful momentum for change had been building in China both inside and outside the Party. In 1989 Deng Xiaoping labeled the Tiananmen movement "counter-revolutionary turmoil," and you would think that would have scared people. Yet most Party, government, and military officials in Beijing—probably 70 percent or more—supported the protesters anyway. Some even joined them in the streets.

Q: With these large, long-term trends undergirding the Tiananmen movement in 1989, why did it fail? Why has political change remained beyond reach?

A: Several reasons. Most important, I think, is that there was nothing for the movement to believe in at that point in history. This was a global problem. The revolutions of the twentieth century had failed, and the socialist movement was in tatters. As of 1989 the great majority of Chinese intellectuals looked to America and to capitalism for models, but what Deng Xiaoping was advocating then already was—to put it bluntly—capitalism, so how could capitalism be a rallying cry for an alternative? This vacuum in thought, theory, and strategy was the major reason for the failure.

Q: What about the intellectuals? Isn't it their job to supply thought, theory, and strategy?

A: In my view intellectuals—and especially writers—must bear a major responsibility for the failure. On the whole the role of China's literary elite over the last twenty-five years is not very pretty. In the 1980s some writers did push for reform, but only in a superficial way. More often than not, "reform" boiled down to more social status, material comfort, and creative freedom for themselves. They were not very interested in moving the larger society forward.

Q: What do you mean by "not very interested in moving the larger society forward"?

A: After 1978 no one in China had more freedom than writers, especially fiction writers. No one had a better opportunity to influence society. But what did they do with this opportunity? Mostly they pursued wealth and fame, while questions of social justice, especially for society's downtrodden, drifted into the background. A few leading fiction writers led young writers down the road of modernist escape fiction. One of these senior figures, sometimes called "China's most clever writer,"[9] was clever enough to become a minister in the central government, where he wrote fiction that indirectly supported the Communist Party while at the same time enjoying the cachet of "dissident writer" both inside and outside China.

Q: And you feel that writers' neglect of society contributed to the failure at Tiananmen?

A: Yes. Writers in the 1980s did not dig into society to reveal and clarify the large popular trends that were taking place. As a result, when spring of 1989 came, both the students in the square and the political intellectuals who were helping them were largely out of touch with those deeper social trends. The great tide of popular discontent that underlay the nationwide protest movement was beneath their feet but largely invisible to them, so they were unable to use that strength to tactical advantage. Student leaders appeared time and again before the television cameras of the world, brimming with their youthful confidence, but what was in their minds? Only a few catchwords about "freedom" and "democracy" borrowed from the West. Their self-conception as the originators and cutting edge of China's democracy movement, the heroic leaders whom all the workers and farmers had been waiting for, was extremely naïve. How could they possibly not have lost out to the pack of wily old scoundrels whom they were up against?

Q: And after Tiananmen the intellectual elite has done no better?

A: Worse. In June 1989 few people thought the regime could hang on much longer. But it has. Part of the "credit" for this must go to a craven intellectual elite that has made a bargain with the regime: political support in exchange for personal privilege. The regime has bought off other social groups, too—notably the bureaucratic class and the new business elite—but no group, if you think about it, has gained as much from the bargain as the literary intellectuals have. Their material standards have risen sharply; their social status, which under Mao had hit rock bottom, has skyrocketed; and the expanding latitude for creative writing (a life-or-death matter in their line of work) has been another special bonus for them. It is hardly surprising that they feel grateful to the regime and are ready to grovel before it. Some even say the June Fourth massacre was justified—after all, it kept China "stable" and avoided the chaos that one sees in Russia. They say that Jiang Zemin, despite the repression, rampant corruption and polarization that came to China during his years in power, has been cleverer than Zhao Ziyang.

And whatever their views, they tend to see only the elite events —demonstrations at Tiananmen or the jockeying leaders in Zhongnanhai—and see nothing of the big changes deeper in society. They think the Communist Party is just a matter of struggles between conservative and reformist leaders at the top; they overlook its deeper role as a foul, reactionary force that pervades society and feeds resentment at all levels.

Q: There was a kind of "Mao nostalgia" in the 1990s. Where did that come from? Why would people feel nostalgic?

A: For Mao everything depended on "thought." He exaggerated the importance of thought and downplayed or ignored the flesh-

and-blood side of life. The Long March survived on "spirit," and the Great Leap Forward was supposed to run on spirit, too. By now, though, China has swung to the opposite extreme. Now everything is material, nothing spirit. This leaves people who remember the Mao years feeling odd, yearning for something to believe in. Mao led China to disaster, but at least he gave you something to believe in.

Q: Do any Maoist ideas still survive in popular thinking?

A: Yes—equality, for example. Mao said workers were "masters" of the country. This was never more than half true in his day—because workers never really did have their own unions or their own power—but merely championing the slogan at least raised the status and self-respect of workers. Peasants, too, were never treated equally by Mao, but the slogans about "people's communes," "learn from the peasants," and so on at least promoted the idea of equality—and it still survives. In the thinking of Chinese people today, you can have more money or status than I do, but if so there had better be a good reason for the difference. You're not supposed to be born better.

The importance of equality can also be measured by looking at suicide. There was a lot more suicide in China in the 1990s than in the 1940s. Is that because material conditions were much worse in the 1990s? No, for the most part. The difference is that in the 1940s destitute or despised people accepted their fates more easily. They did not expect social respect. In the 1990s, though, to be laid off or unemployed had become a tremendous loss of face. The idea of equality gave people pride, and when the equality was snatched away, it brought unprecedented shame.

Q: Your view of these "deeper" movements toward political change in Chinese society are fresh and interesting. Western China-watchers seldom speak in these terms.

A: That's because they can't see what's happening under the surface. You have to spend time in the grassroots in China in order to sense them. Even in my own case, I discovered these trends without really meaning to.

Q: What do you mean?

A: I mean what happened to me in 1957. Being labeled a "rightist" was a disaster for me in many ways, but it also caused me to learn a lot about China that I hadn't known before. As of 1956 I was part of socialist China's new elite: I had a good job as a reporter and a certain fame as a writer. My salary was 158 yuan per month, about five times what an ordinary worker got, and pay for individual manuscripts came on top of that. I was on my way to the new upper class. Then, as a "rightist," I was forced to go live in the countryside and mountains among some of China's poorest people. That was new to me. Always before I had lived in cities. I learned a lot about the ordinary people and came to respect their gutsy struggles with life.

In the mid-1980s, on three trips to Shaanxi as a reporter, I was startled once again at the feistiness of China's ordinary people. People formed lines outside my door waiting to tell me their grievances. They kept coming and coming. At dinnertime someone brought me food so that I wouldn't need to take a dinner break. These were ordinary folk, not intellectuals; no one needed to lecture them on democracy; they knew what was right and wrong, fair and unfair, and were very articulate about it.

Q: *The Chinese government argues that the Chinese people are not ready for democracy because their "quality" [suzhi] is too low.*

A: (*Laughs*) Ridiculous! The opposite is nearer the truth. Chinese workers and farmers for a long time have been more ready for democracy than their counterparts in Russia and Eastern Europe—and maybe many other places, too.

Q: *Why do you think China has been different?*

A: Mostly because of the Cultural Revolution. It is a mistake to view that huge event one-dimensionally. It brought beating, smashing, cruelty, and torture, to be sure. But it also had the unintended consequence of jolting people into thinking for themselves. People like Wei Jingsheng and Zheng Yi were forged by the Cultural Revolution. They didn't go to college; they learned from life—from sharing the lives and sufferings of ordinary people. They learned to challenge authority, and they set a goal of changing the system. The "big-character posters" of the Cultural Revolution truly did give people a new sense of power.

How could Deng Xiaoping have turned Maoism around so fast in the 1980s if he had not had strong popular sentiment on his side? If the Cultural Revolution had not happened—if China had continued with the system it had in the mid-1960s—I'm afraid China today would look like North Korea. Socialist China and North Korea both started with a basically Confucian society combined with a Mao-style (or Kim-style) dictator. The only major difference was that China was too big and couldn't be sealed and controlled as North Korea was. China's slide into the Cultural Revolution was neither accidental nor really very abrupt. It was the culmination of a rising popular distaste for Communist Party control. The history and effects of the Cultural Revolution still need a lot more study.

Q: So this popular rebellious spirit rose out of the Cultural Revolution and continued until when? Through the 1980s?

A: At least to the 1980s, for sure. Remember that the 1989 demonstrations were not just in Beijing. They were in hundreds of cities across China, and millions of people took part. And this happened—can you believe it?—without any political organization or publicity equipment. Could it all have happened because a few student leaders at Tiananmen were waving banners and giving interviews to CNN? No. It came out of a deep, long-term recoil from Maoism.

In the same month as the Beijing massacre—June, 1989—the literary magazine *Reportage* published a piece by Mai Tianshu called "Worship of a Living Legend." It tells about a deputy mayor in Yueyang City, Hunan Province, who in the late 1980s required his officials to go on television every month to answer questions from representatives of ordinary citizens. The bureaucrats were so embarrassed by the questions that they decided to frame the deputy mayor and get him fired. That, in turn, led to two full days of spontaneous street demonstrations by thousands of indignant commoners. Such populism was not unusual in China then. It was the true background of the Tiananmen movement.

Q: Did the June Fourth massacre stop this whole trend?

A: It certainly slowed it down. In the 1990s people pulled back. Jiang Zemin's policy of using economic incentives to buy people's consciences began to work at many social levels. Here we can see a less attractive side of Chinese popular responses. The Chinese people sometimes show a weakness of conviction, a herd mentality.

Q: What do you see as the state of the popular mind since 1989?

A: Many people have embraced a simpleminded response that says, well, if the socialist road didn't work, then the capitalist road must be correct. To them, the end of Eastern European socialism and the collapse of the Soviet Union reinforces the message that there must be only one way out. Moneymaking becomes the only value because nobody can come up with anything better. There are no public ideals, nothing to believe in. On the surface, the Chinese people seem once again, as in the early twentieth century, to be a "tray of loose sand." But if you look more closely, you can see that those grains of sand have changed. They have their own assertive power now; they won't suffer oppression passively, and under the right conditions could become strongly cohesive.

Q: What would your own wishes be for China's "path" into the future?

A: I often wonder what Czechoslovakia would have been like if the Soviets had not crushed the Prague Spring in 1968. That phrase that the Czechs used—"socialism with a human face"—appeals to me. I think a formula of political democracy combined with some planned social ideals is something the world should still try. If "reform" means jettisoning ideals and not replacing them with anything else—no, that's not the answer. You can see this problem of the "two extremes" even in the way words are used.

Q: What do you mean?

A: Through all of the Mao years, there were certain words that never—and I do mean almost literally *never*—appeared in an official document.

Q: Like what?

A: Like *ziyou* [freedom] or *kuaile* [happiness]. Things like "happiness" just weren't on the agenda. Even *ren* [human being] and *wo* [I] were rare. But if you look now at official documents, there are certain other words that never appear. *Geming* [revolution], *dou-*

zheng [struggle] and *jieji* [class] used to be everywhere, but now—nowhere. Even worse, *lixiang* [ideals] is never used—it's just not in the official vocabulary.

Q: So you still hope for a middle way, somewhere between Maoism and where China is now?

A: It was right to repudiate Maoism—in fact even today we still haven't done enough to repudiate it. But that doesn't mean we need to go to the other extreme, as some of today's dissidents do. Some of them look at history and conclude, for example, that since the Communists were so horrible, everything the Guomindang did in the 1930s and 1940s was right. That's too simple. One of these good people, for example, wrote an essay called "Anti-Communism Is Not Patriotism, But a Patriot Must Be Anti-Communist."[10] I would love to ask the author exactly where he finds any "communism" at all in today's China or today's Chinese Communist Party. What precisely is he wanting to oppose? What could his sweeping statement really mean? The Chinese Communist Party in the 1940s was hardly the same thing that it is today. It had a lot of popular support back then. Some of the problems it solved in the early 1950s—corruption, crime, unemployment, gambling, prostitution, drug abuse, foot binding, illiteracy—had been intractable problems in China for a long time. The Party used force, yes; but I'm not ready to say that a certain amount of coercion, in working on problems like that, is always a bad thing. And my question is this: Would a "patriot" have to reject all of those activities just because communists carried them out?

Q: Back in the 1950s people in the West didn't see much of the positive side of Chinese communism, either.

A: The West's mishandling of China at mid-century is one of the saddest aspects of the Cold War. Stalin and Mao had their differences in the 1940s—as some U.S. diplomats knew, and said, at the time. Communism was not an international monolith, and even if it had been, the Soviet Union after World War Two was in ruins, hardly in a position to launch a takeover of the world. The U.S. could have dealt with Mao separately, and could have compromised with him. Mao would probably have accepted some kind of sharing of power, either geographically—north and south of the Yangzi River or something like that—or politically in some kind of multi-party arrangement. In retrospect, the only real chance for China to avert the disasters that befell it came in 1946–47 with the peace talks between the Nationalists and the Communists. If those talks had succeeded, and the Communists had not gained their monopoly of power, Mao Zedong would not have dared to go berserk in the way he did. But the U.S. leaned all the way to the Nationalists' side, driving the Communists into hostile opposition in Korea and elsewhere, and inadvertently creating the conditions that paved the way for Mao. The history of the Cold War is another topic that deserves a lot more study and reappraisal than it has had.

Q: The whole Cold War?

A: Yes, the question matters right to the present day. The Cold War helped to cause the "terrorism" that we see today. Where does today's terrorism come from? It comes because people feel resentful. The Cold War led the U.S. to prop up anti-communist governments around the world—and even engineer coups, sometimes. Social and political reform usually ground to a halt wherever such governments were propped up. The U.S. pounded small countries like Nicaragua and Panama; when the tiny country of Grenada wanted to build an airport it got invaded. These are the kinds of things that drive people toward martyrdom. I remember a story in a Chinese newspaper in 1954 about Cheddi Jagan, a leader of the Marxist People's Progressive Party of Guyana, who won a national election in 1953 but was deposed and imprisoned the next year by British and American agents. In 1992, when Guyana was finally able to hold another election thirty-eight years later, guess who won? Cheddi Jagan. See? People have memories. The Cold War led the U.S. to do a lot of things that hurt its reputation in the world, and that have to do with terrorism today.

Q: And you feel that, absent the Cold War, China's communist movement could have taken a different path.

A: At least it's possible. Without a Cold War, China would not have used the Soviet model as much as it did, and a "human-face" socialism would have had a better chance.

Q: You were hoping for a revival of that possibility in the 1980s, no? Your reportage piece "The Second Kind of Loyalty" seems to say so.

A: Yes, and quite a few people shared that hope in the 1980s. The two I wrote about in "The Second Kind of Loyalty" were not Party members, but there were people inside the Party very much like them. They wanted a better kind of socialism and were still ready to work for it. "The Second Kind of Loyalty" made a splash when it appeared. It kept getting republished. Meanwhile I began taking criticism from two very different sides. Party hard-liners of course did not think a "second" kind of loyalty was necessary. The first kind was fine. But from the other side came the view that because the Party was so rotten, I should have opposed it outright— not go looking for another way to be loyal. In my view all-out confrontation was a mistake. It overlooked those idealists who, despite everything, still wanted humane socialism to work.

Q: Do any ideals survive today?

A: Ideals are submerged today. The popular desire for values is not well articulated or organized, but it's obviously still there. You know it's there because complaint and criticism remain so audible. Farmers and workers protest almost all the time. Among the long-repressed liberal intellectuals, a new left wing that criticizes injustice toward the poor and underprivileged has emerged in recent years. Criticism, by its nature, must be grounded in a belief that things can be better than they are. It implies ideals. The Chinese people are groping for something better, so there is hope that today's cynicism won't last forever.

Q: Does that "something better" include democracy?

A: I think so, but survival is still the first question for people.

Q: What do you mean?

A: I remember, as a young man the 1940s, seeing refugees crowding the railway station in Harbin. They were fleeing poverty in the "free areas" of north China and coming to Heilongjiang, which was under Japanese control. I wrote a poem about them in which I bemoaned their new bondage to the Japanese. But later I thought about it and realized survival comes before freedom. Before you can live free, you first have to stay alive.

Q: Today Communist Party leaders use this argument to oppose the spread of human rights in China. They say China needs more wealth first, before it can "afford" freedom. You agree?

A: I agree that survival has to come first, but completely deny that that is what the leaders in China are doing today. Look at China: suicide and other violence are on the rise; AIDS, schistosomiasis, and other diseases are increasing, and where do people turn? The public health-care system has collapsed from lack of funds. Even poor little Cuba can provide free education and medicine, but China, now much richer, does not. Wealth grows, but so does the number of people living in poverty. Education used to be basically free in China, but today is available only to those who can pay their own ways.

Q: So you think these problems need to be solved before China can turn toward democracy.

A: I think the problems need to be addressed *at the same time* that democracy comes. Too many Chinese intellectuals these days think that all you have to do is to insert Western models of democracy into textbooks, send Chinese people to go study them, and—presto!—you've got Western democracy. These people should take a look at a recent survey I saw of nineteen Latin-American countries. It shows that when democracy changes only the political mechanisms while leaving social or economic injustices in place, it doesn't mean very much to people. They don't pay it much attention. I think China is similar. When you look at the huge social problems that have exploded in China since the 1980s—corruption, inequality, cynicism—I'm afraid that "one man, one vote" alone is not going to do much.

Q: What are you working on currently?

A: I am working on a book that is largely on the topic of this interview: how the Chinese people have changed in several ways between the 1940s and now. Other people have written extensively about China's political and intellectual elites, and these topics of course have their place, but I want to describe trends that are deeper in society, in the daily experience of ordinary Chinese people.

NOTES

1. *Liaozhai's Record of Wonders,* stories of the supernatural by Pu Songling (1640–1715).

2. "Zai Qiaoliang gongdishang," *People's Literature* no. 4 (1956): 1–17. The story was a main piece of evidence for the attack on Liu as a "rightist" the following year.

3. Mao Zedong's classic statement of literary policy. See Bonnie S. McDougall, *Mao Zedong's "Talks at the Yan'an Conference of Literature and Art": A Translation of the 1943 Text with Commentary* (Ann Arbor: University of Michigan Center for Chinese Studies, 1980).

4. In 1957, a year after Liu's "On the Bridge Construction Site" appeared, Mao delivered a long speech on "Correct Handling of Contradictions Among the People" in which he distinguished between criticism of the enemy from criticism among the people.

5. Translated by Howard Goldblatt as "Six Chapters from my Life 'Downunder,'" *Renditions*, no. 16 (Autumn 1981): 6–61, and by Geremie Barmé and Bennet Lee as *A Cadre School Life: Six Chapters* (Hong Kong: Joint Publishing, 1982).

6. Lin Biao, a longtime leader of the People's Liberation Army and Mao's "second in command" during the late 1960s, died in September 1971 when an airplane he was riding in was shot down over central Asia. The official story is that he was attempting to flee to the Soviet Union after a failed coup attempt against Mao.

7. In a movement "to oppose the right-leaning tendency to reverse correct verdicts."

8. Steel balls to manipulate in the hand to promote general health.

9. Wang Meng.

10. Xu Shuiliang, "Fangong budengyu aiguo, dan aiguo bixu fangong," *Baijia zhengming*, February 29, 2004. http://www.boxun.com/hero/xushuiliang/122_1.shtml, accessed December 4, 2004.

PART ONE

SPEECH TO THE CONGRESS OF LITERATURE AND ART WORKERS

Listen Carefully to the Voice of the People

Translated by Kyna Rubin and Perry Link

On November 9, 1979, Liu Binyan gave a startling speech at the Fourth Congress of Chinese Literature and Art Workers in Beijing. Repeatedly interrupted by spontaneous applause, the speech eventually became famous not only as a clear exposition of key problems that had been facing Chinese writers in recent times, but also as a courageous statement of thoughts that had occurred to many intellectuals but that few had dared to mention in public.

The speech has never been published as originally spoken. Excerpts were published in *People's Daily* on November 26, 1979, under the title "Listen Carefully to the Voice of the People" ("Qingting renmin de shengyin"). The present translation is based on this version, although we have restored some deleted lines. The *Literary Gazette* (*Wenyibao*), in its November–December issue of 1979 (nos. 11 and 12), published a fuller and more extensively edited version of the speech under the title "The Call of the Times" ("Shidai de zhaohuan").[1] —ED.

Face Life Squarely, and Listen Carefully to the Voice of the People

Of the middle-aged writers present at our Fourth Congress on Literature and Art, the most active and prolific in the past two years have been comrades such as Bai Hua, Wang Meng, Deng Youmei, Gong Liu, Shao Yanxiang, Cong Weixi, and Liu Shaotang. Considering their actual age, they should not look as old as they do. Just look at Bai Hua, with his head of white hair, and Gong Liu—who has entirely lost his hair. Whose fault is this?

If mistakes have been made, I must ask why it is that scientists are permitted their mistakes, and so are politicians, while writers alone are forbidden to make mistakes. It is said that the mistakes of scientists are forgivable because they produce no "social effects";[2] but then what about the mistakes of politicians? Which is larger—the consequences of a politician's mistake or the consequences of a writer's? How many times larger?

Those of us here today are fortunate to be alive and well, to have had our "rightist" labels removed,[3] and to be able once again to serve the people with our pens. But we mustn't forget all the young people who were implicated with us twenty-two years ago. They were also labeled "rightists." Some of the verdicts on them have not been reversed even today. I am thinking of our comrade Lin Xiling, whose fate has been even worse than ours.[4] I hereby appeal to all those in authority, including the leadership of People's University, to expedite the rectification of these cases. These "rightists" have lost more than twenty of the most precious years of their lives, and don't have very many more to go. The question of their exoneration simply must not be allowed to drag on any longer.

But looking back over the last twenty or more years, I feel we have gained certain things in spite of our losses. Fate brought us into intimate contact with the lowest levels of the laboring masses; our joys and worries became for a time the same as their own. Our hopes were no different from theirs. This experience allowed us to see, to hear, and to feel for ourselves things that others have been unable to see, hear, or feel.

In my own personal experience, the most unforgettable years were 1958–1960, when I shared a bed and even sometimes a quilt with poor peasants. The things I saw in the villages, and the plaints I heard from the peasants, were all vastly different from what was being spread by the authorities and the press. Whom was I to believe? I had resolved at the time to obey the Party and to remold myself from the bone marrow outward. But there is no avoiding the fact that objective, material things are more powerful than subjective, spiritual ones. However great my will to reform, it was no match for the continual onslaught of certain plain incongruities. For example, the higher authorities told us that our impoverished gully of a village ought to build a zoo and a fountain. Now, what were peasants who hardly ate meat all year supposed to feed to lions and tigers in a zoo? With no water source—with man and beast still drinking rainwater—how were they to build a fountain? A struggle began to rage deep inside me: how could two diametrically opposed "truths" coexist in the world? The longings of the peasants were one truth, and the policies of the higher-ups and the propaganda in the newspapers were quite another. Which should I follow? Not until 1960, when Party Central issued its "Twelve Points on Rural Policy,"[5] did I finally get my answer. It was right to uphold the interests and demands of the people. Anything that ran counter to their wishes was ultimately untenable.

This year we have seen the appearance of Ru Zhijuan's "The Misedited Story" and Liu Zhen's "Black Flag," both of which are stories about these same years I have just been speaking of.[6] We should ask ourselves what the "social effects" would have been if stories like these had been permitted publication twenty-one years ago. Would the masses have risen in opposition to the Communist Party? Would the peasants have rebelled? History tells us they would not have. The effect of these short stories would have been quite the opposite: they would have helped the Party to see its mistakes while there was still time to make changes. Such changes would have heightened the Party's prestige, strengthened the collective socialist economy, and stimulated the peasants both economically and politically. Recent experience has taught us time and again that true harm to the prestige of the Party and socialism is done not by literary works that describe problems, but by the problems themselves, problems that have been caused by our own mistakes and by the destructiveness of our enemies.[7] Had writers during the years 1958–1960 been able to hold their heads high, to speak out in behalf of the people, to uncover mistakes, and to expose the destructiveness of our enemies, this would, in fact, have been the best way they could have upheld the Party and socialism. Yet in 1958 no one was writing works such as those by Liu Zhen and Ru Zhijuan, and even in 1962, when Party Central summed up the lessons of the 1958–1960 period, no one could write stories that told the truth about peasant life. Not for twenty years—not until the third year after the "smashing of the Gang of Four" —did *People's Literature* and *Shanghai Literature* publish these two stories, thereby reclaiming for literature some of its rights to tell the truth about life. Even today we have to admire the political courage of these two editorial boards.

We should try to learn from our experience, and I have three points to offer in this regard.

First, writers should face life squarely and listen carefully to the voice of the people. The policies of the Party must pass the test of practice and be corrected when they are wrong. When faced with the "two kinds of truth" that I referred to a moment ago, we writers must maintain a strong sense of responsibility to the people in reaching our conclusions. Our thinking must be dead serious, never rash, and always independent. We must never simply follow the crowd. The test of time has shown that all those literary works about peasant life in the late 1950s are dead today, whereas stories like those by Liu Zhen and Ru Zhijuan live on.

Second, some comrades apparently feel that literature's "delving into life"[8] is simply a matter of writing about the dark side of society, to the exclusion of heroes or progressive characters. This is a misunderstanding. In varying times and under varying historical circumstances, progressive people must confront varying social problems. A writer cannot portray life separately from actual society, even if he limits his heroes to model workers and war heroes. A writer cannot avoid taking a stance on the great social questions of the day. The several heroic characters that Ru Zhijuan and Liu Zhen have created in the two stories just mentioned are all assertive and courageous in protecting the interests of the masses—which are the same as the interests of socialism—and they all meet with some temporary setbacks. These heroes, who are genuinely part of the tide of history, have won the power to survive; the heroes in those other [overly romantic] literary works have by now lost this power.

Third, literature is a mirror. When the mirror shows us things in life that are not very pretty, or that fall short of our ideals, it is wrong to blame the mirror. Instead we should root out and destroy those conditions that disappoint us. Mirrors show us the true appearance of things; literary mirrors speed the progress of society. Smashing a mirror is no way to make an ugly person beautiful, nor is it a way to make social problems evaporate. History has shown that it is better not to veil or to smash literary mirrors. Isn't this truth all too clear from the extended period of time in which our realist tradition in literature was dragged toward an evil dead end? To forbid literature from delving into life, to deprive writers of their right to reflect on the problems of real life, and not to allow writers to speak for the people harms not only literature but the people and the Party as well. The period of literary history in which such things could happen has now come to an end, and a new chapter has begun. We hope no one will be pulling literature backward any more.

Answer the People's Questions

Our differing views on literary issues have always been bound up with our differing views on politics. And these two kinds of differing views have always derived from the question of how to interpret society and reality.

For example, as some comrades see it, Lin Biao and the Gang of Four did not actually wreak much havoc, and in fact there was no "ultra-leftist line." Others feel that the havoc and the criminal line of the Gang of Four have followed them into collapse and final extinction, and that the only problem remaining today is to get everybody to be productive together.

My view is that the tragedies brought on us by the Gang of Four have yet to be fully exposed, and that what has been exposed is yet to be fully comprehended. The Gang's "residual perniciousness"[9] must not be conceived as something lifeless or static—something just standing by, waiting to be swept away. It is a living social force, and it has its social base.

The perniciousness most worthy of our attention is the invisible kind. The Gang of Four has disrupted the organic workings of our Party and has damaged our social relations. They have created a highly abnormal relationship between our Party and the masses. What makes this matter so difficult to deal with is that many people, while not bad people themselves, either knowingly or unknowingly have been protecting bad people. Superficially they are all Communist Party members or Party cadres; but every action they take serves only their vested interests and comes only from their own habits of thought. This is the very problem I have pointed out in "People or Monsters?" It is not going to go away unless we deal decisively and finally with it.

At this point I would like to bring something to the attention of those comrades who feel that the primary duty of literature is to portray heroes. We are faced today with the ironic fact that heroes are in an awkward position. To do good deeds one has to offend people. One has to take risks and even make a bad name for oneself. When I did newspaper work in the 1950s I always found it hard to initiate criticism of a person. Now, in the late 1970s, I suddenly find it has become hard to praise a person. Take, for example, the case of Liu Jie, an inspector of the neighborhood registry in the Daxing'anling district of Heilongjiang, who was praised in the press for sticking to principles. She also had the support of the Provincial Party Committee. But it was precisely the commendation of the Party newspaper that brought calamity upon her, and the support of the provincial leadership was of no use in breaking the siege that befell her. There were even threats on her life. Now, if a true writer of the people were to interview this progressive young woman, there can be no doubt that he would soon find himself taking sides with her. He would join the battle against wickedness and help her to win a more advantageous position. Only then would he turn to writing up her story. I feel strongly that only this kind of writer deserves the name "writer of the people."

To another group of comrades, those writers and critics who hold that it is the responsibility of literature to introduce modern-

ization and construction, I would like to offer a different observation. The modernization of industry and agriculture is by no
means simply a matter of adding new machinery. Human beings
are still the mainstay of all productive forces, and the enthusiasm
of people today still suffers many artificial constraints. This question deserves notice and additional study.

Methods of enterprise management that are modeled after the
patriarchal family system, or after medieval practices or the ways
of Genghis Khan, cannot possibly sustain a lasting rise in production. Militaristic methods and political incentives can, it is true,
motivate workers over the short term; but as time wears on this
approach is also doomed to failure. It is simply incompatible with
the nature of modern industry. In history, the birth and development of modern industry has gone hand in hand with the liberation of human beings. This was a qualified liberation, of course. It
grew out of the feudal serf system, in which people were bound in
their social places. It gave to individuals freedom of their persons
as well as certain political rights and legal guarantees of equality.
As the individual came to feel that he was an independent person,
a free person, a person with a certain dignity and worth, a person
equal with others before the law, gradually the ideas "personal
character" and "individuality" came into being. Only when the individual attained this kind of status and this kind of consciousness
did he begin to rely on himself and devote his talents to the improvement of his lot. The result was that productive forces in the
period of capitalism exceeded those of the feudal period many
times over. For socialism to exceed capitalism in productivity, it
can and must provide even better conditions for human development and advancement. Management principles modeled on the
feudal patriarchal system are a step backward from capitalism;
they constrict people, inhibit them, and block their abilities and
potential. It should go without saying that socialist modernization
gains nothing from this.

It may seem that what I've been talking about falls into the
realm of economics, but this is not the case. All this has to do with
people, and therefore with literature. There are only two ways in
which the feudal patriarchal style of leadership supports and ex-
tends itself. One is by coercion and command, and the other is by

attack and retaliation. And both these methods, because they have, in contemporary political life, become common ways in which a minority can subdue the masses, warrant our closest vigilance. "Power corrupts, and absolute power corrupts absolutely." Without the supervision of the people, a good person will turn bad, and an honest official will turn corrupt.

We must answer the people's questions. We have no right to be auditors in the courtroom of history. The people are the judges, as well as the plaintiffs. We must help supply them with scripts. But before we provide answers, we first must learn. We must understand more about social life than the average person does.

One serious problem is that we still lack an accurate understanding of our own society. Our efforts to understand it have been suspended for many years. In recent times we have not had any sociology, political science, or legal or ethical studies worthy of the name "science." The kind of investigative research that Chairman Mao used to advocate has also been shelved for many years. A vast unknown world lies before us. Consider a few examples.

First, "class struggle." Everyone accepts that class struggle has "expanded" for many years, but in fact, for a long period of time, the target of class struggle was completely misconceived. Its content and methods were also wrong. (In fact, it has been a distinguishing feature of our current historical period that mistakes continually repeat themselves.) Recently a new question has been raised: do classes really exist in our society? Some say they do not. Some say of course they do—just look at Wang Shouxin.[10] Her case shows that after more than twenty years of "struggle," we still haven't figured out whom we ought to be struggling against.

Second, we have worked for more than twenty years at "socialist construction." Yet innumerable problems have dragged on without resolution, and in fact have gotten worse over time. This year our economists have identified the crux of the matter by raising the question of the goals of production under socialism: are we, in the final analysis, producing steel for the sake of steel, and petroleum for the sake of petroleum, or are these things for the people, aimed at satisfying their ever-increasing material and spiritual needs? It seems there are some individuals who do not agree that the goal of production should be to maximize satisfaction of the constantly increasing material and cultural needs of society as a whole.

Third, for many years now we have assigned top priority to "the human factor" in an unending political and ideological revolution. But after many years of this, people's enthusiasm not only has not increased—it has actually declined. This is another question to ponder. It is mystifying that this piece of land called China, always so inhospitable to the cultivation of "rightist opportunism," has nonetheless allowed revisionism with a "leftist" tag to grow so wild.

On "People or Monsters?" and Other Things

Our readers need literature with many different themes and styles. But they especially need writers who will serve as spokesmen for the people, writers who will answer their questions and express their demands by confronting the major issues of the day. The welcome for such writers is clearly evident in the spirited applause that plays like "Harbinger of Spring" and "Power Versus Law"[11] have received, and in the wide readership that "People or Monsters?" has had. Some readers worry that "People or Monsters?" which exposes such massive problems, creates a negative or pessimistic mood in readers, causing them to lose faith in our Party and our system. I have received a great number of thought-provoking letters from readers of "People or Monsters?" and judging from these, there is no such danger. The reader response is positive. The work triggers a burst of righteousness in people; it arouses the ardent wish of everyone who cares about our country to cure our illness and save our society. Some readers have even gone to Chairman Hua[12] with concrete proposals for reform. But the opposition to "People or Monsters?" of course has been fierce, too. I have awoken to a hard fact: in today's China, if one speaks or writes and does not incur somebody's opposition, one might as well not have spoken or written at all. One has no alternative. The only alternative is to cower in a corner and fall silent. But if we do that, why live?

I have never been good at mathematics. Ever since I was a schoolboy it has been my weakness. But there is one math problem I have figured out for sure, and it is this: writing a single article can equate to making a person a "rightist," but writing one hundred similar articles equates to the same thing. So should I keep on writing?[13]

We are writing in the particular time and circumstances of China at the juncture between the 1970s and the 1980s. The needs of the times and the demands of the people must be our commands. Our role is necessitated by the inexorable development of history. We have no right to sidestep the immensely complex problems of our society. We must help our readers to understand our society more profoundly and accurately, and help them to rise in struggle for the complete realization of the great historical task of the Four Modernizations![14]

NOTES

1. An earlier version of the present translation will appear in a collection of translations of Chinese literature from 1979 to 1980, edited by Mason Wang (University Center, Mich.: Green River Press, 1983). The version of the speech that appears in *Literary Gazette* is translated by John Beyer in Howard Goldblatt, ed., *Chinese Literature for the 1980s* (Armonk, N.Y.: M. E. Sharpe, 1982), pp. 103–20.

2. "Social effects" here means undesirable social consequences. The phrase has been widely used in post-Mao China to maintain a subtle yet sometimes strong pressure on writers to conform with official policy.

3. Liu refers to labels applied during the Anti-Rightist campaign of 1957, when hundreds of thousands of intellectuals who had criticized Party policies were punished for anti-Party or anti-socialist thought.

4. Lin Xiling was a young lecturer at People's University in Beijing when she was arrested in 1957 and charged with being part of the "Zhang (Bojun)–Luo (Longji) Alliance," a group who objected to the one-party system, to ignorant Party officials "leading" non-Party specialists, and to the political campaigns forced upon the nation after 1949.

5. The "Twelve Points on Rural Policy" was an emergency classified document aimed at rectifying serious economic dislocations that had resulted from the overly idealistic policies of the Great Leap Forward in 1958–59.

6. "The Misedited Story" ("Jianji cuole de gushi") was published in *People's Literature* (*Renmin wenxue*) no. 2 (1979). "Black Flag" ("Heiqi")

was published in *Shanghai Literature* (*Shanghai wenxue*) no. 3 (1979); an English translation appears in *Chinese Literature* (Beijing), May 1980. Both stories attack the excesses of the Great Leap Forward and the decline from previous years in the Communist Party's concern for the peasantry.

7. "Enemies" here refers to the domestic enemies who conceived and directed the Great Leap Forward (1958–1960) and the Cultural Revolution (1966–1972).

8. The phrase "delve into life" (*ganyu shenghuo*) stands for a principle that Liu Binyan adopted in the 1950s from his friend and mentor the Soviet writer Valentin Ovechkin. The principle is that a writer should investigate life for himself and tell the truth, both the good and the bad, about social issues. "Delving into life" has been opposed, in both the Soviet Union and China, by literary officials who prefer that only the rosy side be published.

9. *Liudu,* literally "coursing poison," was a standard and politically approved term for the Gang of Four's legacy in 1979.

10. The mastermind of massive embezzlement in "People or Monsters?"

11. "Harbinger of Spring" ("Baochun hua") by Cui Dezhi appears in *Drama* (*Juben*) no. 4 (1979). Set in a factory shortly after the fall of the Gang of Four, it explores a controversy over whether an outstanding employee can be named a "model worker" despite her bad, i.e., bourgeois, class background. "Power Versus Law" ("Quan yu fa") by Xing Yixun appears in *Drama* (*Juben*) no. 10 (1979), and is translated in *Chinese Literature* (Beijing), June 1980. The play criticizes officials who abuse power for selfish purposes.

12. Hua Guofeng (b. 1921) was Chairman of the Communist Party of China from October 24, 1976, until June 29, 1981.

13. These four sentences were omitted from all versions of the speech published in China. They drew unusual applause from their live audience in 1979, however, so we have restored them here.

14. "The Four Modernizations" is a program to modernize industry, agriculture, national defense, and science and technology by the year 2000. First enunciated by Zhou Enlai at the Fourth People's Congress (January 13–17, 1975), the plan became the dominant policy of the Deng Xiaoping regime in the late 1970s.

PART TWO

REPORTAGE

People or Monsters?

Translated by James V. Feinerman

"Reportage" (*baogaowenxue*) is a modern Chinese genre that falls
between literary art and news report. Good reportage differs from
ordinary news reporting in several ways: it is longer and more
carefully written, and while it may begin from an event in the
news, its author seeks to uncover aspects of the social background
that are more basic and enduring than the news event itself.

"People or Monsters?" is reportage and cannot be properly ap-
preciated unless viewed that way. The story of Wang Shouxin's
massive corruption in Bin County, Heilongjiang Province, was
widely known in China before Liu Binyan ever went there to do
his investigation. Hence he does not bother, for example, to introduce his characters in ways that are conventional for Chinese fiction. His contribution—and it is a formidable one, given the barriers and risks involved—was patiently to gather and check facts,
and then to piece them together into a single mosaic whose unity
lies not only in the logical coherence of the whole, but also in the
steady moral presence of the author. He could easily have treated
Wang Shouxin as a scapegoat, as so many others were treating the

Gang of Four; instead, he has coolly analyzed the basic social conditions that had allowed her corruption to grow. When these conditions were documented and published, readers everywhere in China recognized them, to a greater or lesser degree, in their own environments. It is this fact that made "People or Monsters?" so widely popular, and also this fact that brought the wrath of certain political critics upon Liu Binyan. The reaction in Heilongjiang Province, where some of the characters in "People or Monsters?" were still in power, was particularly intense. Some even charged that Liu Binyan had written the piece in order to make a fortune by selling it to Americans.[1]

We must not overlook the importance to contemporary Chinese writers and readers of the simple truth-stating function of literature. To do so can lead us toward literary judgments of a piece like "People or Monsters?" that are beside the point. For example, when Liu Binyan documents corruption at some length and does not cover the fact that the Communist Party itself is complexly involved in it, he sometimes appears to condescend to his readers with brusque "authorial intrusions," such as the famous line "The Communist Party regulated everything, but would not regulate the Communist Party." But it is wrong to say that readers are here receiving a simple-minded summary, or that the author arrogantly supposes that they need one; the point for readers—which was exhilarating—was that here, finally, in print, with the prestige of publication in People's Literature and the moral authority of a writer who was famous for his conscience and his courage, was a statement that many had had in mind but never dared, save in the most secure confidence, to utter. Writers like Liu Binyan know and respect their readers' feelings. What they are doing by putting their punch lines in black and white is the very opposite of condescension.

In October 1979, Liu Binyan spoke out in defense of the student literary journal Our Generation just before this "unofficial publication" was shut down by the authorities. In January 1980, Liu published "Warning," which was subsequently declared to betray "a lack of faith in Party central." Under increasing pressure, Liu wrote a letter to the Central Propaganda Department in spring 1980, in which he set the record straight on some rumors about him, but also apologized to the Party. "I've always had the problem of being insufficiently serious," he wrote, "and I have said some inappropriate things. I have also allowed my biases to emerge. . . ."[2] In the months following delivery of this letter the political pressure on Liu Binyan seems to have abated; certainly it was much lower by fall of 1982, when Liu was given permission, after earlier denials, to accept a long-standing invitation to the International Writers' Workshop at the University of Iowa. —ED.

The courtyard of the Party Committee of Bin County had long been the center of attention for the people of the entire county. During the ten years following land reform, people constantly came and went, as casually as if they were dropping in on their relatives. Whatever problem or circumstance brought you to the town market, or somewhere else in town, you could always go to the county hall to pass the time for a while, chatting with the cadres who were in charge of that year's work teams in your village. After a time, however, the courtyard walls seemed to grow slowly taller and thicker, so that when commoners passed by, or popped in for a look, they felt somewhat afraid, somewhat awed by the mysteriousness within. By the early 1960s, when people who hurried past the courtyard's main gate could smell enticing odors of meat, cooking oil, and steamed bread, they felt that something wasn't quite right. Their mouths would contort into bitter smiles. Being an official isn't bad at all, they would think to themselves.

In November 1964, a crowd of people gathered at the gate of the courtyard, where a jeep had just driven in. The people had heard that a new Party secretary was coming, and they wanted to see for themselves what kind of person he would be. Their intense curiosity was mixed with eager anticipation, and not a little worry, too: the present County Party Committee had run through three secretaries already—would the new one be able to make it?

From the moment he arrived, Tian Fengshan, a tall, ruddy-cheeked outlander, became the object of everyone's attention. Before long people began to say, "*His* Communist Party and theirs are quite different."

At that time, Bin County in Heilongjiang Province had just begun recovering from the three years of economic hardship.[3] The people had paid a great price for these years, and there were quite a few problems that now required the serious consideration and reappraisal of the Party Committee. Yet at the meetings of the Standing Committee of the County Party Committee, and at the study classes for Party members at Two Dragon Mountain, all the talk was about women.

Tian Fengshan was taking over from a rotten bunch of leaders. While the people were living off tree bark and leaves, making food from a "flour" of crumbled corncobs and cornstalks, the children of the county Party secretary were amusing themselves by tossing meat-filled dumplings made with fine white flour at dogs in the street. Peasants, carrying small packs of dried grain with them, would trek more than thirty miles to present petitions to the County Party Committee, only to be met with icy stares. This is why people seldom approached the County Party Committee any more; those with problems went straight to the provincial capital at Harbin. And so it came about that the county Party secretary and members of the Standing Committee had even more time to relax in their armchairs and discuss their favorite topic.

Tian Fengshan began personally receiving petitions from the masses and he personally took care of ten important unjust cases that had dragged on for many years. People would begin arriving at his door before he had even got out of bed. He would chew on dried grain as he listened to their complaints. He also went around to all the restaurants and stores in the county seat checking the quality of their goods and services. He rescinded the title "Advanced Enterprise" that had been given regularly each year to the food products factory. "True, you earn tens of thousands of dollars[4] each year," he told them, "and true, you save tens of thousands of pounds of rice, oil and sugar. But you do this by cheating the common people—what kind of 'advanced enterprise' is that?" Having inquired into housing conditions, he lowered rents. He brought cadres to see the more backward production brigades, and immediately the poorer brigades began to change for the better.

But history allotted him a mere two years! In November 1966, Red Guards stormed the courtyard of the County Party Committee. Within two hours the man who had been honored by the people of Bin County as "Honest Magistrate Tian" retired forever from the stage of Bin County's history.

As the lonely, looming figure of Tian Fengshan fell into obscurity, a new star began to rise in the Bin County seat. This fellow was thin and small and quite ordinary in appearance; but because of his military rank he quickly became all-powerful, a great figure who held sway over the five hundred thousand people in Bin County. Even today, thirteen years later, the political achievements of this leftist Commissar Yang are felt in the daily lives of the people of Bin County; people often think about him and discuss him, always sharply contrasting him with their fond memories of Tian Fengshan.

The first impressions Commissar Yang left with people were of his quacking voice and his inflammatory public speeches. Yet while people were still sorting out these first impressions, one thing had already aroused everybody's interest. Whenever Commissar Yang's jeep drove by on the dirt road from the county seat, raising a cloud of dust, people felt puzzled: "Why was Commissar Yang running around with that woman?"

The woman with Commissar Yang in the car was shortly to become an important figure in Bin County and would, thirteen years later, shock the entire country. She was Wang Shouxin.

Enter "Leftist" Wang Shouxin

On the eve of the storm, things were just a little too quiet at the tiny Bin County Coal Company. Party Branch Secretary Bai Kun and Manager Teng Zhixin, both from poor peasant backgrounds, had been keeping this little enterprise of a few dozen workers in apple-pie order. The spirit of the time was to learn from the heroic soldier Lei Feng; cadres were honest and labored for the public good. Yet peering back through the murky clouds of the past thirteen years, it probably cannot be said that there were no problems at the coal company. For example, Zhou Lu, the person who had been nominated by the Party to succeed the Party branch secretary that year (we here pass over the question of whether it was right to designate this person in advance, since Party secretaries are supposed to be elected), later became an accomplice in Wang Shouxin's massive corruption scheme. By contrast, Liu Changchun, one who was reckoned at that time to be ideologically backward, later fought tirelessly against Wang Shouxin, and never did yield to her.

Wang Shouxin began as the company's cashier. She was full of energy, but unfortunately all of it was directed outside the company. One moment she would be sitting there and the next— whee!—she had disappeared. She was always first to find out who had been fighting with whom in public, which couple was headed for divorce, or what new goods had just arrived at the department store. She always took it upon herself to spread around whatever she could learn, and her old-biddy gossiping often set her comrades against one another.

When the great billows of the Cultural Revolution rolled along, they stimulated God knows which ones of Wang Shouxin's animal desires, but in any case brought out in her political urges that had lain dormant for many years. At first she tried to establish herself in commercial circles, but no one would have her. She tried the students, but had no luck there either. She finally got some support when she reached Commissar Yang of the Munitions Ministry; then she returned to the coal company and tried to build an organization. When no one would cooperate, she went after Zhang Feng, who was a former bandit. "Let's team up," she said. "Let's bash them to smithereens! We'll call ourselves the 'Smash-the-Black-Nest Combat Force'!"

She also drew aside the driver Zhou Lu, a Party member, and prodded him gently in the ribs with her elbow. "You've been oppressed, too," she wheedled, eyebrows prancing and eyeballs dancing. "Why don't you seize the time and rebel?"

This person Zhou Lu was, unfortunately, afraid of his own shadow, despite his huge frame. He was afraid that rebellion could lead to misfortune. Yet if he didn't rebel, but just watched as Wang Shouxin became the trusted lackey of Commissar Yang, he feared even worse consequences. He thought long and hard, and finally decided that the old bunch of officeholders like Bai Kun would never return. Bucking up his courage, he climbed aboard Wang Shouxin's bandwagon. Wang had often taunted him: "Marry a hawk and eat meat; marry a duck and eat chickenshit." Zhou Lu finally made up his mind that he had to have meat.

The first person obstructing Wang Shouxin's way was Liu Changchun. This man had been a handicraft worker, a weaver; now he was the planner and accountant for the coal company. His dependents included five of his siblings in addition to his wife and children, and he could hardly stretch his salary to support all of them. After a long day's work, when others were going home to relax or going out to amuse themselves, Liu Changchun had to moonlight. He made use of his weaving skill by mending socks, and he sometimes sold bean sprouts in the market. He would earn scarcely a couple of dimes for one night's work. He tried occasionally to raise a piglet that he would buy at the market; but he didn't know how to feed piglets and could even end up losing money when he sold them. In sum, he refused to join in all the framing and the fawning, the stealing and the sneaking. He just carried on, repeatedly managing to muster energy from his thin and withered frame, never bemoaning his sorry lot. He wouldn't curse the fates for not favoring him, or turn into a sourpuss; and he seemed always able to keep his spirits up.

Probably because of his suffering as a child, or perhaps because of the obstinate disposition that is typical in craftsmen, Liu Changchun would not bow and scrape or put up with scurrilous talk. He would stick his neck out, glare with a pair of eyes that took no account of the reaction of the person glared at, and say things that offended people. Moreover, in order to take care of his family, he had to spend time every day on his "private plot," and this, in the eyes of the Party leadership, removed him even further from favor.

Wang Shouxin's "Smash-the-Black-Nest Combat Force" challenged Liu Changchun's "Red Rebel Corps" to a debate.

Liu Changchun could not conceive of Wang Shouxin as a serious adversary. But he was viewing her only as an individual and failed to see the influence that she had already accumulated. At the outset he had committed the mistake of underestimating his enemy.

At the public debate that followed, a short, thin fellow took the platform. Hands behind his back, he squared his shoulders and puffed up his chest. At first Liu Changchun was dismayed, thinking him to be some leader from Harbin. But when he looked more closely he burst out laughing: "It's only *that* little bastard. He's been the rebel leader only three days, and he's already trying to act the part."

The man was Wen Feng, director of the "United Program to Defend Mao Zedong Thought." He was coming out in support of Wang Shouxin, and he didn't have to say very much. It was enough that he flap his lips a few times, using his deep voice and clear enunciation to show off for a moment his long-dormant ability as a public speaker. Most important was the slogan that he tacked on at the end to intimidate everyone. "Follow Commissar Yang closely," he said. "Resolutely make revolution; sweep away all ghosts and monsters!"

Commissar Yang was standing next to Wen Feng and Wang Shouxin. One's attitude toward Yang had become the new acid test that separated revolutionary from counterrevolutionary.

Up on stage, Wang Shouxin was wearing her shiny black hair cut short and pulled back behind her ears. Although she had been wearing less makeup since her decision to become a rebel, her fair-skinned face appeared lively and pretty, making her look younger than her forty-five years.

Commissar Yang had specially deputed an officer of his to take charge of the debate. The deputy's word was law on every question. "Liu Changchun," he pronounced, "your Red Rebel Corps has allowed the powerholders to get away with things: you let them stress production and suppress revolution. You still go to them to 'study the problems of production.' Where do you show the slightest bit of rebel spirit? Your group is rightist! Your whole direction is wrong! You are ordered to disband beginning today!"

Liu Changchun was furious. This was absurd! Convicted before he even had a chance to say anything! Liu had always liked to read newspapers and think for himself. He was proud of his ability to understand policies and to address them. Now he scrambled onto the platform clutching the "Sixteen Points" and the "latest directives"; clearing his throat and assuming a bold stance, he was all set to tie into them. He was too naïve to realize that the scriptures he possessed were already out-of-date. He was met by a deafening uproar of slogans; then he was jostled, and there was punching and kicking as well. This special modern form of "debate" used in our ancient, civilized country is most efficient. Within two minutes Wang Shouxin's political enemy had been "refuted" beyond any hope of recovery.

Any number of struggle sessions were held, but Liu Changchun refused to bow his head. Once when his head was physically pressed down, he still laughed and looked around the room, as if seeking someone to share his joke or hear his sarcastic comment. Zhou Lu, who was in charge of this session, shouted himself hoarse, only to find Liu Changchun still fighting to raise his head and answer back. "Hey, Zhou Lu, you really are a goddamn bumpkin! Why do you have to shout your pisser voicebox dry?" This comment put Zhou Lu on the spot, and greatly amused all who heard it.

The day after the debate, when Wang Shouxin had seen there was no one around but the two of them, she stole up to Liu Changchun and whispered into his ear: "Let's work together, Changchun. I am not very literate, and I need you as my military adviser. I'll be in charge, and you can be number two . . ."

Liu Changchun's eyes widened. "You can knock that off right now!" he replied in a voice as hard as nails. "I'd rather be the stable boy of a gentleman than the ancestor of a bastard! You'll get yours—just wait!"

That was precisely his style—refusing to give in even when he was butting his head against a stone wall. Most other people had already gone over to Wang Shouxin, and her influence was growing greater and greater. Meanwhile the Red Rebel Corps was falling apart. Yet Liu Changchun tried to rally the spirits of those in his faction who had still not fought back. "Don't worry," he said, "if you land in jail I'll bring you your meals."

He never imagined that, within a few days, he himself would be taken off to jail in handcuffs, charged as an "anti-Army" active counterrevolutionary.

The World Turned Upside Down

In poor and backward areas the fragrance of the flower of political power has its greatest allure. Were this not so, the "rebel" leader

Wen Feng could never have been up front shouting, "Follow Commissar Yang closely," nor could he ever have benefited from doing so. To be perfectly fair, when Commissar Yang first heard the slogan he was taken aback and asked someone around him, "What's he saying?" The person who was asked had been clever enough to reply, "Weren't you sent here from Chairman Mao's headquarters? Of course we must follow you closely!" Commissar Yang then assented. "Yes, yes," he said, nodding his head. "You should follow me closely."

Close behind "following closely" came loving and adoring. One day when he came to the office, Commissar Yang found he had left his keys at home; without saying a word, his female secretary immediately hopped onto a bus to fetch the keys. Separately and simultaneously, his driver showed up at his home too. Each was hiding his motives from the other in order to be the one to return the keys. After arguing each other to a standstill, they finally agreed to bring them to the commissar together and share the praise.

In brief, the force of Commissar Yang's prestige in Bin County was the same as the force of the potential of bullets to kill people. When Wang Shouxin accompanied Commissar Yang on an inspection tour of a commune late one night and informed the commune cadres that "Commissar Yang's favorite dish is boiled meat with pickled cabbage and blood sausage, but the meat must be lean," it was obvious that she was savoring the taste of real power, and that she liked this taste at least as much as that of the famous Manchurian dish.

One day in August 1968, Commissar Yang strode briskly and boldly into the planning office of the Bin County Commercial Revolutionary Committee. He looked around the room at the committee members, all of whom had risen out of respect. Then, in his customarily firm voice, he shocked everyone by saying, "Wang Shouxin must be allowed to join you on this committee."

The committee members all looked at one another without a word. At last one of them courageously asked, in a low voice, "If she joined, what could she contribute?" What he meant was that she couldn't read a character the size of the big dipper. Then there was her reputation . . . for sleeping around.

Commissar Yang was pacing around the office, as though lost in thought. When he heard this objection he stopped short and glared fiercely at the officials before him. He knit his brows and then spoke irritably, in words as clear and immutable as boldface type: "The question is not whether she should join, but whether she should be the vice-chair!"

This was an order, and as such as it was adopted immediately and unanimously by the committee, who did not bother to wait for a referendum among the commercial workers of Bin County. For those days, this was normal. If it hadn't been, why would Commissar Yang have had to knit his brows? That scowl admits several interpretations: "You hopeless boneheads!" or "What's this? You people are anti-Army?" or "Maybe you didn't mean it when you all shouted 'Follow closely'!"

Actually Commissar Yang had worries of his own. Wang Shouxin had been begging him for a position since 1967, insisting that she be made head of the Women's Congress. This puzzled the highest authorities. She wasn't even a Party Committee member, so how could she be the head? Impossible. Wang Shouxin was greatly put out. She had "rebelled"; she had been running around with Commissar Yang; she had, for the first time in her life, come to enjoy the taste of power in this society of ours. So many people obeying a single voice, playing up to you, flattering you! What power! What fame! How much more honorable this was than her former ideal—to be the wife of a collaborationist policeman or a landlord.

But now she had become deeply disappointed, and went around complaining about Commissar Yang behind his back. "Commissar Yang, my eye! He's less than a prick hair! And those bitches at the Women's Congress are all sluts!"

After that Commissar Yang again ordered the Commercial Revolutionary Committee to "receive" Wang Shouxin into the Party. A number of members opposed her; even the Commercial Committee chairman, Zhao Yu, who had resolutely opposed and smashed Tian Fengshan (in those days, the degree to which one opposed Tian Fengshan separated "revolutionary" from "nonrevolutionary" and "counterrevolutionary"), found it hard to "follow Commissar Yang closely." Hence the entire committee bore the brunt of the commissar's wrath: "Still needs training? Will you kindly tell me in what way she needs training? Isn't the Great Cultural Revolution the test of a person? As far as I can see, she's the only person in Bin County fit to enter the Party!"

A month later, in an address to the Workers' Congress, Commissar Yang told more than five hundred people that "some people still have misgivings about the rebels. They find minor faults, but fail to see the big picture. Here are all these rebels and no one seeks to cultivate them. Instead, you cultivate easy-going types for entrance to the Party." In the end, despite the opposition of 70 percent of the Party members, Wang Shouxin joined the Party as a member "specially endorsed" by Commissar Yang.

This happened in September of 1969. In the very same month, a fine Party member named Zhang Zhixin was arrested in Liaoning Province by a dictatorship organ of the Communist Party.[5] One had joined and one had been kicked out. Tian Fengshan had fallen and Commissar Yang had risen. Were these merely insignificant accidents in their implications for communist organization in China?

Ten years had to pass before anyone could even raise questions about this massive inversion of justice.

Wonderful Exchange

On the day that Wang Shouxin first took over as manager and Party secretary of the coal company (which was later called the fuel company), some workers were digging trenches for oil pipes. Some members of the county work team were playing chess in the office. When she saw this Wang Shouxin flared up. "Well I'll be damned," she yelled. "You play chess while others work. What kind of work team is this?"

Zhou Lu, now the assistant manager, was shocked; Wang Shouxin had never yelled at anyone like that before. What he didn't realize was that someone at that very moment was observing him, and that this person was also shocked by certain changes. The observer was the old Party secretary at the coal company, Bai Kun, and there was something he couldn't figure out: this guy Zhou Lu had never been very good at his job—once when he was driving a car he had lost a wheel and didn't even notice it. That I can forgive, mused Bai Kun, but—though I always thought highly of his character and even felt I could train him to take over for me— suddenly he appears to have changed entirely. He fawns over Wang Shouxin like crazy, patting the woman's ass whenever she speaks. It must have been the same, all this flattering and fawning, when he worked for me. But because it made me feel comfortable, I always felt it was a virtue. How could I have failed to see through him all these years?

There were many things that had not been seen through. Just look at Wang Shouxin—she too had seemed to change completely. Formerly she had been lazy and useless, but now she was the first one on the job and the last to leave. Even her clothing changed drastically—she wore a cotton jacket and rubber shoes. All day long she would be running in and out of the office, busy as a bee, laboring along with the workers who were unloading coal or cleaning up.

Over the years Wang Shouxin had come to know this tiny coal company thoroughly, and to become thoroughly bored with it. Yet once she became boss, all that changed; everything now seemed to take on a strange radiance. Jet-black coal piles, glistening lumps of coal—how delightful! No longer was she bored with those who were busy unloading the coal, weighing it or collecting payment for it. Everything now belonged to her, and everybody obeyed Wang Shouxin's orders.

Of course Wang Shouxin supposed that she was "serving the people." But "the people" were various: they differed in quality and rank. The first reform she carried out was to sell coal according to a person's position. She arranged to have the top-grade coal picked out and packed in waterproof straw bags for delivery by truck directly to the doors of the county Party secretary and the members of the Standing Committee. This was coal that caught fire quickly and burned well—just right for cooking dumplings at New Year's. And payment? "What's the rush? We'll discuss it later . . ."

As for the people's armed forces, no question about it—nothing was nearer and dearer to Wang Shouxin's heart than the brown padded coats of the military. Soldiers were on the top rung of her class ladder. Right below them came the Organization Department. These people were sent the best grade of coal, delivered in special trucks, and were treated to meals to boot. Next in line were those concerned with personnel, finance, and labor.

Wang Shouxin was a warmly sentimental woman with clearly defined likes and dislikes. Her tens of thousands of tons of coal and her nine trucks were the brush and ink that she used every day to compose her lyric poems.

The distilleries and provisions factories produced the sweet, enticing smells of famous liquors, pastries, and candies. Wang Shouxin was not a glutton; no, what she sought from these sweet smells was only the smiling faces of provincial-, prefectural-, and county-level "connections." For this reason, such factories could rely on a never-ending supply of fine-quality coal at low prices. Wang Shouxin couldn't care less about the bearings factory or the porcelain factories. These produced nothing but cold, hard little knick-knacks. Who would ever want gifts like that? So these factories got low-grade coal, with prices jacked up at that. What if a factory was losing money? Going bankrupt? What if the coal could not burn hot enough to heat large vats? None of *that* had anything to do with the great Wang Shouxin!

One year in January the county hospital ran out of coal. A man was sent to seek out Manager Wang. After looking over his letter of introduction, Wang Shouxin raised her eyebrows and questioned the man. "How come your top man didn't come?"

"He's busy, he didn't have time . . ."

"A man named Gao Dianyou from your hospital has informed against my son. No coal for you!"

The man begged and pleaded, but Wang Shouxin wouldn't give an inch. "Your Gao Dianyou accused my son of adultery," she continued. "The County Party Committee has been investigating for two months already, and my son is still the vice-director of the Xinli Commune, isn't he? Don't think you can slip one past Old Lady Wang! This exposé of my son is the work of Fang Yongjiu of Xinli Commune and was prepared by Director Rong of the Commune's Health Department. Gao Dianyou is just their mouthpiece!"

When word got back to Gao Dianyou, he immediately wrote a letter to the County Party Committee: "There is obviously something fishy going on here. How could Wang Shouxin know so much about my expose of Liu Zhimin? I request the County Committee to give this matter their closest attention and to take measures to assure my physical safety."

This was not the first time, nor would it be the last, that an accusation against Wang Shouxin fell into the hands of Wang Shouxin. It was also not the first or last time that Wang Shouxin brazenly used the coal she controlled as a weapon for revenge.

Trucks were also important instruments in Wang Shouxin's system of rewards and revenge. Every fall people in Bin County had to go up to the mountains for firewood and down to the villages for vegetables in order to get through the winter. And in a county seat with a population of thirty thousand, trucks were hard to come by. Yet this was an ordeal every family had to undergo every year.

Inspector Yang Qing of the County Inspectorate had that year asked a driver to go to the mountains for firewood. His family prepared a complete banquet for the returning driver—no mean feat on a salary of about thirty dollars a month. When it was almost dark, they could hear the truck returning, and the whole family rushed out for a look. The truck had come back empty! The driver's face revealed his displeasure. "Roads were blocked," he said, and drove his truck back home. How would this family get through the winter? They were on the verge of tears. Husband and wife looked helplessly at the banquet spread, which was getting colder and colder.

Then in their hour of despair, who was it that lent them a helping hand?—Old Lady Wang. How could the whole family not be grateful?

Wang Shouxin was deeply concerned about the difficulties of people in Bin County. The county cadres' wages hadn't risen for over ten years, and every family felt the pinch. Many had borrowed anywhere from several hundred to nearly a thousand dollars of public funds. In 1975 the County Committee, on instructions from above, insisted on a deadline for the return of the public funds. Enter Wang Shouxin, the "goddess of wealth." She always carried with her a passbook for an unregistered bank account, and she could produce ready cash just by reaching into the drawer of her office desk.

People she could use didn't even have to open their mouths; Wang Shouxin would approach *them:* "Having problems? Short of cash?" The rebel leader Wen Feng and his pals, as well as the leaders of many important offices, all "borrowed" public funds that Wang Shouxin had appropriated without the niceties of book-keeping, and then used that money to repay their own debts to the public. A new relationship arose from this transfer of the proletarian state's money: first, Wang Shouxin, rather than the state, assumed the creditor's role; second, Wang Shouxin's money did not necessarily have to be returned. In fact, she preferred that it not be returned, because then people would owe her their loyalty and future favors. But even if the money was returned, the debts of favor would remain. The favorite method of repaying these obligations was for the debtor to use his own power for Wang Shouxin's convenience. This caused the debtor no material loss, and for Wang Shouxin it was more than she could buy for a thousand pieces of gold. So why not do it this way, since it had such benefits for both sides?

At bottom, all this was an exchange of goods that was effected by trading off power. One form of this barter involved the direct handling of goods. For example, Wang Shouxin raised a large number of pigs, pork being another item in her power brokering. But where could she get fodder for the pigs? Just seek out the vice-director of the Grain Bureau, of course! More than five tons of corn, bran, soybeans, and husks were sent right over. Later on, Wang Shouxin needed flour, rice, and soybean oil for her partying and gift giving. No problem! Just call the vice-director again! And thus it happened that, in the short span of one year, another five tons of rice, flour, and soybean oil passed into her hands. In return, the vice-director could "borrow" money or bricks from Wang Shouxin, or "buy" complete cartloads of coal on credit. Payment was never required, and in fact no payment was ever made.

In this county, the organs of the "dictatorship of the proletariat" served Wang Shouxin's "socialist" enterprises extremely well. Wang Shouxin would dispatch carts loaded with meat, fish, grain, oil, or vegetables to Harbin, in violation of county regulations. When this happened, the chief of the Section for Industry and Commerce, who was also second-in-command of the "rebels," would give special approval under his own signature. From 1973 on, her vehicles could come and go unhindered. In return, this fellow received a "loan" of four hundred dollars plus a variety of presents. On one occasion Wang Shouxin had to "safeguard" some cash that properly belonged to the central government. She needed it for her private dealings and building, so she couldn't put it in a bank account; that was when the deputy chief of the Finance Section, another of her "rebel" friends, opened account number 83001. To it she diverted hundreds of thousands of dollars, which were always at her disposal in a perfectly legal and protected place. To repay this man, Wang Shouxin arranged to have his son-in-law transferred from the temporary labor force to a permanent job. Then she admitted his son to the "Camp for Educated Youths" she had set up and, after falsifying his credentials, arranged his admission to a university.

For years this trading of influence went on between Wang Shouxin and dozens of officials—perhaps a hundred—on the County Party Committee, County Revolutionary Committee, and at the district and even the provincial levels. Many of these people used their status as the capital for their trade. Once Wang Shouxin, in order to set up a "nonstaple foodstuffs base," needed to take over more than thirty-three acres of good land that belonged to the Pine River Brigade of the Raven River Commune. This infuriated the commune members and local cadres. The head of the County Agricultural Office, who lacked the power to approve this deal, arranged a meal where he brought Wang Shouxin together with the leaders of the commune, the brigade, and the production teams that were involved. This gave the impression that the County Revolutionary Committee supported the discussions and acquiesced in the illegal dealings. Thus a huge tract of arable land changed hands.

This kind of "socialist" exchange does indeed demonstrate great "superiority" over capitalist exchange; neither party has to have any capital of his own, there is no need to put up private possessions as collateral, and no one needs to run any risk of loss or bankruptcy. Everybody gets what he wants.

One thing was completely clear, however. Not a single one of these exchanges could have been made without a departure from

Party policy, or without either causing direct loss of socialist public property or breaking Party regulations and national laws. In some cases all of these violations occurred. Eventually, this had to harm the socialist system and discredit the Party's leadership. Through the incessant bartering, Party and government cadres slowly degenerated into parasitical insects that fed off the people's productivity and the socialist system. The relationship between the Party and the masses deterioriated greatly.

How Can a Single Hand Clap?

Language is a strange thing. When Commissar Yang pointed to Wang Shouxin as having a "completely red family," he had meant to praise her. Yet, in the mouths of the common people, the same phrase—"completely red family"—was said as a curse. When they went down the list of Wang Shouxin's family and asked how each had entered the Party or risen to official positions, they rejected all of these relatives one by one.

Her eldest son, Liu Zhimin, was a lazy oaf who could think only of women. He almost always looked half-drunk. What could possibly have qualified him to become a member of the Chinese Communist Party? And how did he become vice-director of Xinli Commune? When he tried to rape a girl, why was it that he was treated with such leniency, and even assigned thereafter to the County Committee "to make policy"? Wang Shouxin's second son entered the Party from a cadre school that had only a temporary branch, one without the power to recruit Party members. And what about her youngest, that totally unqualified young dandy who got appointed assistant manager of the photography studio? Even stranger was Wang Shouxin's younger sister, who, shortly after being expelled from the Communist Youth League, managed to enter the Party!

Since the people loved the Party, they were of course going to be upset when they saw these shady characters sneak into it! From 1972 onwards, any time a political campaign came along, people would flock to the Party Committee to put up big-character posters with their questions about Wang Shouxin and her "completely red family."

Yet the Party organization of Bin County could not be re-formed until there was a change in the Party leadership. The op-portunity for this came in 1970. Early in the year, because of his success in "supporting the Left," Commissar Yang was appointed head of the security task force for all of Heilongjiang Province. He was succeeded as Bin County Party secretary by an old cadre named Zhang Xiangling. Zhang was a solidly built, middle-aged man, with a pair of big, thick-soled feet. In 1945 he had *walked* all the way from Yan'an to Baiquan County in Heilongjiang. Now he was preparing to make use of his big feet again to take the measure of Bin County. Despite a severe stomach ailment, he could cover as many as thirty-five miles in one day.

But he quickly discovered one place where he could hardly take a single step, and that was inside the courtyard of the Party Com-mittee. For Commissar Yang, even after receiving his transfer or-ders, hung on in Bin County for several months; he had reorga-nized administrative power so that each important position at the section level and above was filled by a "rebel" member. Most of the regular cadres of Bin County were still down in the countryside or were under house arrest.

Whenever Zhang Xiangling tried to free one of these cadres, the "Cultural Revolution Group" would inform him that they planned to hold a criticism and struggle session concerning that cadre the next day, and they requested Zhang's attendance. The power of the "Cultural Revolution Group" was much like that of the Beijing group of the same name [headed by Mao Zedong and his wife Jiang Qing]; its deputy leader also happened to be a woman—Wang Shouxin's daughter-in-law.

This woman was in her twenties, not very tall but slender and pretty. Her smile disclosed a pair of comely canines that made her even more attractive. As a typist at the County People's Commit-tee she was fine. But once Commissar Yang appointed this poorly educated, minimally capable woman to be deputy head of the Cultural Revolution Group, she suddenly became another person altogether.

Nothing causes self-delusion quite so readily as power. The very day this woman achieved power, she began—mistakenly—to con-vince herself that she had the education, the moral stature, and the ability that such a position called for. The vanity, narrowness, and jealousy that had lain dormant in the typist's heart were all suddenly awakened. Her lovely eyes now flared with suspicion and hatred, as they followed and searched out her potential enemies. The tears she had shed at the departure of Commissar Yang now changed to enmity for Zhang Xiangling. Whenever a meeting took her to Harbin, she always went to see Commissar Yang, and in this way Bin County remained subject to Yang's will through a kind of remote control.

For a while Zhang Xiangling had only this one power: he could absent himself from criticism and struggle sessions. His situation bore a startling resemblance to the position of Chinese magistrates under the puppet regime of Manchukuo [occupied northeast China, 1932–1945], where real power lay in the hands of the Japanese. Yet unlike those days, when there was only one Japanese deputy magistrate, now there were "Japanese" all over the place. The "rebels" who held the deputy positions in each of the sections had greater power than that of the formal section heads.

In order that readers have no misunderstanding, I must do a little explaining about the "rebels" of Bin County. The Bin County high school students who had been "Red Guards" had long ago been quelled by the "Unified Program to Defend Mao Zedong Thought." The Red Guards' crime had been that they were "anti-Army." Those who took over the power also called themselves "Red Guards" at first, and wore red armbands. But actually they were stubble-bearded cadres, many of them well over forty and old enough to be grandparents. They belonged to the generation of the Red Guards' parents. The important distinction, however, was not that of age. It was primarily that they all had families to feed and were much more interested in economics than the youngsters had been. Second, many of them had "rebelled" because of the frustration of having failed, after many years in officialdom, to enter the Party or to be promoted. These people could think of nothing but their desires for material improvement, political power, and influence.

What worried Zhang Xiangling most was that not only the leadership but the whole Party organization was growing more corrupt daily. One married couple who entered the Party in 1969, right after Wang Shouxin had, were overheard fighting with each other in this fashion: "What're you so uppity about? A few bottles of good liquor were your ticket of admission to the Party!"

"Goddamn it, you're worse than I. You think you could have joined without that pretty face of yours?"

Only by doing his utmost, and at the risk of his own Party membership, was Zhang Xiangling finally able to remove from office a few of the most detested "rebel" leaders. In 1970 there was a resolution to reinvestigate the pack of rascals who had entered the party in 1969. Yet, when he left Bin County in 1972, Zhang had to admit that he had failed to change the balance of political power in Bin County. Not long thereafter, those he had removed from power came back; his resolution to purge bad elements from the Party was never put into effect.

Zhang Xiangling left behind several newly constructed factories in Bin County. He could hardly have imagined that these factories would lose money year after year and would make little contribution to the central government treasury, but would help line the pockets of grafters, thieves, and powerholders.

"A Heroine of Her Times"

Many differing accounts of Wang Shouxin's character circulated among the people of Bin County. "Old Lady Wang is straightforward; she doesn't hold anything back." "Wang Shouxin is the world's greatest phony, and she's also a bare-faced liar." "Old Lady Wang is good hearted, warm, and concerned about people." "Wang Shouxin is vicious and hounds people to death."

All these descriptions were true. She could be straightforward one moment and phony the next. Two months earlier her heart might have bled for you, but two months later she'd be hounding you. All of this was not incompatible. It may seem so, but we shall gradually see how it all fit together.

When she found a worker crouching in the office, furtively eating some sugar, she set upon him and boxed his ears. Yet a moment later she came back saying, "Why are you making a hog of yourself? Don't you have any sugar at home? Take this bag with you and get going!" Her manner had changed completely within a few minutes, but this was not being phony. What she sought was compliance, together with a clear display of her power. Her heart-felt concern and scolding attacks were not in the least inconsistent.

Wang Shouxin had not had an easy life. Her father had been a horse trader, with no property to fall back upon and no regular job. The powerful could cheat and oppress him; yet honest people would also shy away from him. Wang Shouxin grew up with a fear of the Japanese, the collaborationist police, and everyone who owned wealth or land. Yet using her womanhood, which included a certain measure of good looks but excluded a sense of shame, she developed the weapons she needed for self-protection and for attack. Her environment taught her not to be shy, and she learned how to develop contacts with people whose social status was much higher than hers. She was obliged to adjust to hardship and could endure even inhuman living conditions. She became familiar with the lives of people at the lowest stratum of society. This was all very useful to her in the 1970s, when her life changed drastically.

After 1970, Bin County suddenly began to build all sorts of factories; the use of coal increased dramatically, while coal production remained the same. This phenomenon set the stage for Wang Shouxin to display her talents.

First she had to go to the appropriate prefectural and provincial offices to fight for the necessary allocations of coal and transportation facilities. No matter how high the official, she had a way of putting him at ease. She could summon every charm that a woman of fifty could muster without being disgusting. "Ahem, I say, Secretary Wang (or Manager Gao, or Secretary-General Nie, or whatever), we common folk in Bin County are in quite a fix. We have to queue for coal and can only buy small baskets of it. If you don't increase our allotment, we might have to burn our own legs . . ."

She'd cajole you, pester you, flatter you no end. One minute she'd laugh, the next she'd cry—all entirely in good faith. Still no answer? Fine, she had yet another trick: she'd undo her pants and give you a look at the scar on her abdomen, making it clear that Old Lady Wang was braving illness to come fight for the people's coal. Now how about it? Hadn't you better figure out a way to get her to pull up her pants? Worried, angry, you'd want to get rid of her as quickly as possible. But then you would think again—she *had* come for the public good, after all. And you had to hand it to her: her local flavor, her common touch, her ingenuousness (pants half-down, etc.), and her intimate manner did have a certain charm for men her age.

"OK, I'll approve two thousand tons for you." As long as coal was for sale, it was all the same whether it went to Bin County or to Hulan. Old Lady Wang would leave overjoyed.

A few days later, someone would show up at the same official's office carrying a few things: ten pounds of fish, twenty pounds of pork, several dozen eggs, and a few quarts of soybean oil. At first the official would have no idea where they came from. But as the saying goes, show me the official who flogs gift-givers. What's more, these were all things that were hard to come by at any price. "How much a pound? How much should I pay altogether?" The bearer would only laugh—"What's your hurry? We'll take care of it later"—and leave.

At first all these things had to be purchased, and at high prices. A pound of fish cost over a dollar. But Wang Shouxin had vision. Buy it! She even had her own underground cold-storage cellar specially built, so that she could store things and have them at her disposal. Eventually things came by means of barter: a commune or a production brigade that made bricks would be given coal and, in exchange, would give her hogs, each one of which had to be at least 220 pounds with thin skin and lots of meat. As the scope of Wang Shouxin's exchanges widened, and as her needs increased, she had to figure out a way of increasing her sources of goods while lowering their cost. So she set up fishing teams of four men to a net, then constructed a hog farm, and then a "nonstaple food-stuffs base" that occupied the land of an entire production team and allowed her to produce fruits and vegetables for her private use. But Old Lady Wang still wasn't satisfied; she finagled a bull-dozer that spent days noisily digging a great hole that she converted to a fish-farming pond.

Wang Shouxin's requirements kept on increasing as the County Party Committee gave her responsibility for buying cement, fertilizer, and tractors. Her responsibilities required ever more contact with higher and higher officials. Other than giving gifts, what means had she to "ignite" these people's "revolutionary zeal"?

Wang Shouxin was a keen observer of the lives of leading cadres both inside and outside the county. She knew their thinking and their needs. "Aside from eating," she mused to herself, "what other problems most worry them? What are they most concerned about?" Then, slapping her thigh, this extremely clever woman cried out, "I've got it! Their sons and daughters! They're always thinking of how to keep them from being sent down to the countryside, how to bring them back to town as soon as possible, how to get them into college or get them a better job!" Since so many places were setting up "camps for educated youths" who had been sent down to the countryside, why couldn't her fuel company set one up in the name of the production brigade? It could be, in effect, a transfer station. With Wang Shouxin's extensive network of connections, it would be no problem at all to get dozens of sons and daughters into college, or into good jobs, or transferred back to the city.

The location she decided upon was the Pine River Brigade of the Raven River Commune. There she had ten or so tile-roofed houses put up, and the scions of leading cadres at the provincial, prefectural, and county levels came in droves. Some didn't bother to come but had their names put down anyway. In either case these children drew a salary of thirty or forty dollars a month. Commissar Yang's daughter, whose name had been entered in this way, never worked a stitch but did get admitted to the Party and was later "transferred" back to Harbin.

While some laughed, others wept.

For example, here is one of the many letters of accusation that were written over a number of years by the peasants of the Pine River Brigade:

> Wang Shouxin and her parasitical ilk have used their influence for years to oppress us; they have forced us to sell, or simply give to them, the most productive land of four of our production teams; they have destroyed as much as 143 acres of our forests. Our production brigade's brick kilns use her coal, so she had us in a stranglehold if we didn't give her the land. She and the others cut

down over ten thousand of the pine trees we had planted with ten years of arduous labor. The twenty-five acres of terraced fields we carved out of the hillsides have been turned into her melon patch. And still they have the arrogance to boast that if they order production teams to be ploughing their fields by 6:00 A.M., even our Party secretary won't dare to miss an hour! The production team had to neglect their own land because they didn't dare to ignore Wang Shouxin's. Her people also sank a well near the terraced fields, and then locked it up, refusing to let the local peasants have any water! Because they've taken our good land and stolen our labor, we've been driven to the point where we get only forty cents a day in pay. They never pay the agricultural production tax, nor any tax whatever on all their income—everything we produce is used for giving gifts to rotten cadres and throwing parties for them.

Yet Wang Shouxin's conscience was clear. All these activities of hers were "for the public good." Why else would every county Party secretary she worked with praise her so effusively? "Old Lady Wang is really great!" they would say. "She's come up with so much coal!" "Old Lady Wang really gets results! Of all the five counties bordering the river, Bin County has shipped the greatest amount of coal!"

But there was one question: her money. Where did it come from?

There were two kinds of coal. Coal produced by the state-run coal mines had a sale price fixed according to the cost of producing it, and was supplied "under the state plan." Coal supplied "outside the state plan" was small-pit coal, and transport and miscellaneous charges were added to its price. From 1972 onward, Wang Shouxin hit upon an extremely simple scheme for making money: take a portion of the state coal and charge small-pit coal prices for it. This would net from three to nearly ten dollars per ton. She made out two sets of invoices: one bearing the original prices and another with transport and miscellaneous charges added. The latter were not entered in the accounts, nor was the extra money ever paid to the state.

Wang Shouxin let only two people in on her great secret. One was her accomplice Ma Zhanqing, director of White Rock Enterprises, which was part of the fuel company. The other was an accountant named Sun Xiyin. Both of them had been brought into the Party by Wang Shouxin. Sun Xiyin came from a family of small businessmen, and the only human relationship he thought possible was essentially that between shopkeeper and shop clerk, or perhaps between a Japanese and a collaborator. It was natural that he now treated Wang Shouxin with the same obsequiousness and loyalty he once gave to his shopkeeper. He was ever grateful to Secretary Wang for bringing him into the Party. He knew her orders were that income from the surcharges on small-pit coal be set aside in a special account and not be paid over to the state; invoices for it were to be destroyed. His own job was fourfold: making up invoices, collecting payment, keeping the books, and distributing coal. Thus, carrying out the secretary's orders came quite naturally to him.

One day, when Wang Shouxin had finished her instructions to him and Sun Xiyin had turned to go, she told him to stop. "Wait a minute. I hear you're going to tie the knot again? Tsk! You're all of fifty years old! Why bother with something like that? Forget it!" This was an order, but Sun Xiyin felt it had been well meant; the secretary was so concerned about him. In point of fact it had been nineteen years since his wife had died, and only after careful consideration had he decided to seek another companion.

What really concerned Wang Shouxin was her secret. There was nothing to be gained in involving another pair of ears and another mouth. Who could tell what kind of person Sun Xiyin had hooked up with? What could she do if this woman turned out to be as loose tongued as herself?

Her Party

Even after justice finally caught up with her, Wang Shouxin was known to have boasted. "Go to Bin County yourselves," she said. "Old Lady Wang was tops at looking after the welfare of the masses!" This was not untrue. At her behest, her staff's coal and food was always delivered right to their homes. And there was always something extra at festival time. At Mid-Autumn Festival everyone got two pounds of moon cakes, but these Wang Shouxin delivered personally so that everyone would believe that Secretary Wang was favoring only him. This made one especially grateful. On a trip to see a doctor in Canton, Wang Shouxin was careful to remember to buy everyone a synthetic-fiber sweater. And the fuel company had built more worker housing than any other enterprise in the Bin County seat.

But Secretary Wang had another method of dealing with people: oral abuse. She could chew someone out so utterly, "to the depths of his soul," that after a few sentences the person would be in tears. Take Zhou Lu, for example—assistant manager, second-in-command, a tall, strapping fellow. Wang Shouxin abused him as if he were her child. She swore at him "as if he were a clove of garlic," as they said in the local dialect, or "as if he were an eggplant." When the staff showed up for work, one look at Zhou Lu's face would let them know if Secretary Wang was in or not. If Zhou Lu was busily going about his business, then Wang Shouxin was not in. If he had a straight face and acted as if he were scared of his own shadow—then Secretary Wang was definitely in. "I have come to this pass," Zhou Lu thought to himself, "because of only one thing—fear. Dealing with her I'm like a piece of bean curd that has fallen into a pile of ashes; you can't brush the ashes off, you can't blow them off—nothing works. My only hope lies in her age. How much longer can that candle of hers burn? Once she's dead I'll be all right."

Despite her tremendous capacity to terrorize, Wang Shouxin still could not rest easy. She always worried about who might be out to get her, and she had an extraordinarily sensitive intelligence network. At one point Zhou Lu, no longer able to put up with Wang Shouxin's temper, decided to resign as assistant manager and go back to driving a car. The next day Wang Shouxin took him to task. "So you want out, do you? If you want out, I'll give you your walking papers right now. Out! Get out right this minute!"

Her intelligence network had, of course, required painstaking cultivation. By crowding some people and getting them transferred out, then wheedling others and getting them transferred in, finally the staff of the fuel company was almost all people in whom Wang Shouxin could have complete faith. She simultaneously set about building a Party organization of foolproof reliability.

When Wang Shouxin discovered someone of acceptable obsequiousness, she'd drag him in and say: "Blind enthusiasm isn't enough; you must coordinate with the organization."

When the Party met to discuss the first person she nominated, some members disagreed with her choice. This made Wang Shouxin blow her stack. "He withstood the test of the Great Cultural Revolution! He's stronger than any of you! Look at you Party members! A bunch of capitalist-roaders and monarchists! Not one of you is worth a damn! If this man isn't fit for the Party, none of you is!"

She got her way. The second person she advanced was Ma Zhanqing. His credentials: "exerts himself to the fullest, shouts slogans all day long, is very good at dispensing coal, is not too self-seeking, watches over public property like a hawk. I think he's all right, fit to be a Party member." Again some people opposed him, and Wang Shouxin's jaw dropped in disbelief. "If everyone in the fuel company were like Ma Zhanqing," she said, "we'd all be a lot better off!" Having spoken, she picked up her tobacco basket and left. This signaled that Ma Zhanqing had been accepted and that the meeting was adjourned.

Wang Shouxin single-handedly recruited eleven Party members. The special qualifications of each one merit careful scrutiny.

A driver: obedient, simple, straightforward. When ferrying Wang Shouxin around to deliver gifts, he continued to be simple and straightforward. Clearly he had some reservations, but he never leaked a word. And never asked any questions. He just stuck to one principle: "Nobody can question Secretary Wang's activities. Do what you like, but that is that."

Another: hard working, honest, obedient, eager to get into the Party. When Wang Shouxin was building a house for her sister, he sawed a publicly owned pine gangplank into six pieces and procured a case of glass that had been cut to proper size. He delivered these by truck to the building site.

A carpenter: hard working, honest, obedient. He took care of all the work that Wang Shouxin needed done on her own house. He was also adept at delivering gifts.

With one exception, the eleven Party members were all "hard working, honest, obedient." Obedient to whom? To Wang Shouxin, of course. According to the logic that says that closely following the secretary is closely following the Party, and that protecting the secretary is protecting the Party, how far wrong were they, actually?

In short, Wang Shouxin had a rear guard in the fuel company upon whom she could depend. And in the County Party Committee and the County Revolutionary Committee, she had thirty-some "rebel" cohorts working for her like bees. From the County Party Standing Committee, and from the Party secretary personally, she had nothing but praise and trust. What more could Wang Shouxin ask? She was entering the prime of her career.

Of course, when she remembered her illicit treasury with its more than forty thousand crisp, new ten-yuan [about $6.70] bills, she became slightly nervous. At these times a certain image would appear in her mind and give her strength. "Ha, come to think of it, what do we little guys matter? Aren't the top cadres in the province always sticking their hands into the till?" She was thinking of the assistant manager of the Provincial Fuel Company, Guo Yucai. She had been going to him since 1971 whenever she needed coal; in return he received quite a lot of chicken, fish, meat, and eggs. Finally she invited him to White Rock Harbor, where she held a banquet especially in his honor. Having drunk and eaten his fill, Guo Yucai lay down on the bed-platform. "Remember those two trucks I got you?" he said. "I'm out of pocket quite a bit on them!" Wang Shouxin caught his drift immediately, wrapped up two hundred dollars, and handed them over to him. A few days later he came back again. "The last time I was in Beijing on business I was short of cash." Another few hundred made their way to him. Over a four-year period Guo Yucai took over thirteen hundred dollars in bribes; in return he assigned Bin County six trucks, a refueling machine, and a large amount of coal.

This man was precisely the type for Wang Shouxin. What she feared most was that other Communist Party members would prove to be unlike her, to have no greed. The more important the cadre, and the more gifts and money he took, the more elated she was. By going through Guo Yucai, Wang Shouxin was able to throw a banquet for a deputy head of a department in the Ministry of Commerce. When she saw him off at Harbin, Wang Shouxin presented this man with a set of sofas, a bed-wardrobe combination and tea tables, as well as one hundred cubic feet of lumber and several gunnysacks of soybeans. He accepted everything. Wang Shouxin was now more at ease than ever. "Even in Beijing cadres are like this," she observed to herself. "These articles weren't Old Lady Wang's private property—he must have known that!"

When the Gang of Four fell from power, Wang Shouxin and her "rebel" comrades-in-arms felt a momentary quiver of fear. But for Wang Shouxin, the long trip she took in 1978 was evidence enough that, even though nearly two years had elapsed since the smashing of the Gang of Four, Old Lady Wang's position was not only as impregnable as ever, but even continuing to rise.

This long trip in 1978 was a show of strength, a demonstration of her power. It had been arranged for her by Vice–Secretary-General Nie of the Heilongjiang Provincial Economic Committee and was intended as thanks to Wang Shouxin for her help in arranging for his three children to return from the countryside and take jobs in the city. He had bought airline tickets for her and sent his son to accompany her. When this embezzler extraordinaire took off from Harbin airport, three department heads of the provincial government showed up to see her off. When she arrived in Canton, three units were there to receive her. In Shanghai, someone was specially sent to take her to a first-class hotel.

Wang Shouxin had reached the pinnacle of wealth and fame. Her influence "at the top" was growing daily. The car of some provincial, prefectural, or county official was always in front of her house. Her status had skyrocketed because of the many things she had been able to procure for Bin County, and as her status rose, she became ever more fearless, arrogant, and oppressive. In tiny Bin County, whom should she fear?

"All-out Dictatorship"

At the beginning of 1975, while it was still winter, Wang Shouxin and some workers climbed the mountains of Gaoleng in search of timber. They headed into the hills with pork, hard liquor, cigarettes, and soap in their trucks. At each checkpoint Old Lady Wang would go in for a friendly exchange, while her henchmen outside began giving out all those things that were normally so hard to find. At some checkpoints Old Lady Wang would go in, put down her carryall, and say with generosity and concern, "Didn't I hear that you were short of batteries here? Here, I've brought some flashlights to go along with them!"

In the hills she and her henchmen paid off the inspectors. Old Lady Wang feared no danger or difficulty; she led her troops without mishap up slippery heights of snow-covered piles of logs, picking out the best and calculating her total as she went. When her trucks returned full, all the checkpoints along the way let them pass without inspection once they knew it was Old Lady Wang. In this manner she got more than 1750 cubic feet of top-quality pine for just over $330.

This was a happy event, and Wang Shouxin planned to celebrate it. She could hardly have known that big trouble awaited her in Bin County. Inspector Yang Qing, of the County Disciplinary Inspection Committee, was looking for her. He revealed to her that a member of the County Standing Committee had received an anonymous letter accusing Wang Shouxin of the crime of corruption. That night Wang Shouxin went to Yang Qing's house with two bottles of superior liquor and took possession of the accusing letter—so that, she said, she could check the handwriting.

The next day, as soon as Wang Shouxin arrived at work, she threw the letter down in front of Zhou Lu and began swearing at him. "Goddamn it to hell! I go to Gaoleng for twenty days to get timber and everything here turns upside-down! . . . What the hell have you been doing here? Didn't I tell you to keep your eye on these people?"

Inspector Yang Qing (who later became vice-chairman of the Disciplinary Inspection Committee) also came in, and together with Zhou Lu tried to identify the handwriting by comparing it with that used in other criticisms and complaints. Unfortunately nothing turned up, but Yang Qing picked up the offending letter and reassured Wang Shouxin. "Don't worry who wrote this," he said. "The letter's in my control now, and that will be that!" These words hinted darkly, and also promised, that he was putting on the market the power he had in his hands to shield a criminal. The buyer was there; it did not matter very much at what time the price would be paid.

"OK," said Wang Shouxin, affecting unconcern. "So this letter was aimed at me. A branch secretary has to expect such things. Let's just forget it. If it had been written about someone else, we'd have to be stricter!"

Yang Qing was as good as his word: the letter was never seen again. But Wang Shouxin was not going to leave things at that. She sent three telegrams in a row ordering that the driver Qu Zhaoguo be sent back from the Jixi Coal Mine, saying he was needed for military training. Qu Zhaoguo hurried back that very night. As he entered the room, before he could even take off his padded jacket, he was blasted by Wang Shouxin: "You wanted to grab power from me? You were going to plant a bomb under my ass that would blow me to kingdom come?"

Qu Zhaoguo was utterly floored. He had driven on Wang Shouxin's gift-giving missions a long time now; he even called himself "Old Lady Wang's aide-de-camp." Every parcel, big or small, was personally delivered by this "aide-de-camp." He made sure nobody got the wrong parcel, but never asked any irrelevant questions, either. He was only a silent observer. For example, he noticed that nearly all the houses to which he delivered gifts had telephones. This proved they were occupied by pretty high officials. Wang Shouxin was correct in suspecting that he had been able to guess her secrets. Once when they went to the Provincial Fuel Company seeking coal, he heard an accountant ask Wang Shouxin if she could possibly get him some ready cash, say $3,500 or so. He also heard Wang Shouxin's reply. "Is $3,500 enough? I'll give you $7,000!"

"You can disburse that much?" asked the accountant.

"I don't have to disburse it," replied Wang Shouxin. "There's that much at White Rock."

Qu Zhaoguo was surprised to hear this but immediately composed himself and pretended not to have heard it. This was the first time the secret of the illicit treasury at White Rock had leaked out. Four years later, when the Bin County Party Committee sent a work team to the fuel company to investigate, three months of hard work failed to disclose Wang Shouxin's fatal secret.

Once Wang Shouxin sent down an order that everyone in the fuel company participate in "study sessions." First they would study those two long articles by Zhang Chunqiao and Yao Wenyuan.[6] And this was indeed fitting, for Wang Shouxin was already quite "dictatorial"—more than that, she wanted to be "all-out" dictatorial. Next they studied Xiaojinzhuang [a model commune], and everyone was asked to write criticisms of the bad people. Wang Shouxin took these to her office and checked them closely, one by one, trying to see whether any matched the handwriting of the accusatory letter.

Next everyone studied Xiaojinzhuang's "poetry contest." Wang Shouxin made the opening statement, which was also a kind of call to arms. "Our fuel company has turned up a Fu Zhigao!"[7] she said, stroking her raven-black hair. She liked to compare herself to Jiang Jie.[8] "What's so bad about our company? Even if something is wrong, can't we take care of it ourselves, without writing secret letters of accusation? . . . I'm a fifty-some-year-old woman, why should I bother to get up early, or burn the midnight oil? Everybody knows this old lady keeps on working, illness or no illness . . ." As she spoke she began loosening her belt, and some men who knew what was coming up next quickly lowered their heads. But she couldn't undo her belt that day, probably because she was so agitated. "Have I, Wang Shouxin, ever failed you?" she continued. She cried, swearing and cursing, "The person who wrote that letter will come to no good end! If he has two sons, may they both die! If he has two daughters, may they both die! Extinction to his family!"

The atmosphere at the "poetry contest" was extremely tense. On one side the drum began pounding fiercely, as if Zhang Fei[9] were about to jump out. As the drumbeats quickened, a handkerchief was passed around. Everyone passed it as quickly as possible, as if it could burn one's fingers; the rule was that whoever had it in his hand when the drum stopped had to compose a poem. Candy and apples were set out on the table, but no one was in the mood to eat anything.

The first set of poems attacked Lin Biao and Confucius. Then they became more and more outrageous, using language that would not pass a swineherd's lips. This poem was among the more civilized:

> His family are Japs, and Soviets, too,
> American bones, the flesh of a Jew,
> And who may this be? I hear you ask,
> His name is Wan, and he ain't worth a screw!

This poem amused Wang Shouxin, and elicited a giggle from her. It was only when she giggled that anyone else dared to.

The next poet clearly had foreknowledge of Wang Shouxin's intentions, since he caricatured Qu Zhaoguo:

> Five-foot-six, tall for a runt, mouth as big as
>   his mother's ——,
> Hatchet-face, pointy chin, turtle's neck,
>   legs long and thin,
> Smiles as though he's hard at work, really only
>   knows how to shirk.
> Carries a notebook in his clothes, whatever happens,
>   the notebook knows,
> And he can use it, to wail and complain, every time
>   there comes a campaign.
> The Party branch he wants to unload,
>   and make his way down the capitalist road!

Wang Shouxin laughed as she listened, then tossed the poet an apple and some candy to show her approval. As soon as the poem had been read, she assumed a serious expression.

"Qu Zhaoguo, stand up!" she bellowed. Qu Zhaoguo drew up his five feet six inches and stuck out that neck upon which so much obloquy had been laid. He moved to the center of the room.

Wang Shouxin still was not finished. "If a man has a good wife at home he won't do anything dumb. Lu Yaqin, you lousy little flirt, stand next to him!"

Lu Yaqin refused to stand up. "Call in the militia!" shouted Wang Shouxin. "The only reason we maintain an army is so we can use it when we need it!" But the militia wouldn't budge.

"You're on her side?" Wang Shouxin turned around and suddenly became pleasant and agreeable.

"Zhaoguo, I say, if you wrote the letter, why don't you just admit it?"

"I didn't write it, so how can I admit it? And even if I had written it, it's no vicious attack, and not directed at Party Central. What is there to fear?"

The beating of the drum began again, and once again everybody began writing poems. Their hearts were beating like the drum, thump, thump, thump. These were people who heaved coal all day long—how could they be forced to write poems? Some of them racked their brains until the sweat poured out; for the rest of their lives they would tremble whenever they heard a poem read. But if you didn't write a poem, if you didn't vilify someone, you would become the focus of suspicion—and that was no laughing matter. Some people stole behind the backs of others to see what kind of poems they were writing. People with no education, who couldn't come up with anything, could only stand up and recite "prose"—usually a string of nasty obscenities.

Oh, motherland, are these the masters of the People's Republic? The proletariat whose dictatorship we have? Is this our working class?

Wang Shouxin—is she in the vanguard of the working class, of the Communist Party?

In what colors should we paint this chapter of our history?

Spinelessness: The Disease of the Times

The fuel company was only 220 yards away from the headquarters of the County Party Committee. If the committee could not hear the sounds of Wang Shouxin cursing and the workers weeping, could they really have missed that beating drum? Not seen the big-character posters, or any of the accusatory letters? What about the letters of complaint relayed down to them several times from the provincial and prefectural Party Committees? Had they never seen or heard any of these things?

To leaf through the minutes of the County Party Committee meetings from 1972 onward is an intensely depressing experience. All sorts of problems are discussed: military conscription, family planning, criminal sentences, sowing plans—but hardly any mention of the problems of the Party itself. The Communist Party regulated everything, but would not regulate the Communist Party.

Nineteen seventy-two certainly was an historic year in modern Chinese history. In Bin County, cadres' banqueting and drinking—and pilfering, grabbing, embezzling, and appropriating—all reached a new high that year. And it was in 1972 that Wang Shouxin launched her corruption on a grand scale. The County Party Committee was officially restored in this same year, and Liu Zhen came to Bin County as the first in the succession of First Party Secretaries after the Cultural Revolution.

Even before Liu Zhen moved in, Wang Shouxin dispatched people to put up wooden screens in his house and to deliver shiny black lump coal and, later, top-quality rice. Since they were neighbors they had some other contact as well, but there is no way to establish that Liu Zhen cooperated in, or tried to cover up, Wang Shouxin's criminal activities. When he left in 1976 for another post, he actually warned the woman who succeeded him as secretary that "you should watch out for this Wang Shouxin—she doesn't play straight."

This shows that Liu Zhen had sharp eyes; he could also figure things out. What he lacked was a certain amount of something else.

The problem was that he was as agreeable as could be. Whether lecturing at a meeting, greeting guests, or simply walking along the street, he always had a smile on his face. His gestures, voice, manner, and walk were all gentle and mellow, as if always and everywhere he sought to show others that "I have nothing against anyone; please don't get me wrong, I wouldn't offend or harm anyone." Even people who were dissatisfied and full of gripes would never lose their tempers at Secretary Liu, because of the deep sympathy that welled up behind his rimless eyeglasses. He would listen to your appeal with the utmost concern and attentiveness, as if ready to do anything in his power to satisfy whatever request you made. In reality, of course, he never got anything done.

Before long he got a nickname: "The Old Lady Official." And another: "Liu Ha-ha." He would always nod his head and say, "Ha-ha, fine, fine, fine." Once he returned home and his wife sadly told him that the chickens they had been raising had all died from a disease. "Ha-ha, fine, fine, fine," he replied.

Was he born with this kind of character? Probably not. If one attributes such things to nature, one has to account for a remarkable coincidence. Why is such nature so concentrated? Why, out of three current members in the County Party Secretariat, were all three notoriously "slippery" and "treacherous"?

When the Cultural Revolution began, Liu Zhen had been the county Party secretary of Shuangcheng County. His soul (not to mention his body) had been a little too deeply "touched"—to the point where he had been badly scarred by the experience. Before he came to Bin County, he had been warned: "That place is very complicated; few have gone in there and come out unscathed"; "Bin County—it's scarcely possible to investigate a single thing there." He had long heard that violent struggle and false accusations had left more people dead in Bin County than anywhere else in the prefecture.

The previous county Party secretary, Zhang Xiangling, had given Liu a detailed introduction to the "rebels" and had warned him pointedly not to rely on rebel leaders such as Wen Feng.

Liu Zhen listened and nodded his head; but his own thoughts were running in the opposite direction: "This guy has offended a good many people. If I don't improve relations with the 'rebels,' how can I establish myself? Isn't this as clear as can be?"

Not long after that, Liu Zhen restored the respectability of the bellyaching Wen Feng, who had been relegated to work in Binzhou by Zhang Xiangling, by putting Wen Feng on the Standing Committee of the County Revolutionary Committee. The rest of Wen Feng's clique were given new positions as well.

In 1972, not long after the County Party Committee had been restored, everyone on the Standing Committee pointed out that one thing was perfectly clear: the greatest problems with current Party leadership were an unwillingness to combat unwholesome tendencies and a lack of fighting spirit. The secretary and Standing Committee even devised such resounding slogans as "Work hard, change quickly; the first to change must be the county head-quarters!" and "Whether we can change or not depends crucially upon whether the county headquarters can change!"

Three years later, the 1975 Standing Committee again came to investigate, and the problem was still the same: nobody dared to fight back. And why was this? "Afraid of getting caught in a quag-mire, afraid of offending others, afraid of stirring up a hornet's nest . . ."

Another four years passed—1979—and Wang Shouxin had finally been indicted. When the Standing Committee came yet again to investigate, there was still the problem of "being afraid to struggle."

Did this reluctance to speak up come from everyone's having been bought out by criminals such as Wang Shouxin? Of the eleven members of the Standing Committee of the County Party Committee, nine had accepted Wang Shouxin's gifts—this was a fact. Nonetheless, there were some among the leading cadres who had never taken any gifts. For example, the chairman of the County Disciplinary Inspection Committee was clean. Among the two or three hundred people to whom Wang Shouxin had given gifts, this woman was the only one who had resisted, the only one who had not been tainted. She was an upstanding com-rade who had been working for the revolution since 1946, and she despised all the pulling and fawning around her. When she saw that people these days "couldn't tell right from wrong" or felt "doing one's job is a cinch, but building up good connections is hard," she was upset. "When will we ever be able to resolve this problem?" she worried. Yet even such a fine comrade as she still "failed to see" that people like herself would have to step forward if the problem was to be solved. She was humble, careful, diligent, conscientious, hard working and plain living—except for her un-willingness to struggle, she was the very image of a "good cadre."

Even though the Gang of Four had fallen, the County Party Committee was as weak and pusillanimous as ever in the face of the "rebels." In Bin County, the campaign to "expose, criticize, and investigate" was not carried out until 1978. This time around Wen Feng couldn't avoid self-criticism. But oh, what disappoint-ments those mass criticism sessions were to the cadres and masses of Bin County! The language, tone, and content of the first self-criticisms were no different from regular reports. Secretary Guan was chairing the meeting, and everyone was waiting for him to give some indication of his attitude. But he wouldn't! With the second batch of self-criticisms it was no different: Secretary Guan still gave no indication of his attitude. This was highly unusual. People in Bin County had all become experts on political movements by then, and they felt that consistency with precedent should require the chairman to exert a little more pressure than this. But he still wouldn't! The third mass meeting was the most puzzling of all. At that time it had already been announced that Wen Feng had been relieved of his job and had handed over the reins; at the meeting, it ought to have been someone else's turn for self-criticism. Wen Feng was sitting at the back of the meeting hall that day. Everyone watched as Secretary Guan sent someone from the Organization Department back to the last row to ask Wen Feng up to the stage. Wen Feng was embarrassed and could not be persuaded to come forward. The next scene in this little drama was something nobody, including Wen Feng, was prepared for: Secretary Guan himself came down from the stage and walked the length of the hall, like an emperor leading his troops, right to the back row to give Wen Feng a personal invitation. He insisted on nothing less than having this worthless clod go up and take his place with the assembled leaders. This set the whole place buzzing. No one could understand it: "Isn't this thwarting the will of the people?" "Isn't this giving support to Wen Feng's clique?" Quite a few people felt concern for Secretary Guan: "Hey, Old Guan," they thought to themselves, "What are you doing? Aren't you afraid of losing face before the entire county?" Everyone felt disappointed and hurt. Old Guan had been around in Bin County since land reform [1945] and was well known for his bravery and staunch resolve in struggles with the enemy. He had been nicknamed "Guan the Ruthless," and this was an honorable epithet. Everyone thought of him as one of the more trustworthy members of the County Party Committee. When the Wang Shouxin affair came to light, everyone said privately that "no matter how many at county headquarters are implicated, Guan the Ruthless won't be one of them." But now, how could he have disappointed everyone by doing what he had just done?

The Standing Committee and the secretaries were full of explanations for their easy treatment of the "rebels," including Wang Shouxin. One of them said in a self-criticism that the "Unified Program to Defend Mao Zedong Thought" had first liberated him and then "joined" with him. He had felt great gratitude for this. Another secretary had offered precisely the opposite explanation. The "rebels" had persecuted him, and he was afraid people would think he was seeking revenge. This had been why he refused to oppose the "rebels." In reality, the basic reason was clearly that the rebels had all along been a political force that no one could take lightly.

In sum, everybody feared offending this group or that group, but was quite happy offending the "masters" of our People's Republic—the people!

Among the various County Party secretaries, one person deserves separate mention because of the special circumstances of his case.

Wei Gao was one of three members of the County Party Committee between 1972 and 1976 whose credentials stood out from all the others. These three were all known for being "slippery" and for their great fondness for wine. At a meeting of the County Party Committee's Standing Committee in 1972, Wei Gao was evaluated as "evasive in all matters, always among the last to make his position known." He was always trying to please every faction; matters of principle could go either way with him; he would always prefer to take one step backward in order to preserve the peace, rather than considering the bad effects such an action would have on important projects. Yet he did have strong points: he could view problems from many angles and was very good at consulting others.

At that time, he was the secretary in charge of the county's finance and trade; as Wang Shouxin's superior, he knew her like the back of his hand. After close observation and considerable thought, he decided to join his family and Wang Shouxin's through matrimony.

Wei Gao and his wife went together to see a matchmaker. His wife spoke first, asking Old Lady You to introduce their daughter

Xiaoxia to Wang Shouxin's youngest son, Liu Zhizhong. But Old Lady You had her reservations. "Secretary Wei," she said, "your official star is shining its brightest; why do you think you need an old lady like me to make a match for you? Haven't you got offers all over the place?"

The couple insisted that they wanted the matchmaker to go ahead, so she said, "Do you know the background of their family very well? . . . Wang Shouxin and I are both originally from Manjing; when she was young she wasn't a very proper . . ."

"That was all a long time ago," Wei Gao interrupted. "Now that she's older, she doesn't act that way anymore."

So Old Lady You finally gave in. "OK, if you really want to hook up with a deadbeat family, I'll go do it for you."

Wei Gao and his wife took the initiative of going with their daughter to call on the Wang family elders. Later the couple went to the photography studio to visit their future son-in-law, who was a vice-chairman of the studio's Revolutionary Committee. Wang Shouxin was ambivalent about the match, thinking that the girl was not pretty enough.

The wedding was held quietly; even some of the county Party secretaries, when they heard of the nuptials after the fact, were puzzled. Why did Wei Gao insist on marrying into Wang Shouxin's family? This was not a good match.

The vice-chairman of the County Planning Committee, Yi Yongquan, once accompanied Wei Gao to a meeting in Harbin and took this opportunity to speak to Wei Gao about Wang Shouxin. "As a secretary you're the ranking official in the county, but you will also be expected to give help to your daughter's mother-in-law. . . . She has quite a reputation, you know, for throwing parties and giving gifts, squandering money and wasting resources. She's fouled the atmosphere with her corruption . . ." Li Yongquan cited many examples, observing Wei Gao's reaction as he spoke. Wei Gao gave no hint of his emotions, but Li could see clearly that he already knew all about these things and that he had basically determined not to concern himself with them. He finally replied by saying, "All this is hard to believe."

Li Yongquan immediately regretted his candor. He now realized that this fellow's reputation was well deserved, that he really was a sly old fox. Just look at that reply of his: he didn't deny that there was a problem with Wang Shouxin, but neither did he affirm that this was the case.

Perhaps it was due to his slyness that for a period of seven long years people were always wont to believe that the marriage match had been arranged by Wang Shouxin for the purpose of securing a dependable fallback. Not until half a year after Wang Shouxin's case had been cracked did the real truth come to light: Wei Gao had set his sights on Wang Shouxin's money.

The Reasons? Right under Our Noses!

The exposure of Wang Shouxin's case shocked the entire country. How could such a crude, shallow housewife muster such boldness and such ability? How could such brazen criminal activity go uninvestigated for so many years? From their common sense and intuition people naturally focused their attention on the Bin County Party leadership: they were at the root of this, they were her accomplices, it was they who had protected Wang Shouxin!

This is, to be sure, the impression one gets when one views Wang Shouxin's case in isolation from the economic, political, and social life of Bin County. But if one looks at the whole living organism, with Wang Shouxin and her criminal activity organically linked by a maze of arterial connections to the rest of life, then the situation appears to be very different.

Viewing the situation organically, one discovers the following: were it not for the illicit treasury in which she held cash amounting to over a third of a million dollars, Wang Shouxin and her activities would never have aroused the attention, or caused the shock, that they did when the full extent of her corruption was exposed.

Instead, what appears, continuing to view things in this way, is only this: a plainly dressed old lady, straight talking and industrious, rushing all day around Bin County and even outside of it, trying to gather coal, trucks, fertilizer, and cement for the benefit of the whole county.

Her party throwing and gift giving were carried out on a grand scale. But what officials were *not* throwing parties and giving gifts? The maxim "Without proper greasing, nothing works" is as true today as ever. Trucks carting nonstaple foodstuffs sped from the fuel company along the highway from Bin County to Harbin. But they were not alone. Trucks from the Bin County distillery, full of "Binzhou Liquor," traveled the same road, as did trucks from the fruit company carrying apples for the higher-ups. Even within Bin County itself, all the economic units would "pay tribute" to each other. Wang Shouxin's nonstaple foodstuffs base, sanitorium, and lavish banquets at White Rock were famous. But practically every section in Bin County had its own small dining hall, guesthouse, and storehouse. Parties with huge meals and lots of drinking went on everywhere! Wang Shouxin may indeed have been the Coal Queen of Bin County, but she most certainly was not alone. Bin County also had an Electricity King, the head of the electricity board, who was also called "the millionaire." This man's gift giving and lavish parties cost in the neighborhood of ten thousand dollars each year. Just as did Wang Shouxin's fuel company, the electricity board had to pay tribute to higher-ups.

Back in 1964, county Party secretary Tian Fengshan had determined to put a stop to this wining and dining, but the result was only a brief interlude between periods of business as usual. After 1970, Zhang Xiangling also took up the cause; yet, ironically, wining and dining actually increased during his term in office. The integrity of these two secretaries and their revolutionary will to struggle were beyond any question. But neither one of them could achieve his end. The County Party Committee had gone so far as to pass a specific regulation, which was in force from 1972, stipulating that for official guests, no meal should have more than four courses and no liquor could be served. This rule was never actually put into effect. Every year the official county guesthouses misappropriated $1300 of their budgets for this sort of entertainment. Each of these guesthouses, which were run by the various departments of the County Revolutionary Committee, used its income to support the lavish gluttony of cadres. And besides serving their own gluttony, the cadres also dipped their hands into the till. It was, moreover, not only the cadres themselves who gourmandized and stole; their families did the same. At one time the County Party Committee ordered that such guest houses be closed, but to no avail.

Obvious as it was that Wang Shouxin had embezzled public funds to build her houses, the bricks and tiles themselves bore no record of her corruption. And there were many other houses built through embezzlement of various sorts. Aren't those who live in these houses resting easily in their good fortune even today, with no fear that they might ever be prosecuted for their misdeeds? A prime example is the new house of Yang So-and-so, Party secretary and manager of the biggest factory in Bin County, the towel factory.

Yang's house had originally been a structure attached to the factory. Because it had been built to purify water, the structure was fairly crude and had a tank on top of it. But Yang, on his own authority, decided that the structure needed major improvements, which would require tearing down the water tank. He then converted this industrial building into his own private residence. The four-room house required twenty-one tons of cement, not to mention other building materials.

This Yang was unlike Wang Shouxin only in that he used the state's materials and labor instead of its currency. In the final analysis there is no difference between the two.

So we can see that Wang Shouxin's criminal activities were, in the first place, covered up by the general decline in social morality, by the gradual legalization of criminal activity, and by the people's gradual acclimatization to the moral decay around them. Even the distinction between legal and illegal had become quite blurred. Where was the borderline between legitimate gift giving and the offering and acceptance of bribes? Was using public funds for wining and dining or for converting public property to one's own use (as in requiring a "test use," or a "test wearing," or a "taste test") any different from corruption and robbery? The former was within the law, even considered morally sound, but in essence was no different from bribery and corruption. And misappropriation of public property was far more widespread than bribery or corrupt conduct.

There is yet more to discover about the residence of this Yang: there was no way his four-room house could have used twenty-one tons of cement, even though it turned out upon further investigation that, in violation of the regulations then in effect, he had had the walls of his house covered with a thick layer of cement so that the white plaster dust would not rub off. What really happened was that the head of the industrial section, a certain Du, was building his own residence at the same time. A large amount of building materials and half-finished articles "got lost" at the site of Yang's building. The two residences were completed one after the other, and the personal relationship between Yang and Du became even more intimate.

This "relationship" needs further consideration and analysis. Section Chief Du had protected, and would continue to protect, Factory Head Yang; Factory Head Yang, for his part, had supported and would continue to support Section Chief Du. But it was more than a two-party relationship; both Yang and Du had cliques surrounding them. And Yang had an addiction: beginning with his work at the county labor union in the 1960s, through several job changes leading to his present one at the towel factory, in each place he engaged in extramarital sex. Yet he could always come away untainted—like a duck waddling out of the water with its feathers dry. How did he do it? Section Chief Du had the same addiction, but he was quite different in the way he went about satisfying it. He cared not whom he harmed if a person blocked his way or knew too much. At least two framings were his doing, and he even insured that it would be a long time before the innocent victims were exonerated. And how did he do it? The same way: people, connections.

Many of the middle- to upper-level cadres in Bin County came from rural villages after the land reform of 1945. By the late 1960s and early 1970s, their sons and daughters were of marriageable age. The county seat of Bin County had only slightly more than thirty thousand residents, and the number from the social levels appropriate for marriage to cadres was even smaller. Thus in-law relationships, and in-laws-of-in-laws relationships, came to overlie relationships that were already doing quite well—such as those of family, clan, friends, former classmates, former colleagues, former bosses or subordinates, or "I'll-scratch-your-back-if-you'll-scratch-mine" partnerships—and invested all of them with new importance. In terms of extent alone, these in-law relationships had become twice as important as they ever were in feudal society.

A change of equal importance (not to say of even greater importance) was the new layer of political relationships imposed upon personal relations by the Great Cultural Revolution. Those who belonged to the same "faction" shared each other's tribulations, shielded each other, and in a few short years became like brothers to people who had started out as total strangers! When they met and greeted each other as "elder brother" or "younger brother," they really meant it; the relationships between Communist Party members and between revolutionary comrades paled by comparison.

"In Bin County, it's hard to figure out how people are related. It's as though they carry special switches with them, and if you get involved with one person, you're suddenly involved with a whole network." When people who had lived in Bin County for a certain time explained their county to outsiders, they would begin with this phenomenon.

In 1972, a member of the County Party Standing Committee who had come from elsewhere expressed his feelings thus: "We must practice Marxism-Leninism, but there are many pitfalls in doing so. How could personal relationships get so complicated! If you try to go by the book, all sorts of difficulties crop up. You're sure to get dragged in by one thing or another. No matter what you do, somebody will take offense, some problem will arise. There are so many riddles, so much to untangle."

When the County Party Standing Committee met, even if it met in some place as confidential as the War Room of the Military Department, any discussion of personnel questions would inevitably reach the ears of the persons involved. This presented major difficulties for the cadres involved in allocating and transferring personnel. If they were still deliberating on someone's placement, or had just decided it, and that person got wind of the decision, he could come to appeal, or to raise protests, or to seek support from friends. Things often ended in a stalemate.

When someone got into trouble, ten people would intercede for him. When a complaint came in, all concerned would seek the good offices of others. If someone were to come and say to you that So-and-so and So-and-so have already agreed to help, and all we need now is you—what would you do? Would you adhere to the rules? And risk offending everyone in sight? Wouldn't it be better to cast a blind eye, give him a little wave of the hand and let him have his way this once? Unless one's Party discipline were exceptional, who would be such an ogre as to refuse?

Some people sum it up by saying that everything in China has been messed up by people who are afraid of offending others.

For the same reason a very strange phenomenon would occur time and again. Something of considerable gravity would take place and raise a tumult in the town. Everyone would insist that something be done about it. Yet as soon as somebody was sent to investigate, the whole affair would evaporate. In 1972, people from Manjing reported that an official named Chen, who was in charge of the supply and marketing cooperative, was constantly being wined and dined and having illicit relations with women. The problem was "serious." Since this cooperative was serving as an official model for the whole province at that time, something definitely had to be done. The local Standing Committee consulted with their secretary and decided to send someone to investigate. After a time the report arrived: "no great cause for alarm." Seven years later it came out that this fellow named Chen was guilty of embezzlement and had indeed been engaging in illicit sex for quite some time.

During this period, political movements were launched year after year in Bin County, but one thing was mystifying. As all these movements, or class struggles, as they were also called, became fiercer and fiercer, the evildoers felt more and more at ease. It was the good people who kept being victimized. Some were unjustly framed; others were subjected to attack and revenge for their exposure of evildoers.

Complex personal relationships, built of layer upon layer of interlocking connections, formed a dense net. Any Marxist-Leninist principle, any Party plan or policy that came into contact with this net would be struck dead, as if electrocuted. When an enterprise got entangled in the net, its socialist design would come undone; when a legal case fell into the net, the dictatorship of the proletariat would get twisted out of shape. Right and wrong became thoroughly confused, reward and punishment turned upside-down. Truth yielded to falsity; the good-hearted were ruled by the vicious.

"Why do good people look bad and bad people look good?" At one time this topic was actually discussed at a meeting of the Party Standing Committee. In reality, of course, much more was at stake than merely looking good or bad. What the masses said was, "In Bin County, the good are cowed while the evil are proud."

Just look at the great pride of that repeat offender Zhao Chun, who always managed to evade the law and go scot-free. From 1969 on, when this man used his relationship with the "rebels" to worm his way into the Party, he began brazenly stealing timber and other state-owned materials, committing crimes time after time. Each of these cases could have been investigated, but not once was he ever punished in any way. The County Party Committee had ruled that no one who owed money to the state could build a private house. He, though, not only owed the state money and lived in state-owned housing; he also was able to use state-owned building materials to build himself a second house. He stole building stones allocated for defense. When a tractor overturned, he siphoned off the compensation money for the dead driver's family, plus the money for repairing the tractor—over five thousand dollars—from the public treasury. He also sold the scaffolding that had been used in constructing this house and pocketed all the proceeds.

To this day Zhao Chun drives his car with reckless abandon. Sometimes he has intentionally aimed it toward Han Cheng, an official in the towel factory's security department, and has slammed on the brakes right in front of him. Zhao Chun's aim has been to threaten and torment this person who was in charge of prosecuting his crimes. "Just watch it, wise guy—remember I can kill you anytime I want!" This has been the unspoken message. The insults and vituperative obscenities he has hurled at Han Cheng have become so common that they are taken as a matter of course. And what about Han Cheng? Not only can he get no support, but he has been relieved of his job as a security official. When this happened he brought all the incriminating material from the many cases involving Zhao Chun to the authorities. He pleaded and appealed in every direction, but no one would touch the case.

Could anything be more blatant, more maddeningly perverse than this? But Han Cheng's was not the only case in Bin County of a security official being bullied by villains.

Why was it that even now, under the leadership of the Communist Party in socialist Bin County, and three whole years after the fall of the Gang of Four, this half-human half-monstrous behavior could continue unabated?

The riddle is easy to solve: Zhao Chun had "connections." Besides his "rebel" cohorts, he had a valuable uncle—Vice-Director Lu of the County Party Committee's Organization Department. Vice-Director Lu and Section Chief Du belonged to the same clique. As we have already seen, Section Chief Du and Manager Yang of the towel factory were also connected. And Manager Yang was the one who relieved Han Cheng of his job. Zhao Chun's several crimes had taken place in the towel factory; the tractor he destroyed and the compensation money he misappropriated were also written off by Manager Yang.

This lovely curtain of fraternal loyalty, sincere gratitude, mutual concern, profound friendship, etc., etc. concealed relationships of out-and-out power brokerage. One side would invest a peach (either a material benefit or the means to obtain one, derived, in either case, from the power in that side's own hands), and the other side would answer with a plum (also a material benefit either directly or indirectly returned).

This is another of the social conditions that created and helped cover up Wang Shouxin, and that continue even now to create and cover up criminal elements.

Little Guys Do Some Big Things

There were two minor figures in Bin County who dared to show their contempt for this all-encompassing, all-powerful net, and even dared to challenge it.

One was Liu Changchun, with whom we are already acquainted. Wang Shouxin looked down on him and often sneered at him behind his back, her mouth twisted in contempt. "Look at that miserable little twit!" she would say, and then spit. But she failed to realize how tough Liu Changchun's tiny, thin body could be. He could not be crushed by the awesome pressure brought to bear on him by the "rebels" and the army, nor was his fighting spirit worn down by long years of hard living and suffering. Liu Changchun's contribution to the final victory over Wang Shouxin cannot be underestimated.

First he was jailed as "anti-Army" and an "active counterrevolutionary"; later the charge was commuted to "bad element," and he was moved to a cell under the "civil administration" of his original unit. When he got out he had to do more than ten hours of hard labor per day, and was given only $14 a month for living expenses. His wife stayed at home, bedridden with acute heart disease. (The hospital denied her both medicine and doctors' services, a policy that had been ordered by Wang Shouxin's son Liu Zhizhong, who was vice-director of the Xinli Commune.) Finally, Liu Changchun was ordered to report to the countryside along with the cadres who faced elimination as "extra personnel." Liu Changchun was now up to his neck in debt and could borrow no more, so he had no alternative but to sell off his only remaining property—a two-and-a-half-room house. He got only $265 for it. After he was sent to the countryside his wife's illness worsened, and not long thereafter she died. He labored in a rural village for four and a half years, and of the more than one thousand persons sent there with him, Liu Changchun was the very last to get permission to return to Bin County.

By then Wang Shouxin had become a major figure in Bin County. Her home's furnishings and her standard of living were as good as those of a provincial Party secretary. She was constantly besieged by people bringing her gifts and asking her to do things. Liu Changchun had been left alone in the world—his wife dead and gone, his property wiped out, not a penny to his name.

Liu Changchun's life had come to this pass because of his stubbornness. He had already become unpopular during the fifteen or so years before the Cultural Revolution. He had always liked to speak up—about anybody.

When he returned from the countryside he was amazed at all the new houses Wang Shouxin had built. "Where'd she get this much money?" He began to investigate. He sought out Qu Zhaoguo, who liked to gossip; Qu revealed that Wang Shouxin had once lent $6,500 in cash to the provincial fuel company. When Qu was about to leave he scrutinized Liu Changchun carefully. Perceiving Liu's intentions, this smoothie Qu quickly calculated the balance of power involved.

"You think you can really get her?" he asked.

"That depends on whether she's done wrong!" Liu Changchun had not changed from earlier years. To see his spirit of determination and self-confidence you would have thought he was a prefectural Party secretary.

By this time Liu Changchun already suspected Wang Shouxin of corruption; his problem was to get reliable evidence. He had experience as a planner and statistician and knew that she could not have embezzled so much money merely through fraudulent "supplementary wages." He went looking for Old Battle-ax, the one who kept the fuel company's accounts.

"When you marked up the cost of nonstate coal," asked Liu, "how did you indicate it on the books? Was it obvious how much small-pit coal was sold on a given day?"

"No, it wasn't," replied Old Battle-ax. "Generally, they reported only the price of $16.50 per ton. There was no mention of the additional $10.10." Later he said, "In the accounting report that they made every ten days or so, they wrote at the bottom of each column: received, such-and-such an amount for transport charges of small-pit coal."

How were the invoices for coal made out? A person who had been employed at White Rock explained this to Liu Changchun. Two kinds of receipts were made out when coal was sold—one for the price of the coal and another for transport and miscellaneous charges. The latter receipts were never turned in; no one knew where they went.

"What, was it all embezzled?" Liu Changchun was beside himself.

"Who knows? They never let us find out . . ."

"That clinches it!" Liu Changchun did some mental arithmetic: ninety thousand tons of coal a year, perhaps ten thousand tons of it sold as small-pit coal. That would generate an extra one hundred thousand dollars per year—in five years that would be half a million dollars! But how to check this? Easy! Cast the net wide—ask each unit in the entire county to examine its receipts for coal purchases.

Liu Changchun's discovery encouraged him immensely. He pressed his investigations across the whole of Wang Shouxin's empire. How many potatoes and soybeans did she get from those hundred or more acres of land? How many fish did she get in one year from a labor force of four men? How much money could she embezzle from the supplementary wages of her temporary and seasonal labor?

At this point Yang Qing, vice-chairman of the Bin County Disciplinary Inspection Committee, betrayed Liu's activities to Wang Shouxin. As a non-Party member of the masses, Liu had been pursuing his work purely out of a sense of duty. He had given no thought to any personal gain from his endeavor and as later events made clear, he not only gained nothing but suffered a good deal because of it.

Liu Changchun was not alone. A second "little guy" to stir up the hornets' nest around Wang Shouxin was named Shi Huailiang, a worker in the pharmaceutical company.

Back in 1972 he had put up a wall poster entitled "Wang Shouxin Is the Key to Solving the Problems of Bin County." Where Shi Huailiang differed from Liu Changchun was in the somewhat broader scope of the questions he worried about and analyzed. He would occasionally come out with something quite surprising, but without much fuss beforehand. In 1972, for example, a brainstorm inspired him to mail seven dollars to Chairman Mao. "Enclosed are my Party dues," he wrote on the remittance form. "Please accept them, kind sir. Shi Huailiang."

This was indeed a strange act, and afterwards it brought him to the brink of disaster, because the remittance form was later sent back by some office. The leaders and Party members of the pharmaceutical company took Shi Huailiang to task. "Everybody knows you're no Party member, what do you mean trying to pay Party dues?" "What's the idea of sending Party dues to Chairman Mao?" The questioners supplied their own answers: one, "You're just itching to join the Party, and have itched yourself into a hopeless frenzy!"; two, "You are mentally ill."

How can "itching to join the Party" count as a crime? Only, obviously, if the applicant is joining for private gain rather than for the public good. But what possible basis could they have for assuming that Shi Huailiang wished to join for promotions and lucre rather than to devote himself to the cause of communism? They were seeing their own faults in someone else. But perhaps not. Perhaps their speculations accurately reflected a certain feature of objective reality: that joining the Party really could become, and in fact already had become, a well-known means to realize personal gain.

But wasn't this precisely what was worrying Shi Huailiang, precisely what made him send his Party dues directly to Chairman Mao? He had been applying for years to join the Party. But in the meantime there were certain things he couldn't understand. A person in the Xindian granary had been expelled from the Party only three months after joining, charged with illegally purchasing more than ten tons of state grain. A person in the County Grain Section had been expelled from the Party four months after joining, charged as a neo-bourgeois element. Another person had been detained for interrogation in solitary confinement three days after joining the Party. When the truth came out, it became clear that all these people had committed crimes before entering the Party. Then how was it that this sort of person could get into the Party? Once, during an official trip to Harbin and elsewhere, Shi Huailiang learned that quite a few who joined the Party did not go through proper channels but entered as "specially approved" members, all via "connections." "If this goes on for long," he mused to himself, "won't all these people inevitably change the nature of the Party? This is serious!" But how could he get this message to Chairman Mao? If he wrote a letter, Chairman Mao probably wouldn't receive it. Besides, think of the trouble if the letter fell into the wrong hands! He thought long and hard and finally came up with the idea of mailing his "Party dues" to Chairman Mao as a hint. Chairman Mao would surely wonder why this fellow hadn't paid his dues to the County Party Committee. "If he mailed them to me, there certainly must be some problem with the local Party." If Chairman Mao were to realize this and send down his instructions, Shi Huailiang could then let fly all his charges without fear of reprisals. He could send the authorities a report that would tell everything about the whole Bin County Party organization.

He had dreamed a lovely dream. But nothing came of it, and all he actually got for his efforts was a flurry of denunciations. The problems never reached the ears of the higher-ups. Yet this only reinforced Shi Huailiang's belief that the Party structure had suffered a breakdown that had to be corrected. His concern for things outside his purview was one of the symptoms of his "mental illness."

Shi Huailiang was different from Liu Changchun. Shi was much steadier, simpler, and more good-natured. He typically wore a silly grin on his face and did not look at all like the combative or cantankerous sort. His "mental illness" showed in his extraordinary sensitivity to the suffering of the masses. He seemed to reserve an extra nerve in constant readiness to pick up signals from strangers in need. He was a man of few words, unflappable and unhurried. The energy that others spent on talking he would devote to thought. Why was it, he wondered, that in 1976, when Bin County had had only one drought, a drought that hadn't even caused lower productivity (then still over 1130 pounds per acre) they were already suffering from lack of food, clothing, and fuel? Why did there have to be national emergency allocations of money, food, and coal? Why was there a big drive in the county seat for contributions of winter clothing? Why, even with these measures, did so many peasant families have to burn the thatch from their roofs and the frames of their bed-platforms to get heat? How could it be that, after so many years of socialism, both collectives and individuals were as poor as this? Every evening he spent a bit of time studying the works of Marx, Lenin, and Chairman Mao. Since his income was so low, he was able to buy only the thinner volumes. Yet he was already well versed in the *Anti-Dühring*.[10] Despite his poor education, he liked to write occasional reports on investigations of social phenomena, or the like, as if he were a researcher from the Bin County branch of the Chinese Academy of Social Sciences. This was no joke. There were plenty of people in Bin County more learned and literate than he, and plenty who were better writers, but Shi Huailiang was the only person anyone had ever known who considered unpaid social research to be his personal responsibility.

This being the case, it was quite natural that his attention should come to focus on the internal workings of the pharmaceutical company. As soon as it did, his life opened a new chapter whose title might have been "The Tragedy of Independent Thought: The Price of Concern for Country and People is Sacrifice of Oneself," or "A Good Person Almost Always Comes to Grief."

The first thing he observed at the pharmaceutical company was one aspect of the problem of "connections" that we have already discussed. From the time Secretary Pan arrived there, he began building his own little circles and cliques within the leadership. He drove out the old leadership one by one. Four of the five people in the new leadership weren't even members of the labor union! Then, after he had been secretary for two years, Secretary Pan suddenly struck it rich. When he arrived he had owed the public treasury more than $850, and two years later he had returned it all. Not only that, his son had bought a moped and a hunting rifle, and his family had turned up with expensive radios, clocks, watches, and so forth. Yet his salary was only $36.30 a month. Shi Huailiang continued to observe the personal relationships within the company, then gathered all his findings and wrote a wall poster:

> [H]ow strange it is that a certain leader in our company, though he lives in a socialist society in the eighth decade of the twentieth century, dreams the dreams of an eighteenth-century feudal monarch. His doctrine is "I am king," and whoever disobeys him is in for trouble. The workers in the pharmaceutical company have none of the rights of citizens. They have become slaves. The leaders are doing whatever they please to the workers, and are subverting the nature of a collectively owned company.

When Shi Huailiang was preparing another wall poster, this one about Wang Shouxin, some people tried to dissuade him by saying, "Forget it—you can't do anything about them." But he only laughed and replied, "So what if I can't? History will record that there was somebody who opposed Wang Shouxin. That, too, has its uses."

On September 15, 1978, he wrote yet another wall poster that he took personally to glue up inside the County Party building. It was a very unusual poster, entitled "A Satellite for Social Science." It began thus:

> In the eighth decade of the twentieth century, several leaders of the Bin County Party Committee successfully launched a satellite for the "social bourgeoisie,"[11] thereby benefiting China's social sciences. The satellite not only provided valuable material for the scientific research of the Chinese Academy of Social Sciences; every socialist country in the world could, in my view, learn from its data. Wang Shouxin was in possession of neither factories nor land nor shops—no private means of production. Nonetheless, she was able to accumulate as much as $276,500 in cash and nine hundred kinds of material supplies. This qualifies hers as a rich and powerful family. In my view the phenomenon of Wang Shouxin has to have its scientific explanation; otherwise it would not have come into existence. I conclude that a dissection and analysis of it will promote the development of human society and of social science. Accordingly I call upon all the successive leaders of the County Party Committee who have been implicated with Wang Shouxin (but I exclude Zhang Xiangling), plus the various section and bureau chiefs who are also involved: Do not be afraid, and lift your sights above the question of your own culpability. Consider the fate of Party and country. Report the whole story, in simple, unadorned truth, to the provincial and central authorities. Summarize the lessons to be learned.

This was a most beneficial and necessary wall poster.

Joy Lined with Worry

In 1978, Bin County began its "Double Strike" campaign.[12] On August 1, the first wall poster attacking Wang Shouxin for corruption appeared. This was the work of Liu Changchun again!

On August 5, a work team from the County Party Committee stationed itself at the fuel company. This time it seemed the

County Party Committee really meant business. Yet while the battle was ending in victory, it was also revealing some problems.

When a Communist Party county committee dispatches a work team to look into the problems of an enterprise over which it is charged with leadership, how can this work team receive no support from the local Party organization? From start to finish, not a single Communist Party member came forward to expose Wang Shouxin to the work team.

The work team leader, Gu Zhuo, was a clear-headed and capable comrade. He and many of his team worked so hard that they gave up sleep and lost weight. Yet even after three months they could uncover no material that conclusively proved Wang Shouxin's corruption.

Comrade Gu Zhuo acknowledged that the only important information supplied to his work team during the investigation came from the same Liu Changchun. Liu was also the only one to take the initiative in providing information. Flush with excitement, he had told Gu Zhuo that "Wang Shouxin's den is at White Rock." (Later, hundreds of thousands of dollars did indeed turn up in her illicit treasury at the White Rock Business Department.) "She sells state-enterprise coal as small-pit coal and marks up the price. You can have my head if she isn't guilty of corruption! I think she may be the biggest embezzler in the entire country."

"Enough, enough!" Gu Zhuo had been thinking to himself, quite unconvinced. But the facts eventually showed that every word Liu Changchun had said was true.

Gu Zhuo had bridled at what Liu Changchun said next. "I've told all this to Secretary Guan and to the provincial and prefectural leaders. If you don't clear things up here you'll have to pay for it. I'll get you indicted!"

Liu Changchun's old shortcoming—of not caring whom he offended—had riled Gu Zhuo. "I'd be perfectly happy if you went to the County Committee and got me recalled! You think this job is a piece of cake?"

Gu Zhuo later recalled something that Liu Changchun had said. "If I can't topple Wang Shouxin, I'm not going to close my eyes when I die!" Gu wondered how anyone could talk this way. Wasn't this personal animosity? It never occurred to him to ask what was wrong with a bit of personal animosity directed at the forces of evil. The social forces represented by Wang Shouxin had completely destroyed this man's family. Could anyone marvel that the White-Haired Girl hated Huang Shiren?[13] But the Party members in the fuel company not only felt no personal animosity toward Wang Shouxin—they didn't even feel any "public" animosity toward her.

This, however, was not Comrade Gu Zhuo's fault. For many years the commonly held view had been that the collective and the individual were separate and opposed. Personal wishes, feelings, and inclinations, no matter how proper and reasonable, or even high-minded, had all been trampled into the ground as "individualism."

The various prejudices against Liu Changchun deterred the work team from assiduously following up the important information he gave them. Another piece of important information that turned up was also ignored. This was a letter of August 28 written "to County Party Secretary Guan in confidence" by the peasants of the Pine River Brigade of the Raven River Commune. The letter raised nineteen important questions about Wang Shouxin for the County Party Committee to consider. Each question was solidly backed by supporting evidence. Moreover, the first of the nineteen points was, purely by coincidence, the same matter that Liu Changchun had pointed out—the "small-pit coal" surcharges that had provided Wang Shouxin her opportunity for embezzlement. The letter clearly pointed out the existence of the problem and could have given the County Party Committee some concrete leads with which to begin their investigation.

But it seems the work team never saw this letter, or at least paid no attention to it. How else could they have spent all of September and October "so vexed we could not eat or sleep well" and still have failed to determine whether or not Wang Shouxin was indeed guilty of corruption? And why would they have worried about the possibility of falsely accusing Wang Shouxin, making it "a terrible pity to have to reverse her verdict sometime in the future"? All they needed was a direct raid on her base at White Rock. Interrogations of Ma Zhanqing and Sun Xiyin would have provided the necessary breakthrough in the case.

The problem with the work team was the same as that with the County Party Committee. Both were divorced from the masses and therefore divorced from reality. The work team's attitude toward Zhao Yu, chief of the Commerce Section, shows the laughable proportions this problem could assume. It was obvious from the time they arrived on the scene that Zhao Yu ought to have been an important lead, so they went to him for information on Wang Shouxin. Yet the connection between Zhao Yu and Wang Shouxin was an open secret. Because of his public opposition of Tian Fengshan, Commissar Yang in 1969 had made Zhao Yu number-one man in the Party organization of the Commerce Bureau. Wang Shouxin had been his second-in-command. Zhao Yu had intercepted all the letters of accusation the masses had written about Wang Shouxin, neither investigating them nor questioning her. When Wang Shouxin pushed a large group of workers out of the fuel company, he gave her his backing. And it was also he who praised Wang Shouxin at a mass meeting called by the Commerce Bureau; she was "strict in the administration of her enterprise, ruthless in checking unhealthy trends, and correct when she revoked the licenses of certain drivers!"

In 1976, when Zhao Yu was doing political indoctrination at the Raven River Commune, he lived at the hostel of the White Rock Business Department. The commune's cadres, the workers at White Rock, and members of neighboring communes all rushed to him with exposés of the violent tyranny, the extravagant waste, the fraudulent pricing practices, the disruption of the economy, and other offenses perpetrated by Wang Shouxin and Ma Zhanqing. All of this Zhao Yu suppressed. "Don't try and mess with Old Lady Wang!" he threatened. "You'll only get yourselves into trouble!"

In 1977 there was an ideological cleanup of Party members in the Commerce Section. Shi Huailiang, as a worker in the pharmaceutical company, wrote four wall posters that were right on the mark in exposing Wang Shouxin. But Zhao Yu would not allow them to be posted.

When Liu Changchun put up his poster attacking Wang Shouxin, Zhao Yu, who could see that Liu did this at great risk, took pleasure in the prospect of Liu's suffering. "This guy Liu

Changchun is quite a go-getter! The only one out of half a million people to speak out—he'll get what's coming to him sooner or later, just wait!" When Shi Huailiang wrote posters supporting Liu Changchun, Zhao Yu ordered the work team that was stationed at the pharmaceutical company to cause trouble for Shi Huailiang. More than ten struggle sessions of various sizes were held in an effort to have Shi Huailiang branded a counterrevolutionary.

It was precisely at the time Zhao Yu had ordered this persecution of Shi Huailiang that the Party work team at the fuel company came to him inquiring about Wang Shouxin's crimes. How absurd can you get?

But absurdities were everywhere. Here there was a work team sent to the fuel company by the Communist Party's County Committee, and at the same time cadres of the Communist Party were busy frustrating that work team as well as the whole Party Committee. While one of them was running to Wang Shouxin to warn her that she was the target of the campaign, another was concluding a pact with her to cover up each other's crimes. Yet a third was busily scheming with her about how best to evade the imminent attack. Let's look at a conversation between Wang Shouxin and the County Revolutionary Committee's chief of agriculture in August 1978, five days before the work team moved into the fuel company:

"I've come simply to warn you that a work team is on the way. You are the target; they're going to put you on the stand. . . . Now, about that incriminating material I gave you . . . I want it back before it incriminates me."

"Impossible. Ours is a proper relationship. . . . Can you arrange to have Liu XX be appointed leader of this work team?"

"I only handle agriculture; I have no say in such things."

"If you could arrange to have a woman sent, I could run her ragged, completely wear her out. Can't you figure out a way to have a woman sent?"

"Don't try to choose who'll be sent. Whomever they send will be tougher than Xun Hongjun, and that old geezer really gave me a hard time last year. Meng XX is all right, more stable. . . . Liu Changchun once came to my house urging me to attack you, but I wouldn't."

Two days later, this fellow nevertheless went looking for Liu XX. "Do you have a work assignment?" he asked. "If not, come to the fuel company!"

Ah, connections! Such is the nature of those endlessly magical connections!

The final cracking of the case of Wang Shouxin was complex and exciting, especially in the way several hundred people were mobilized to track down and recover all the money. But I cannot use space here for all these interesting details, because there is a more important point that deserves our attention.

The more important point is that after Zhou Lu told the work team of his and Wang Shouxin's embezzlement, he begged the work team to protect him. "You have to be responsible for my safety," he told Gu Zhuo. "If she finds out I've told you everything, she'll move heaven and earth to get me killed. What if she comes to my door in the middle of the night to do me in—what am I going to do?"

In the case of Sun Xiyin, the work team had assigned guards to him beginning the very night he confessed. This had delighted him, for he also had feared that without such protection Wang Shouxin would kill him.

Liu Changchun's circumstances were somewhat different, but some well-intentioned people went out of their way to warn him, too. "Be careful when you go out after dark from now on," they said. "Wang Shouxin despises you. She'd part with a small fortune to see you dead."

Even reporters and investigators who came to look into the whole story of Wang Shouxin and Bin County had people come to them with warnings as they left. "When you come next time, you'd better look out for your personal safety. Don't take any comfort from the fact that Wang Shouxin has been locked up; the situation in Bin County is rather complicated."

The situation in Bin County was indeed complicated. And who can wonder that this is so? All ten of the people jailed in the case of Wang Shouxin were members of the Communist Party.

The former Bin County Party Committee secretary, that so-called sly fox who married into Wang Shouxin's family, tried to conceal Wang Shouxin's embezzled funds for her. He also came up with a scheme for her. "Get yourself one of those giant earthen jars, put the money in the bottom, and cover it with something else. Then bury it as deep as possible . . ."

The "complications" did not end in Bin County. Wang Shou-xin's eldest son, Liu Zhimin, was under investigation in Harbin by the Sungari River Prefectural Party Committee. His corruption and criminal activities had become quite obvious. Those "bud-dies" of his, who had arranged for him and his wife to get job transfers and who had removed incriminating material from his files (getting, of course, quite a reward for this) were still doing all they could to help him. Even when Liu Zhimin was "under surveillance," he wined and dined himself just as before; those charged with watching him helped him to while away the time by playing chess and poker with him. He could even hop into a lim-ousine and ride to Acheng County, over thirty miles away, in or-der to conclude a mutual-protection pact with an accomplice.

The case of Wang Shouxin's corruption has been cracked. But how many of the social conditions that gave rise to this case have really changed? Isn't it true that Wang Shouxins of all shapes and sizes, in all corners of the land, are still in place, continuing to gnaw away at socialism, continuing to tear at the fabric of the Party, and continuing to evade punishment by the dictatorship of the proletariat?

People, be on guard! It is still too early to be celebrating victo-ries . . .

August 1979, Shenyang City, Jilin Province

Author's postscript: For reasons that my readers can well under-stand, the names of certain characters in this piece have been changed.

NOTES

Originally published in *Renmin wenxue* (Beijing), no. 9, 1979.

1. *Wenyi qingkuang*, no. 9 (1980): 13–15.
2. Ibid., pp. 13–15.
3. Bad harvests in 1959, 1960, and 1961 were the results of natural calamities in addition to man-made calamities caused by the policies of

the Great Leap Forward, a highly impractical effort to get instant results in industry and agriculture.

4. Here and throughout this book, "dollars" refers to the equivalent of 1979 U.S. dollars. Measures of length, area, weight, etc. are converted to miles, acres, tons, etc.

5. A campaign was under way in 1979 to praise the young woman Zhang Zhixin, who spoke out against repression during the Cultural Revolution and paid for it with her life.

6. Presumably "On All-out Dictatorship Over the Bourgeoisie," by Zhang Chunqiao, in *Red Flag*, no. 4 (1975), and "On the Social Basis of Lin Biao's Anti-Party Clique," by Yao Wenyuan in *Red Flag*, no. 3 (1975). *Red Flag* is the theoretical journal of the Central Committee of the Communist Party. Zhang and Yao were leading Party theorists, and two of the Gang of Four.

7. A traitor in the widely read novel *Red Crag* (1961) by Luo Guangbin and Yang Yiren.

8. The martyred heroine of *Red Crag*.

9. Fearless military hero in the *Romance of the Three Kingdoms* and other stories, whose entrance in Peking operas is always announced by drumrolls.

10. *Anti-Dühring* is the brief title for Friedrich Engels's *Herr Eugen Dühring's Revolution in Science* (1878), an important work in clarifying basic theories of Marx.

11. "Social bourgeoisie" refers to people who act like the bourgeoisie within the socialist system. It is not a standard term, but is parallel to "social imperialists," which in the 1970s was a standard term for the Soviet leadership, who were charged with acting like imperialists within a socialist system.

12. The name of the campaign also rather callously means "playing doubles," as in ping-pong.

13. In the famous story "The White-Haired Girl," the heroine's hair turns prematurely white as a result of oppression by the landlord here referred to, Huang Shiren.

Sound Is Better than Silence
Translated by Michael S. Duke

The title of this piece of reportage, which carries in Chinese the connotation of "after all, sound is better than silence" (*bijing you-sheng sheng wusheng*), is immediately recognizable as a dramatic reversal of the famous line "at that time, silence was more powerful than sound" (*cishi wusheng sheng yousheng*) from a Tang Dynasty poem by Bo Juyi (772–846) called "Song of the *Pipa*." Bo Juyi's line evokes the poignancy of pure silence when the sound of the *pipa,* a stringed instrument, ceases. The protagonist of Liu Bin-yan's piece, Zhou Jiajie, speaks in neither the sweet tones of a *pipa* nor the glass-shattering shrillness of *die kleine* Oskar in *The Tin Drum* by Günter Grass, but he refuses to talk in the same way that Oskar refuses to grow during a twenty-year period in which his country and its leaders are pursuing ever more disastrous policies. In the end, his patience and his labors are rewarded; but clearly he will have to speak up loudly for what is right, because his former critics still hold powerful positions. —TRANS.

The cacophony of gongs and drums, the earsplitting explosions of firecrackers, and the elated laughter and shouting of the populace filled every corner of the small county seat of Xinjin County in Sichuan Province. It seemed as though all 203,000 county residents had descended on the county seat on the same day, and everyone was quite obviously willing and able to express his emotions through the tumultuous noisemaking. Perhaps percussion instruments and even firecrackers were invented for precisely such occasions, when speaking and singing cannot fully express the intensity of people's emotions.

I really don't know at what time the people began to fear the sound of their own noisemaking and chose to remain silent. . . . But during the New Year's Festival of 1980 in Sichuan everyone was talking and laughing to their hearts' content. During the New Year's Festivals of recent years, all of the well-wishing was essentially over by the fifth day of the first lunar month, but this year people were still visiting back and forth even after the fifteenth.[1]

In both the county seat and the commune, several groups of dragon and lion dancers burst forth on New Year's Day. The entire populace turned out to squeeze in around the wildly dancing dragons and lions and to catch a glimpse of which group would be the strongest and most daring in climbing up the tall pole to retrieve the prized red paper package hung there by a local shop or government office—this was an ancient custom, probably a rite of spring. Everywhere the older people could be heard to exclaim nostalgically, "Haven't seen this in over twenty years . . ."

It was an all too familiar refrain. Had not even the County Committee secretary and the commune and production brigade secretaries, describing the changes in the people's lives and production in 1979, remarked that "this hasn't happened here since 1957"? No question about it: in only one year the peasants' net income had increased an average of 40 percent, and town and country bank savings had increased more than 50 percent, not to mention a large increase in the rations of grain and edible oils. In what previous year had such good things ever happened?

For some thirteen hundred plus families, however, the greatest jubilation was not on that account. During many repeated campaigns since 1957, the heads of these households had been repeatedly branded as this or that sort of "bad element," and their families had had to suffer through ten to twenty gloomy and miserable years. This year marked the first time that these people could stand forth in the light of day and celebrate New Year's on an equal footing with their neighbors. Relatives and friends who had been forced to break off all relationships for ten to twenty years in order to "draw a clear line"[2] were once again able to visit together. They were constantly repeating a single refrain: "We never thought we would see this day!"

One person in the crowd received particular attention. The people crowded around the Fangxing Commune's lion-dancing troupe, continually pointed to a certain lion, and happily yet quietly exclaimed: "He's the one, he's the one, Zhou the Mute . . ."

I

In 1968, at the season for making grain deliveries to the state, an insignificant person from a small village in Sichuan's Xinjin County took sick. The illness was very strange: all he did was trip and fall, but it made him deaf and dumb.

The sick man's name was Zhou Jiajie, and he was a member of Production Brigade Number Eight of the Fangxing Commune. At that time, following the entire nation, the county seat was a flurry of activity—busily clearing out the class ranks.[3] As his family was helping this mute man along the central street in the county seat, they were met by a gaggle of people, among whom were some unfortunate ones done up with various colored streamers, clothes, and makeup to represent "class enemies." The former village elder was dressed up in a long Confucian robe, carried a water pipe, had a sword hung at his side, and was followed by a retinue of young village men. The getup of the GMD [Nationalist] army officers made them look as if they'd just stepped down from a movie screen. A "female spy" was so rouged up that she looked, a little too unrealistically, like a prostitute. . . . The booming of gongs and drums, the chanting of slogans, and the repeated shouts of derision by the crowds who had gathered to join the fun and enjoy themselves laughing and yelling at that group of despicable enemies all blended together. The ink was not yet dry on their long banner, and Zhou Jiajie could only make out the last line, "The struggle between the Chinese Communist Party and the Nationalist Party continues," as he was helped down a narrow little lane.

That was a particularly noisy era. The sounds of slogans, drums, speeches, arguments, laughter, sobbing, bloody battles, and explosions being emitted from the Chinese mainland fiercely shook the apathetic and unfeeling world of men as well as the dark chaotic universe, announcing the beginning of an unprecedented period in history. Not only was the Chinese nation to be wrenched off of its historical track, but the entire world was to be remade. The whole world concentrated its gaze upon this homeland of our ancient civilization and awaited with joyful expectation or fearful trepidation the advent of a great miracle.

Living in the midst of this world revolution, Zhou Jiajie must be considered most unfortunate! It was right then that he suddenly lost the ability to speak or hear.

He spent his meager savings on a month in the hospital, but his illness was not in the least improved. His family was most anxious and the villagers felt completely confused, but only Zhou Jiajie himself appeared quite unconcerned by his illness; and that was because he knew that his was an absolutely incurable malady. At that time, he was only worried about one thing: "I must never never let anyone find out that my deafness and dumbness are feigned."

The autumn in West Sichuan had been quite lovely. All the grasses, trees, and various argicultural crops were greedily breathing in the sunshine in anticipation of the coming six-month-long season of darkness. The year's harvest had been fair, and one could more or less make it through the fall and winter; as for the coming year, in those days there was no reason to make any plans, and no way to carry them out even if one made them.

It was during that time that Zhou Jiajie took his son to deliver his grain allotment to the state. Father and son had each walked about seven miles carrying their load on shoulder poles. On the way home, their shoulders felt much lighter, and they should have been talking and laughing, but Xinqiang noticed that his father was frowning darkly without saying a word. Just as they were passing by a burial ground and the sky was already growing dark, Xinqiang suddenly heard the sound of something very heavy dropping on the ground. Turning back quickly, he saw that his father had fallen down by the side of a grave. The ten-year-old boy was scared to death. Later on the villagers brought a wooden door and carried the still unconscious Zhou Jiajie back home.

When Zhou Jiajie finally woke up it was already after midnight. He still had a slight headache. He tried to think back on how he had happened to fall down. If he had not had a head full of worries, had not been imagining all sorts of troubles as he walked along, he probably would not have taken such a tumble. A thought that had been pounding in his head constantly for the past few days now mercilessly drove out every other idea, even overriding the sporadic throbbing of his headache: "What am I going to do? They are going to beat me to death. . . . Not even those leading cadres could escape . . . and that school principal lady . . ."

He had already seen many other people tied up and beaten, but this one he remembered with particular clarity. He knew her, that school principal lady. She had her hands tied behind her back and was hung there on a tree. Her attackers used a three-foot-long wooden club with a length of coarse rope tied to the end; the rope seemed to have been carefully soaked in water first. In the beginning the woman cried out sadly, but very quickly lost her breath and grew completely silent. Zhou Jiajie could see only the faint twitching of the twisted little finger of her right hand (either a birth defect or the remnant of a childhood accident); only that slight trembling of one limb showed that she was not yet dead. He had secretly wiped away his tears and quietly stolen away.

"They will force me to explain[4] everything. But I'm not an escaped landlord at all and I've never cheated anyone. Starving other people to death was never my mistake, but all of that is impossible to explain, and talking about it will only increase the weight of my crime. How *can* I explain it all? But if I don't explain myself, they'll beat me . . ."

This man of thirty-six years of age feared only two things: being humiliated or causing others humiliation; being beaten or beating others. He was too sensitive and could not bear to feel himself or others suffering either mental or physical pain. It was precisely this mortal weakness of his that made him quite ineligible to play the role of a hero of that age. If his heart had only been a little harder during those years, he would not have fallen into his present plight.

He felt a loud buzzing in his ears. Some people said that sort of a fall could bring on a stroke, one so bad a person might die or become an invalid or even become deaf and dumb. "Mute?" Zhou Jiajie's heart beat faster: "If I really became mute, that would be fine. If I could not talk when they beat me and 'struggled'⁵ against me, then they wouldn't beat me half to death."

In this manner, then, this Chinese Communist Party member, this excellent rural cadre, this man who had given his entire youth to the great enterprise of socialist transformation, on this piece of land that he had watered with the sweat of his brow, in order to allow himself and others to go on living, was forced to make a final resolution to seal up his own mouth!

Early the next morning when his son Xinqiang called him for breakfast, he did not answer. Thinking he was still sleeping, his son came over and patted his blanket, but he still did not move. His son grew agitated and shouted at him, but he only opened his eyes slightly, shook his head, and made a gesture to indicate that he could neither hear nor speak. When his wife ran in and saw the way he looked, she was so anxious and afraid that she began to cry.

The villagers helped to take Zhou Jiajie to the county seat, but in the end they carried him back again without any appreciable change.

Feigning muteness was just a hasty expedient to deal with a pressing problem. When he "became" a mute, he did not even have time to think about what sorts of situations he would have to deal with once he "really was" a deaf mute. He had quietly contemplated that once this campaign was over he would just open his mouth and start talking again. But who could have imagined that the rape flowers would bloom and fade, fade and bloom again—that this particular campaign would last longer than the Anti-Japanese War?

Actually, when the Cultural Revolution began, Zhou Jiajie had long since become a "political corpse." In 1960 he was expelled from the Party, deprived of his position as production brigade branch secretary, and branded an escaped landlord and alien class element. In those days he worked very hard and was even given a model-commune-member evaluation, but he was still a nonentity as far as political and social life were concerned. Eight years as a political mute was no doubt very good preparation for actually "becoming" a complete mute later on.

He had originally thought that the storm of the Cultural Revolution would pass over such a political invalid as he was then. He never imagined that he would be unable to avoid trouble. The village Rebel Faction leader, Wang Quan, came to visit him, urged him to join their "organization," and promised, "We can settle your case." Zhou Jiajie knew very well what sort of a character Wang was and so he diplomatically declined his offer. Of course he hoped to get himself exonerated, and he never gave up hope that some day he could return to the Party ranks, but that was an internal Party matter that had nothing at all to do with the likes of Wang Quan!

A short while later, Zhou Jiajie went to market and saw a bulletin listing twenty targets of the class "purification" campaign. He immediately tensed up and an inauspicious premonition seized hold of his mind. Just as he expected, in a few days' time big-character posters appeared reading, "Drag out the alien class element Zhou Jiajie!"

In 1960, when he had been expelled from the Party and branded an alien class element, Zhou Jiajie believed that that was the final blow. He thought that he had fallen to the lowest level of society. Who could have imagined that they would have to "continue the revolution"? This new attack made it impossible for him to express his hopes, desires, opinions, or feelings, or even to associate with other people.

This was not the end of his troubles, however; misfortune itself seemed to possess the ability to grow naturally. When you are forced to pretend to be deaf and dumb, you in fact leave yourself open to even greater calamity: if it is ever revealed that you are only pretending, then you will never be able to escape even greater punishment. That a class enemy like you could have the effrontery to escape from struggle and trick the revolutionary organization! Redoubled humiliation and heavier blows from revolutionary clubs might descend on Zhou Jiajie at any moment!

Zhou Jiajie could do nothing less than prepare himself thoroughly for whatever circumstances might arise at any time. Living among other people, he had to sever all natural relations with them. That was no easy task!

When he walked down the road and people approached him, he ignored them if he could; if not, he simply nodded his head. If he met a close acquaintance he could smile a little. That became Zhou Jiajie's only opportunity to smile. A smile in any other situation could give rise to suspicions that he had heard something.

Most frightening were sounds that came from behind; there was almost no way that he could guard against them. Once when he was cutting bamboo and a woman came up close behind him and gave a fierce shriek, Zhou Jiajie shuddered all over. The woman began to wonder: How could this deaf man hear my shout? Luckily, his nephew, Zhou Zhongci, was sitting beside him and spoke up, "How could that be?! I've tried it many times, he simply can't hear. When he moved just now it was only because he wanted to move." In that way the woman was just barely mollified.

While working in the fields together, people like to banter back and forth and come out with humorous quips. Everyone could laugh when this happened—everyone except Zhou Jiajie. Not only could he not laugh; even if his face twitched slightly or the expression in his eyes changed, he could be giving himself away!

Zhou Jiajie was not being overcautious. He had already heard people angrily exclaim many times, "He's faking pretty well all right, but if we dragged him down to a struggle session we'd see if he could talk or not!"

Sometimes Zhou Jiajie actually envied true deaf mutes. "I'd be a lot safer if I were really deaf!" Sure, he could close his eyes and not see, he could cease to sniff with his nose, and he could keep his mouth shut; but how could he stop up his ears? How could he hear something and yet have no reaction? Nevertheless, Zhou Jiajie knew in his heart that he had to succeed at this. He knew that his own ears had already changed from an indispensable organ of life into a dangerous threat, a tool that other people might use to harm him.

II

His new life was not completely without compensation. After he had broken off all associations with other people, he found that he had more time to think about himself and his past experiences. The one thing that he kept pondering over and over again was how he, Zhou Jiajie, had come to such a sad pass.

At Liberation the seventeen-year-old Zhou Jiajie was still in school, but from the time Land Reform began he was an activist. He led the way in setting up Mutual Aid Teams. When others chipped in one or two thousand square feet of land, he threw in a whole acre. And when the autumn harvest was counted up, his team had the highest productivity, with an average of thirteen hundred pounds more per acre than all the other teams—one acre produced over two tons of grain, a feat that was not to be repeated for more than twenty years. It created a sensation throughout the district and people came to the grain distribution station to learn from them, asking them to summarize their experiences. Young Zhou Jiajie's organizational skills and economic abilities became apparent that year.

In 1953 Zhou Jiajie joined the Youth League and the Communist Party. He was the first middle peasant Party member to be recruited by the rural Party branch office. Naturally, this could not have been without good reason.

Zhou Jiajie also led the way in organizing early Agricultural Producers' Cooperatives. When these were transformed into advanced APCs, his responsibilities increased, and his economic abilities were given even greater scope to develop. His cooperative organized a collective pig farm, a noodle factory, and an apiary, all of which were well administered and made a great deal of money, once again becoming the most outstanding enterprises in the district. Everyone said that Zhou Jiajie was the district elder's "big-headed hammer," and that was the simple truth.

How could he help becoming the district elder's "big-headed hammer"? For every campaign, mission, or important undertaking, the district leaders called upon Zhou Jiajie to strike the first blow; and he really could strike a resounding blow. All the Party had to do was put out an appeal and he, Zhou Jiajie, was certain to respond. Whenever he made promises or issued challenges to other cooperatives, he always had a very practical plan in mind and never made idle boasts or went off half-cocked.

It was really quite hard on Zhou Jiajie to continue to press forward as single-mindedly as he did. At that time his family consisted of his old father, a widowed sister-in-law, and his wife; he was the only able-bodied male laborer. But so much of his time was taken up just attending meetings! It was often three or four in the morning before the meetings let out. When he returned home, the cooperative members were already preparing to start work. His family always complained. With his strength he could easily make three or four thousand work points a year, but as a cadre he only received a four- or five-hundred-work-point subsidy. Besides that, he didn't really think about his own family; if the cooperative lacked for anything, he would often take it from his home and give it to them. One time the cooperative needed some lumber and Zhou Jiajie simply told them, "Cut down my willow trees; cut down my pine trees!" His old father was so angry when he saw him light the lamp at night that he yelled at him, "What the hell are you reading? Put out the lamp!" The old man felt that their family had already suffered enough losses and was unwilling to add lamp oil to the list.

The pressure from his family had occasionally given Zhou Jiajie second thoughts: "Maybe I'd do better not being a cadre, just working my farm instead. . . . A lot of people have gotten rich these last few years." But then as soon as he considered that he was a Party member, considered that the local people trusted him and put the heavy responsibility for all of their property on his shoulders, and then remembered the commitment he had made to the Party and the local people—when he considered all of these things, his enthusiasm was rekindled and he began to work even harder.

That period seemed like a long, long time; it was actually no more than five short years, but what exciting years they were! Year by year life was improving right before one's eyes, and everyone worked with great enthusiasm. In Party meetings one felt just like a child beside its mother; you could say anything you thought and never worry about offending the leadership. When the state monopoly of purchasing and selling began, the leadership had criticized Zhou Jiajie as part of their effort to fulfill the state purchasing quota; but it was only a gentle reprimand and nothing came of it later.

Actually, Zhou Jiajie had been wronged even in that situation. When the state monopoly began in 1953, he made a careful estimate and decided to sell 1,650 pounds of his own grain, no small amount at that time. But the "work cadre" Han who was sent out from the county seat tapped his pencil on that 1,650 pound figure, mulled it over a few minutes, and then sort of mumbled out loud, "1,650, that's a little short, isn't it?" When Zhou Jiajie heard that, he felt hurt and immediately blurted out, "Then I'll sell 2,200 pounds!" as if he had really done something to let the Party down. In his eyes everyone sent down from the leadership ranks was the embodiment of the Party itself. If the Party felt the figure was too small, it must be because the revolution needed the grain. One result of his action was that his family complained bitterly to him. They had to live on short rations for several months that year.

Everyone says that 1958 was a turning point, but actually, many things were beginning to happen much earlier; it was just that no one really understood them.

Nineteen fifty-eight was certainly a historically unprecedented year. For a few months a carnival atmosphere prevailed. And how could people help being ecstatic? Suddenly they discovered that the communism they had thought was still in the distant future was right there before their very eyes! Everyone, even the Chinese Communist rural cadres so long noted for their extreme practicality, was caught up in the foolish intoxication of those days. Even Zhou Jiajie was slightly influenced in that direction.

Everything in those days had to break with convention—immediately, as quickly as possible, and as thoroughly as possible. Take Party meetings, for example. This most familiar activity of rural cadres took on a new form that year. Party meetings themselves were regarded as a magnificent method of "production." You see, every time a meeting was held, the per-acre grain production could shoot up several times. This kind of labor should not be slighted; it wasn't easy. The leadership had to apply great pressure; the grassroots cadres had to squeeze for all they were worth; then more pressure; then squeeze again . . . over and over until the production figure reached unprecedented levels and could be gloriously announced—say ten tons or even thirty tons per acre—and then their great work was accomplished and the meeting could be adjourned. Until they came up with a "big increase in production," the grassroots cadres could not even dream of leaving the meeting.

After a meeting in those days (when a meeting occupied many consecutive nights), even a strong young man in his twenties like Zhou Jiajie staggered down the road on the way home. When he got back to the production brigade at two or three in the morning, he still had to wake up all those commune members who had just closed their eyes after the nighttime struggle for production in order to announce where the next day's ceremonial "battle in the fields" was to take place, how all the tools and implements were to be arranged, etc. By the time everything was arranged properly, it was time to go to work again.

Zhou Jiajie's commitment to communism was beyond question; he wished that it could be realized tomorrow morning. With his great faith in the Party, he carried out every directive with his usual alacrity; but there was one thing that was very different from previous years: he often felt a struggle going on in his mind. There was one voice that accused him of being too conservative, backward, and unable to overcome superstition. This was an extremely gruff and frightening voice, though somewhat abstract. Another voice kept saying other things: The crops are sown too close together, aren't they? The production target is set too high, isn't it? We're going too fast, aren't we? Is this right? Can it be done? . . .

This voice was rather weak and timid, but it accorded with Zhou Jiajie's experience and the things he understood so well. For some reason, the more the conflict continued, the more he began to listen to the second voice.

At first, when the leadership asked him to do something, no matter what it was, he would carry it out, just as in the past; but gradually his faith in them weakened. Finally, he began to hold back a little and even to resist them in varying degrees. The orders he carried out were to collectivize hogs, to collectivize furniture and tools, to abandon work points, and to take meals in big communal mess halls. When the leadership went on to promise that everyone would soon move into "big buildings," each with an upstairs and a downstairs, electric lights, and telephones, he completely approved in his heart, but at the same time he felt somewhat confused. Where were the bricks and lumber to come from? When the order was issued to tear down the old houses, he couldn't do it. Although the houses were not his, he knew full well how much bamboo, wood, and labor it had taken to build them. He just couldn't do it. He couldn't help feeling skeptical: Why all this haste? If we tear down our old houses before we have any way to build new ones, where are we going to live? But he had to tear them down—it was a question of his attitude toward the "Three Red Banners."[6] Zhou Jiajie had to be resourceful; he chose only the oldest and most dilapidated houses for destruction. After he did that for a while, his conscience began to trouble him: was he not merely feigning compliance with the leadership? He should rightly report his own opinion and the actual conditions to the Party.

Recalling that period of history ten years later [1968 recalling 1958], Zhou Jiajie was much more aware of what had happened. The seeds of his present calamity had been sown mostly at that time. His thinking had been, and still was, too "conservative." He could not break the habit of "seeking truth from facts."[7]

At the district meeting called to report production figures, Zhou Jiajie screwed up his courage and reported, "Our commune production this year will average thirty-three hundred pounds per acre." Before he'd even finished speaking, he could see that Party Secretary Cai's expression had changed abruptly. His heart sank and he knew he'd never get away with it. As expected, Secretary

Cai pounded the table. Not long ago a county investigating team had discovered that Zhou Jiajie's commune was not planting the rice sprouts close enough together. They had criticized Zhou on the spot and made things embarrassing for District Branch Secretary Cai. And now Zhou Jiajie was reporting this disappointing figure; no wonder Secretary Cai was angry. He bellowed out: "Zhou Jiajie, you must be sleeping! Commune Number 21 has already reported six and a half tons per acre, and a progressive commune like yours comes up with less than two; how can that be?" Zhou Jiajie bowed his head and remained silent. Of course he knew if he reported six and a half tons he would win a prize—he could take home a brand-new bicycle and make a good impression on the leadership. But what would they do at autumn harvest time? He was responsible for over 130 families, with more than 500 mouths to feed; after the state grain purchases, could he ask them all to go hungry? . . . Later on, a female cadre from the county office told him: "You'd better report at least five tons; otherwise you'll never pass inspection." Zhou Jiajie hardened himself as much as he could: All right, if I have to report, I'll report three tons. How could he have known that the next day the ante would skyrocket again? One commune secretary actually reported a figure of thirty-three tons per acre! Zhou Jiajie once more became a midget. County Work Organization Director Zhang was extremely dissatisfied and kept staring at Zhou Jiajie. Not long after that meeting, the rumors began to fly: Zhou Jiajie used to be an outstanding district worker, and always understood the leadership's plans very quickly, but now he's no good: there's no question that his feelings about the Great Leap Forward are wrong. Zhou Jiajie did not know that he was already being closely watched.

There certainly were many "new things"[8] that year. For the previous few years Zhou Jiajie had always taken the lead in developing "new things," but that year he could no longer do it. He could no longer lead the way in burning up the people's firewood in order to scorch the earth and carry out full scale "militarization," in ordering old women to perform morning calisthenics and running, in making everyone sleep in their fields at night, in wasting perfectly good trees in order to make "wooden tracks" and carry out full-scale "vehicularization," in eliminating work points and changing to a fixed-wage system,[9] and even in smashing all private household cooking utensils in order to secure the "changeover to communal eating without any thought of turning back."

Zhou Jiajie felt extremely perplexed. Wouldn't he be happy to enter into communism tomorrow? That was why he joined the Party in the first place, but now he felt a certain uneasiness and suspicion. His keen insight into agricultural problems, handed down to him by generations of his ancestors, automatically made him respond negatively to those formalistic work methods that did not pay close attention to practical results: using up so much firewood to scorch the earth, tearing down the commune members' walls in order to fertilize the fields,[10] cutting down perfectly good bamboo for use in the mess-hall cooking fires . . . was all that worth the effort? What were they trying to accomplish? Why did they want the commune members to smash up their perfectly good pans and dishes? Were they supposed to eat out of their hats in the mess halls?

His greatest anxiety concerned the food supply. As a leader of mutual aid teams and agricultural cooperatives for several years, he had always had a certain balance sheet in mind: one acre can produce so much grain, one person can eat so much, and the state will purchase so much. Therefore, no matter how much the leadership kept on shouting, "What do we do if there's a surplus of food? Loosen your belts and eat up; build up your enthusiasm and produce," he continued to separate the food rations into three parts and ordered the mess hall to supply reasonably measured amounts. That only made the commune leadership angry again, and they sent down an order abolishing measured amounts. What could he do? Zhou Jiajie watched the commune members consume more than two pounds of grain per person each day, and he grew terribly anxious: when the autumn passed, what would they eat in the spring? A short while later it was time to pay the commune salaries. Where was the money to come from? The leadership sent down an order: cut down the commune members' bamboo and sell it in the marketplace! When this was done there was barely enough for each person to receive $1.30. The "communal mess system" had been in effect only two months, but the food ration was already exhausted. The best they could do was return to the system of rationing. By this time each person was to receive only three and a half ounces [two Chinese *liang*] per meal. But even these rations were not available. Originally over seventeen acres of red potatoes had been planted, but Secretary Cai did not have them harvested. He said, "Don't be so short-sighted; there's more rice than we can eat, so who wants those damn red potatoes?" But Zhou Jiajie continued to have some people secretly dig up a few and store them; in that way he could barely fulfill those "three and a half ounce" rations.

More and more things grew incomprehensible to Zhou Jiajie, and he became increasingly depressed. His production brigade was located at a road that everyone had to use to go from the commune center to all of the other production brigades. Consequently the leadership asked them to give a particularly large number of "performances"—night tilling, close planting, deep plowing . . . Even Zhou Jiajie, a grassroots cadre who had always been a devout believer in the leadership and in every directive they issued, finally arrived at a day when he simply could not take it.

One day another investigation team arrived from County Central. Commune Secretary Cai ordered Zhou Jiajie to take the deep-plowing team to the east side of the village to perform and then, after the investigation team had passed, to rush his people to the west side of the village so that the investigators could witness the performance again on their way back to the commune center. Before the commune official had finished conveying the order, Zhou Jiajie lost his temper and yelled at him, "What are you trying to do? Treat us like actors? We've got water buffaloes and plows and there are so many ditches to cross over—you know how much work it is to move from one side to the other? . . . You tell Secretary Cai we're not going to do it!"

A short time later, Zhou Jiajie lost his position as production brigade branch secretary and was sent to be a substitute principal at the production brigade's agricultural middle school.

III

By the beginning of 1959, a famine had already developed. Zhou Jiajie's Fifth Brigade could sell to the state only half the grain that they had been obliged to promise. This was hardly surprising, since, according to the inflated quotas, Fangxing Commune was supposed to complete a grain sale to the state of 4.4 million pounds. But that year's harvest amounted to a total of just over that amount—where were they to find all the "surplus" grain? According to the false production reports there was still supposed to be more than 4 million pounds in the people's hands even after subtracting their grain rations. If you said there was no more grain, would the peasants believe you? Thus the County Committee issued an urgent order: all of the grain currently stored at the various production brigades could not be moved, but must be gathered up and put into "people's granaries" in preparation for sale to the state.

What about seed grains then? There were no seed grains. The seedling fields had long since been made ready and were only waiting for the seedlings. Mosses and weeds began to flourish there, but there were still no paddies planted with seedlings.

In the last month of that year a struggle meeting was called by the production brigade to criticize and denounce Zhou Jiajie. The meeting was run personally by Ji Weishi, the former Party committee secretary of Dengshuang Commune. As it turned out, Secretary Cai of Fangxing Commune, the one who had believed Zhou Jiajie was too "right," had himself already been declared guilty of "rightist deviation" and deprived of his office. As an expert in class struggle, Ji Weishi had been sent down by the County Committee to rectify this backward commune. He brought along a great troop of people and took over the power and authority of several production brigade branch secretaries and bookkeepers.

"Zhou————Jia————jie————," Secretary Ji poured as much hatred as possible into his enunciation of those three syllables. His booming voice, which belied his short stature, immediately quieted the entire hall and established his authority and status as the embodiment of the Party: "This evil person who has wormed his way into our Party ranks is trying with all his might to topple our great, glorious, and correct Communist Party and ruin the work of socialist construction. We call on him now to confess to the criminal activities he has carried out from October of this year until this moment, activities intended to oppose the 'Three Red

Banners,' to topple the Eighth Production Brigade, and to injure the welfare of poor and lower-middle peasants!"

That was the first time that the twenty-eight-year-old Zhou Jiajie had stood in the accused's box. He was firmly convinced of his innocence and integrity, but the atmosphere of the meeting and Secretary Ji's tone made him feel unusually nervous. He was willing to admit his mistakes, even those mistakes that it was not really his responsibility to admit, but there was no way that he could accept the charge of being an "evil person" and confess to "criminal activities." While he was still trying to figure out just how to respond to such accusations, the agenda was advanced to the stage of "denunciation by the commune masses." He realized quite sadly, "I've been made a landlord!"

It seemed as if everything had been carefully prepared beforehand. The bookkeeper stood up and "confessed" that twenty dollars of the hundred and thirty dollars he personally had embezzled had been taken by Zhou Jiajie. Zhou Jiajie remembered very clearly that this bookkeeper had lent him twenty dollars two months ago when they went to market together. He had asked him specifically if it was public or personal money. The bookkeeper said it was his own money, and only then had Zhou borrowed it, saying very clearly, "I'll pay you back as soon as I sell my hog." Another person stood up to accuse him: "What do you mean only twenty dollars? The cooperative's noodle factory was ruined by him alone with several thousand dollars going into his own pockets; where else would he get the money to dress so well?" Zhou Jiajie laughed to himself: that would be easy to clear up. All the money had gone to buy fertilizer. It hadn't been as much as that, either. Yet another commune member stood up and said that Zhou Jiajie always sat his ass on the side of the landlords. Once he had borrowed a hoe from a landlord, a broken hoe at that, and Zhou Jiajie had made him guarantee compensation to the landlord.

All that was only a prologue. The play proper was just about to unfold.

Wang Quan—who would become a rebel faction leader seven years later—volunteered to reveal Zhou Jiajie's family history in order to supply Secretary Ji's needs. He also incited a crowd of people to join in his accusations. At that moment he jumped to his feet and shouted: "Zhou Jiajie himself is nothing more than a dyed-in-the-wool landlord element!"

This was something one could not afford to be vague about. Zhou Jiajie knew very well the weight of that word "landlord." He wanted to explain before the district people that there must have been some mistake. At the time of the land reform, his family owned only two and two-thirds acres of fourth-class land, a little over a third of an acre per person, which was less than the average amount per person in the village as a whole.

"Tell us, what relation do you have to Zhou Sanma's wife?" Wang Quan asked accusingly.

Zhou Sanma's wife? She was pretty famous. Right, she was Zhou Jiajie's great-grandmother. Zhou Jiajie began to explain that the family fortune completely declined during his grandfather's generation.

Before he could even finish speaking, a loud "thump" resounded through the hall as Ji Weishi took his revolver out and pounded on the table. This was Secretary Ji's favorite ploy for stifling the opposition and encouraging the masses' fighting spirit. He raised his voice:

"Namby-pamby! You won't admit it? Take him away!"

Several guards who were stationed nearby rushed in around Zhou. That was the "organizational conclusion." The next act was the "mass denunciation." Having been a leader for several years, it would be hard not to have offended some people, but even as loudly as a few people shouted and screamed, the general meeting was surprisingly quiet.

It was then time for Secretary Ji to sum things up: the landlord element Zhou Jiajie had wormed his way into the Party, disrupted socialist construction, and committed a multitude of crimes. At this time, in response to the demands of the masses, he would be sentenced to perform supervised labor.[11] His last few words made the greatest impression on Zhou Jiajie: "Zhou Jiajie, listen to me: you can forget about ever returning home in this life—unless every pot in your house rattles and shakes as you do!"

Ji Weishi was famous for his eloquence. A few short and forceful words had expressed everything he felt about struggle with the class enemy. After he finished speaking, he looked over to see Zhou Jiajie's reaction, then waved his arms in satisfaction to indicate that the meeting was over.

Zhou Jiajie was visibly stunned, his face deathly pale. He understood what Ji's words meant, "unless every pot in your house rattles and shakes . . ." He would never return home unless it was as a ghost. Vicious! Even in earlier struggle meetings against the landlords, Zhou Jiajie had never said anything like that. And besides, was it not an announcement of the death penalty? When was that ever a Party policy? . . . As he thought to himself, he looked around the meeting hall; at least his son had not come. He could see only his wife's back; she had drawn in her shoulders and seemed smaller and thinner than ever . . .

In a short while Zhou Jiajie was sent to West Ditch to "assemble for training." At that time he learned that with the exception of Chen Jiaci and a few others who were in college, all of the commune branch secretaries had become "evil persons"—even the commune director and two undersecretaries. All of these people were of poor peasant ancestry.

Everyday life at West Ditch consisted of three routines: hard labor, writing confessions, and holding struggle sessions—"evil people" struggling against "evil people." Confessions were written every day in exactly the same way. Struggle sessions were basically identical too: one person would stand on a bench and explain various "problems" while an audience of a couple hundred others would criticize and accuse him. The next day someone else would go up and the one who was accused the day before would then accuse others. It was certainly a case of "being both the target and the moving force of the revolution." It was nothing less than a theatrical farce, but every one of the "actors" was himself taking a tragic role: when they were chaotically and mechanically shouting, "You're not being honest!" or "Leniency to those who confess, severity for those who refuse!" every one of them felt an enormous sense of pity for the "protagonist" standing up there on the bench.

When no one else was near them, Zhou Jiajie quietly asked Lan Jixuan—a former production brigade branch secretary who had only recently been nominated for commune undersecretary—what his problem was. At the end of 1960, Commune Secretary Ji

Weishi had falsely reported, during a county-wide telephone conference call, a grain sale to the state of 275 tons. But later on he dumped his dirty water in Lan Jixuan's lap by saying Lan had made the false report. In that way Lan was branded a "sub-landlord" during the commune rectification drive.

Lan Jixuan and the recently branded "degenerate element" Liu Nancun (his crime was "placing evil persons in positions of importance"—he had allowed a man who had been a township official for several years before Liberation and another young man who had been pressed into the Nationalist Party's army to occupy positions as production team leaders) had worked together closely ever since land reform days. They had stayed up together many a night during that unforgettable year of 1958: sitting miserably through district and then commune meetings, trying to eke out a production target figure that would satisfy the district or county leadership, then carrying bamboo torches into a "night battle" for production. Finally, they went back to all-night commune meetings when they had to come up with a state grain requisition figure to satisfy county or commune leadership. In order to spur them on, they were brought before on-the-spot meetings: Look at such-and-such a brigade! Their grain stores are full to overflowing. How come you alone have no grain? You must be cheating on production figures and dividing it among yourselves! Everyone knew very well that the stores of the other brigades were full of straw with reed mats thrown over it and a thin layer of grain sprinkled on top to fool people. Someone had made a bitter joke about this: if only people's stomachs could pretend the same way—if filling them up with straw and tossing down a couple of grains of rice could prevent hunger—that would be wonderful.

In the middle of August, Zhou Jiajie's chief worry was this: What is to become of the people now that power in Fangxing Commune has fallen into the hands of a man like Ji Weishi?

Cadres from the County Committee often came on assignments to West Ditch. From fragmentary reports Zhou Jiajie heard, he surmised that rural conditions did not seem to be improving, even though all of the "evil people" had already been locked up. On the contrary, the situation seemed to be growing more serious. Just after all of the "evil people" were overthrown, the "swollen foot sickness" [malnutrition] broke out all over the countryside.

IV

That was precisely the time when the people's beloved leader Comrade Peng Dehuai was toppled from power and Lin Biao took total command of the armed forces after several years of convalescence. It seems that there is a fixed amount of light in the universe. Just after one star falls from the sky, another star shines with blinding brightness.

Ji Weishi was a clever man, but his was a cleverness completely opposite from Zhou Jiajie's. His feelings and thinking in response to external events consistently took a completely different course from Zhou's.

It was right in 1958 that he jumped all the way from credit union director to commune secretary and then carried the "royal sword" of the County Committee into the battle to "rectify" Fangxing Commune. Ji Weishi received the highest commendations from the County Committee in 1958 and 1959. This single fact explains many things.

In 1958—just at the time when cadres like Zhou Jiajie were beset by physical and spiritual anxiety, were suffering from many internal contradictions, going through repeated struggles, coming into direct conflict with and incurring the dissatisfaction of the leadership, and heading step by step toward destruction—Ji Weishi was as happy as a fish discovering water: the "current situation" was molding him into a "hero of our times."

From the tone of voice and subtle facial expressions of the County Committee leaders, he very perceptively sensed the tenor of the times. Thus he lost no opportunity to send up bold and loftily ambitious plans, magnificent production targets, and outstanding figures on the completion of state grain purchases. That was precisely the time when those production brigade and commune cadres who did not understand "the mission of the age" were frowning and sighing all the time and revealing their "right-wing," "conservative," "narrow-minded peasant selfishness." Thus Ji Weishi's character stood out heroically like an eagle among sparrows and attracted the particular attention and respect of the leadership.

At the grassroots level, whatever place Ji Weishi visited was immediately transformed from backward to progressive. His main point was always to get more money and food so that the masses would be easier to manipulate.

There were times, however, when some small misfortune would occur. Ji Weishi reported that the seedlings had been successfully planted slightly ahead of schedule, but when the County Committee investigated, the work was still far from finished. He reported grain sales to the state of 275 tons, but an investigation turned up a shortfall of 93.5 tons. That was easy to explain, of course: it was all the fault of the deputy secretary and the bookkeeper, who were careless with figures; "I did not check" this or "they didn't consult with me" on that. Ji Weishi had a pair of slippery shoulders, and responsibilities just naturally slid off them and onto those of his assistants. Ji Weishi's mistakes never involved anything more serious than "I didn't investigate thoroughly enough."

He only had one irremediable failing: he couldn't stand the scrutiny of thousands of pairs of eyes or the private evaluation and discussion of thousands of mouths. Once he realized what was happening and turned around to look, his expression, voice, and actions were completely different from those seen by the County Committee secretary. In 1959, a Dengshuang Commune member named Yuan Ping'an was eating in the threshing yard when Ji Weishi passed by (he was secretary of Dengshuang Commune at the time). Someone at the table called Ji Weishi over to eat with them, but Yuan Ping'an stopped him: "What're you calling him over to eat for? That bastard takes more and eats more; after he gets through with us, we won't even have enough potatoes to eat our fill!" Ji Weishi heard every word. That night Ji Weishi went to the production brigade to round up a few henchmen, told them to cut some tree branches, and announced that "we simply have to get rid of these unhealthy trends and evil practices!" Then he personally convened a meeting of all commune members and ordered Yuan Ping'an to confess: "What kind of trouble are you trying to stir up with all that fucking talk? What have you got against the People's Communes and the Three Red Banners?" When he didn't come clean, they tied him up. When he tried to explain himself again but did not make a full enough confession, four or five of Ji's henchmen tortured him with whips made of five tree branches tied together. At the same time an old man who had said the wheat was sown too closely together and a married couple who had dropped a few vegetable seeds during shipment received the same fierce beating.

Ji Weishi not only beat or cursed those he didn't like or who didn't like him. He also employed more "civilized" methods. For example, he once ordered a commune member to wear a big mud cake on his head and walk from one production brigade to another, "parading himself through the streets to expose his crimes to others" for five or six miles. The farthest production brigade had to check the mud cake on his arrival to make sure he hadn't moved it.

Actually the masses could see only a very small portion of Ji Weishi's true activities. All the rapid changes in production relations, the wild and chaotic work pace, the constant ups and downs in policy, just like sudden shifts in the earth's surface, naturally produced a number of cracks; and through these cracks Ji Weishi unceasingly sucked up oil and water [i.e., personal advantage]. And he had no qualms about the taste of human blood in what he sucked. During the great movement to produce homemade steel in residential back yards, every family was assessed two dollars. Accordingly, Ji Weishi had thousands of dollars in ready cash. Vast amounts of foodstuffs and material goods, together with several hundred state workers, were also at his disposal. When production brigades fell short on seeds and chemical fertilizer, another large sum of money passed through his hands. Tens of thousands of dollars in relief grain and workers' compensation were also under his control. He knew what sort of contacts he needed, and those people knew what they wanted from him, and thus everybody worked hand-in-hand to one another's advantage. It is still a mystery just exactly how much money he embezzled, how many things he stole, how much relief grain he sold for high prices at the market, or how much rice and lumber he secretly had shipped home. During the first Socialist Education Movement of 1963,[12] he was forced to confess to a certain figure, swearing he was "absolutely honest" and would "pay it back immediately"; but during the second Socialist Education Movement of 1965, he admitted to a much larger figure.

When all of the cadres of Fangxing Commune were cut down like grass and Ji Weishi became the commune secretary, he made an already calamitous situation even worse. It was as if the voices of all those cadres who had been forcibly silenced were concentrated in Ji Weishi's throat, so that this born orator now had a louder voice, a higher pitch, and much greater breath: "There aren't enough rations? Nonsense! The swollen foot sickness is nothing but the swollen foot sickness; it has nothing to do with hunger! State grain sales must be completed, and only ahead of schedule, never behind!"

Ji Weishi measured others by his own circumstances, and thus his words were not entirely lacking in sincerity. From 1959 on— at exactly the same time that the masses entered a state of semi-starvation—Ji Weishi had fresh milk and eggs for breakfast every morning. He went to Fangxing Commune and used their crucible to decoct for himself special medicines that he wrote off as operating expenses, despite the fact that they were a disallowed item. He could go to the commune ponds whenever he liked and take home fresh fish; he could take free pork, duck eggs, and goose eggs; he could go to the old people's home or any of the production brigades and eat with them as often as he liked without paying anything. . . . Matter becomes mind; thus it was quite excusable that he simply could not understand that there was such a thing as "starvation" in this world.

People now say, "If Ji Weishi had not come to Fangxing Commune that year, our losses would not have been so great." Obviously the role of the individual in history should still not be underestimated.

In Ji Weishi's dossier, however, the record of these "historical contributions" is unfortunately too brief. Look at his final evaluation: "This comrade is an activist worker, has great enthusiasm and spirit, and is able to thoroughly carry out the Party's policies and complete his every Party assignment. His class stand is resolute and his class view accurate; he is able to boldly carry out class struggle against evil people and their activities" (of course, that included Zhou Jiajie and those wronged ghosts of the nether world like Yuan Ping'an and others). . . . Ji Weishi's own assessment of himself is somewhat more detailed in its description of his "historic contributions": "standpoint resolute; always struggled against individualistic thought, discussion, or behavior; never wavered on the question of policy direction. While at Fangxing and Hua Jiao Communes, always resolutely struggled against the advocates of the household production contract system;[13] never wavered, never gave in, and took full responsibility for solving such problems."

All of these "resolute struggles" and so forth refer, of course, to his performance during the historical periods of 1958 to 1960 and 1962. But what about his embezzlement, stealing, beating and cursing of the masses, and false accusations of good people? There were two years when his evaluation read "engaged in embezzlement and stealing." This was written in the section on "shortcomings," but a "dialectical" change was also noted, and the "negations" of his various shortcomings also constituted "strong points": ". . . but he was able to confess voluntarily (?) and frankly (?), make just compensation, and make proper self-examination; and his work attitude was always correct (!)."

Thus, whenever the leadership of some commune was not forceful enough, Ji Weishi, "based on his political ability and integrity," would be sent "to strengthen the leadership and give full play to the Party's function as a revolutionary bulwark . . . etc., etc."

None of this is at all surprising, considering that by 1966 Ji Weishi's dossier no longer contained the slightest hint of wrongdoing. His thinking and his virtue were both pure and unblemished; his only minor fault was that "on occasion he is rather one-sided in his evaluation of certain problems; he lacks thoroughness and attention to details in his style of work, etc."

Why did those comrades sitting in their County Committee Organization Office writing such evaluations never go down and look around? Why did they never go to the production brigades, the grassroots cadres, and the commune members and listen to what they had to say? For example:

"Flattering toward the leaders, but arrogant and oppressive toward the workers . . ."

"He's an expert liar; always reports good news, never bad; always reports unfinished work as having been completed ahead of schedule."

"A small man with a big head (a self-important official). His word alone is law."

"Always cursing, beating, and locking people up or sending them to do forced labor for the commune."

The simplest and most devastating evaluation was: "He gets ahead by climbing over the dead bodies of the masses—totally without shame!"

The only weapon that the masses, who could always see things clearly, could use against such a man was to despise and ignore him. They would greet anyone on the street, but somehow "didn't see" this particular corpus of flesh and blood.

The position a man occupies in the hearts of the masses can actually be greatly at odds with the position he occupies among the ranks of officials.

V

Working all day with the commune members and living at home with his family, Zhou Jiajie could not really be considered isolated; but spiritually he was living far away on a very small island, an island so small that there was room only for him alone to dwell there.

Among the masses he was regarded almost as a recluse, and everyone gradually got used to ignoring his existence. Sometimes this made him feel very bad, but it also gave him an important opportunity—he could hear things that other people couldn't, and he was extremely interested in every piece of intelligence about the outside world. Such news was related to his personal security and to his hope of someday returning to normal life.

He had already fallen to the status of the lowest of the low. He was politically equal to landlords, rich peasants, counterrevolutionaries, and other bad elements, but he lacked even their ability to speak and thus suffered more fear and anxiety than they did. He lived in constant fear of falling into some sort of trap. All he wished for was to avoid harassment, accusations, and beatings.

His fears were, of course, not unfounded. Whenever he collected manure with the other commune members, even though he had carried six loads, the brigade leader would mark him down for only four loads while marking everyone else down for six loads. The others would receive four work points, but he, only three. He was extremely angry, but could not speak; he could only force himself to calm down and let it go. Nevertheless, the brigade leader noticed his dissatisfaction and cursed him: "You're only acting crazy!" At that he became over-excited, forgot himself, jumped up, and beat violently on his own chest. The brigade leader took a close look at him, thought a moment, and said, "You're only pretending to be a crazy fool. If we gave you a beating, you'd talk all right!"

He couldn't sleep at all that night, he was so angry with himself for losing his composure. It was clear now that the brigade leader already suspected him of only pretending to be deaf and dumb. He must be extremely cautious.

He went on to consider that merely pretending to be completely deaf and dumb was not sufficient. He had to build the walls of his little island even higher and plan thoroughly for any eventuality. When a couple of close friends who had unreliable class backgrounds paid him one of their frequent visits, he wrote a note to his son: "In the future, these kinds of people should not come very often." After that, in order to protect himself he decided not to associate with three kinds of people: cadres, people with political problems, and people who were too clever for anyone's good.

His wife and son were talking about buying a radio. At first he thought this would be a good idea to liven up his family's silent world and give them some relief from boredom, but when his son wrote him a note asking for his opinion, he wrote down very clearly: "We cannot do it! Didn't you see what happened to Zhou Zhongci?" That was the end of that.

Zhou Zhongci was a nephew. He had been branded a rightist in 1958 because he said the peasants did not have enough to eat. He was later sent to work at the Mianyang Agricultural Machinery Station. There was a radio there with a loudspeaker system attached. On one occasion he tired of listening to a political program and turned the dial to a music station. An alarm sounded for thirty seconds and the security forces immediately came running. Zhou Zhongci was arrested on the spot for the crime of secretly listening to and rebroadcasting an "enemy station." He was relieved of his duties, sentenced to three years in prison, and branded an active counterrevolutionary. When he came out of prison, he was sent back to the countryside to perform supervised labor.

Besides, Zhou Jiajie reasoned, since they already suspect that I am pretending to be mute, they will believe I harbor resentment and will suspect me of sitting at home plotting some sort of activity to get back at them. In those days any radio could be declared to be a wireless sending and receiving set, not to mention the simple fact that if his family bought a radio they would suspect all the more that he was only pretending deafness. He closed his doors to all guests, didn't buy a radio, didn't go to market, and reduced his contacts with the outside world to an absolute minimum. He could do without all things but one—security.

He would close his door at night and sit there weaving basket after basket out of thin strips of bamboo. In two evenings he could weave a pair of baskets, and his son could sell them for a few cents in the marketplace. This was his only recreation and entertainment.

He was the earliest one up every morning. He would first sweep up the entire little yard until it was perfectly clean from wall to fence and outside his gate; then he would start a fire and cook breakfast. He also had to decide when it was time to sell something in the marketplace and what they should buy there as well; he would record everything very clearly in his account book. He had voluntarily taken over the management of all the household affairs and housework. He did so not merely to occupy his mind and relieve some of his depression. In his home he felt like a human being: he could think, organize, arrange, and direct things, instead of silently, passively, and mechanically following everyone else in the completion of this or that labor assignment.

After two or three years he finally became accustomed to being deaf and dumb. People said that he had regained some weight and that his complexion had improved. Of course, he did not have to participate in any meetings and did not have to worry about anything in the commune or the brigade; he was as relaxed as could be. Any very attentive person, however, could see that his expression was becoming duller day by day. Compared to the former Zhou Jiajie, who was full of talk and laughter and whose happiness, anger, grief, and joy were immediately registered on his face, he had become another person.

His own acclimation to the role of being deaf and dumb came more slowly than his general acceptance as such by others. In any public gathering, he himself no longer made any demands for expression or association; but in his heart, his inability to speak up was still a constant source of pain.

The process of being forced to cut himself off from other people and become isolated was the exact opposite of the experience of Sichuan's famous "white-haired girl," Luo Changxiu.[14] When Luo Changxiu escaped into the mountains at the age of fourteen, she immediately cut off all contact with the outside world and became absolutely isolated. She heard only the sound of wind and rain and the cries of tigers and wolves, but not the sound of human voices. She no longer had opportunities to express her thoughts, wishes, or feelings to other people, and thus she naturally came to abandon the desire to do so. Zhou Jiajie, on the other hand, was already a mature adult of thirty-six and had been working in society for many years. He had lived in a rapidly changing society and, as a consequence of his wide contacts with other people, his "social nature" was more highly developed than that of most of the masses. His contacts with other people were abruptly cut off under these quite different circumstances, and yet he still had to live all the time in the midst of the same social group. His ears were continually providing him with various bits of intelligence, which filtered through his mind and immediately became a part of his own thoughts and feelings; but he could not convey any information or express even the slightest reaction to the events of the outside world. Most human beings probably have occasion to endure such painful circumstances only once in their lifetimes—during that brief moment when they are very near death and their mental faculties are still quite lucid but they have lost the ability to speak. Zhou Jiajie, however, had to live under these circumstances all the time. Thus, for him to accustom himself to not speaking was several times more difficult than it was for Luo Changxiu; just as Luo Changxiu could not get used to speaking, did not want to, and was not very good at it once she had returned to the human world.

The written word became Zhou Jiajie's only means of communication with other people, but written words cannot take the place of speech. Whenever an old friend came to visit, Zhou Jiajie naturally wanted to chat a bit with him, yet it was imperative that he not open his mouth. Could written notes possibly serve the same purpose?

When he was feeding the hogs, they knocked over a pail of grain husks, and his wife scolded him at length: "A grown man like you, and you can't even hold the grain pail steady!" He was both excited and angry and wanted to shout something right back at her, but he couldn't. Writing a note was out of the question, because she was illiterate.

He was very upset with his son about something, so he wrote a very short little note: "Silly little fool!" His daughter-in-law saw it, thought it referred to her, and went off crying. He had no way of explaining the misunderstanding; after all, he was not even supposed to be able to hear her sobbing.

Aside from note writing, he could only employ facial expressions and gestures. His wife and daughter-in-law were constantly quarreling. His daughter-in-law, of course, had no compunction about criticizing her mother-in-law in front of her deaf father-in-law. Zhou Jiajie had wanted to interfere for a long time but was completely powerless. One day at dinner when his daughter-in-law was carrying on again, he gave her a dark disapproving look, but it was no use. In a fit of rage, he knocked over the dining table in order to assert his authority as the head of the household.

VI

In 1972, something very important happened.

One day Zhou Zhongci came running over to Zhou Jiajie's house and began gesturing excitedly this way and that. Zhou Jiajie finally understood him: somebody had fallen to his death from a high place. But who was it? Zhou Zhongci pointed to his head, with the meaning that the person was bald. Khrushchev? He had fallen from power long ago; Zhou Zhongci wouldn't be so excited about his death. Zhou Zhongci was growing a little impatient. He tried to imitate the person's facial expression and way of walking, but it wasn't until he pretended to wave the *Quotations from Chairman Mao* that Zhou Jiajie realized who it was: Oh, Lin Biao!

He had not read the newspapers for three years, but from that day on he went out to the roadside every day to wait for the postman and be the first one to see the newspapers.

As his feeling of personal security grew stronger, he gradually began to think beyond his own individual safety and well-being. He felt as if something was vaguely stirring within him, as if something inside him that had been dormant for many years was gradually beginning to reawaken.

It was 1972 already, but the production brigade's per acre grain production had not yet even matched the figures for 1953, when they had developed the first-stage cooperatives! The brigade leader wore out his whistle urging people on to work harder, but everyone was lazy and malingering. They were very good at producing children though! There was not enough to eat then, so what were they going to eat in the future? "If they would make me Party branch secretary, I would . . ." The first time that thought occurred to Zhou Jiajie, it surprised him, but later on his thoughts often tended in that direction.

He turned forty that year. Perhaps it would be his lucky year. He had only worked for the Party six years, but he'd already been a criminal for twelve.

A dark shadow often rose up in his memory and would not allow him to be optimistic. It was something that had occurred in 1962 when he was not yet a mute. He had been cutting down some creepers when a cadre from County Central came up beside him, took his arm, and whispered softly, "I think making you an alien class element was an unjust verdict. They're just beginning to reexamine some cases at the county level. I think there's some hope for you . . ."

From then on, every time county or commune cadres came to the production brigade, Zhou Jiajie would glance at them hopefully. Maybe they've come to find me? Or perhaps they've come to

check up on my performance these last few years? Or to reinvestigate my family's economic condition before Land Reform?

In that year there really were thousands of good comrades
whose cases were reexamined and who were then readmitted to
the Party or given their former jobs back. There were even a few in
Xinjin County. It seems that Zhou Jiajie's case was brought up,
but the only result was that a few more words were added to his
dossier: "A correct decision, no need for reexamination."

A new hope burst forth in 1975. A very great hope indeed, related to the reappearance of the name Deng Xiaoping. News of a
"Party reform" came shortly after that, and there were constant rumors that new rural and personnel policies would soon be implemented. At that point the desire that Zhou Jiajie had nurtured in
his heart for seven long years, the desire to escape from being deaf
and dumb and to speak out once again, was stronger than ever before.

The following year, he passed a note to his son: "Find a good
doctor; I want to be cured."

On the basis of the overall national situation, he had concluded
that if he was "cured" at this time, even if there were some suspicion that he had been faking, no one would investigate him. He
still had a strong hope lodged deep in his heart: one of these days
someone may come to ask about the injustices I've suffered; at
that time, I'll have to be able to speak.

His son and his close friends did in fact go to a great deal of
trouble to make an appointment with a good doctor for him, but
they were unsuccessful. That winter, the situation once again took
a turn for the worse. First came the "counterattack against the reversal of rightist verdicts,"[15] and then the death of Premier Zhou
Enlai plunged the entire nation into deep sorrow and anxiety.

Zhou Jiajie hid in a deserted place for fear that someone would
find him weeping, and the dark clouds weighed all the more heavily on his heart. Why talk about "curing" his illness? What hope
was there to clear up his political problem? China's historical clock
seemed to have stopped again.

Who could have imagined that the pent-up anger, resentment,
and enmity that had been growing steadily in the hearts of all the

Chinese people was just about to coalesce into a mighty force that would sweep the Gang of Four and their followers into the graveyard of history?

VII

After the fall of the Gang of Four, Zhou Jiajie continued to keep silent for almost three more years. Could this be because suffering and apprehension had weighed on his heart so long that his spirit had already become as frozen and numb as the expression on his face? After the slogans "Down with the Gang of Four" and "Liberate the people" had joyfully resounded for so long, why was he still so unmoved that he did not stand up and shout out his appeal for a redress of grievances?

Our wishes always travel in a straight line, while history often prefers a tortuous course. The martyred Shi Yunfeng, who so bravely opposed Lin Biao and the Gang of Four, could never have imagined that he would die at the hands of the Gang of Four element Wang Huaixiang long after the Gang themselves had been smashed.[16] Just think about a few things: Remember when the verdict on the Tiananmen Incident was finally reversed.[17] Remember that as much as two years after the Gang of Four had fallen from the historical stage, some people still refused to allow discussion of the "extreme left" line and many people who had opposed that line were still being punished in prison as "active counterrevolutionaries." Remember again that as late as 1979 the slogan "Practice is the sole criterion of truth"[18] was still meeting a great deal of opposition. When one recalls all these things, Zhou Jiajie's continued wait-and-see attitude of silence does not seem strange at all.

After October 1976 [when the Gang of Four were arrested], he once again waited on the road every day for the postman to deliver the newspapers. He listened greedily to every word people said and carefully and unblinkingly observed every little change in their daily lives as well as their every reaction to these changes and their expectations for even greater and more complete change.

The first joyful event was Comrade Deng Xiaoping's return to work. Many large and small followers of Lin Biao and the Gang of Four were either arrested or removed from office, and that made people feel both relieved and happy. Everyone was talking about Comrade Zhao Ziyang leading a group of Provincial Committee cadres down to the villages to make an extended examination of local conditions and to solicit the opinions and listen to the demands of the peasants and the rural cadres. The people were finally beginning to reap real benefits: whether or not to practice double cropping of rice was no longer an issue of revolution or counterrevolution; they no longer had to hear "If wet rice won't do, plant dry wheat," and "Late autumn is a good time for wheat. . . ."[19] Long-awaited reforms in the cropping system arrived. "Dazhai-style work points"[20] were eliminated, and the principle of more pay for more work was reinstated, as was self-regulation for production brigades. The state put into practice a whole system of reforms that were beneficial to the peasants and allowed them to enrich themselves through their own labor.

"Party Central knows . . ." Zhou Jiajie nodded his head in silent approval as he talked to himself, ". . . knows what sort of errors have occurred these past years, knows how the peasants feel and what they have suffered. Just look, even while the nation is experiencing such difficulties, they're still raising the state purchase price for agricultural products; they're really taking good care of us peasants."

He paid particular attention to the fact that the slogan "Take class struggle as the key" was not mentioned, and that one unjust case after another was being reversed. It looked like they were proceeding from the near to the distant, first taking care of the 1970s, then later the 1960s and 1950s. . . . His heart was slowly warming up, and the flame of hope that had been put out so often before was flaring up once more.

He still did not dare give free rein to his hopes, however, because policies had fluctuated back and forth too many times during the past few years. Who could guarantee that the brakes would not suddenly be applied again? Weren't conditions just like this in 1959, 1962, and 1975? And besides, for so many years every movement had been "anti-rightist," never "anti-leftist." Supposing somebody jumped out again and started shouting, "All of you are rightists and have to be completely rectified!"—wouldn't that be the end of everything? He was also worried that when it came time to exonerate him, since everyone knew he was deaf and dumb someone would say, "What's a person like him worth? Forget him!" One statement like that and he might be confined to oblivion again, just like back in 1962.

Thus he continued to wait and see, continued to remain silent, and continued to stifle his overly ardent hopes. He was afraid of the shock of disappointment.

The Goddess of Fortune finally remembered this man who had been forgotten for twenty years.

On the morning of January 4, 1979, the whole family was in the living room after breakfast when Zhou's eldest son, Zhou Xinqiang, said very thoughtfully, "Something very strange happened. Yesterday afternoon, when I was coming home from work, I ran into Production Brigade Secretary Qin, and he asked me several times, 'Can your father really hear and speak or not?' . . . Something may be going on."

Naturally, Zhou Jiajie "didn't hear" what his son said. He thought the time had probably arrived, but did not dare to act rashly. He had to find someone to consult with and see what was going on.

He immediately thought of Chen Jiaci, a man of similar age, experience, and cultural level, who had been one of his best friends in the early days. He had also been a Party branch secretary in 1959, and if he hadn't gone to study at Dujiang University he would have suffered the same evil fate as Zhou Jiajie. During the most dangerous days of the Cultural Revolution, he was the only one who dared to visit Zhou Jiajie's home and to write notes asking about the well-being of his family and if they had any problems. Zhou Jiajie wrote a note and sent Xinqiang off to find Chen Jiaci. He was a person you could rely on, and it wouldn't matter if you asked him something you shouldn't.

Without waiting for Xinqiang to speak, Chen Jiaci put down his seed potatoes, wiped his hands, and asked, "Did you come to talk about your father's case?" Xinqiang was both surprised and pleased as he quickly answered, "My dad told me to come and ask Uncle Chen if his case could be brought up now." Chen Jiaci was quite positive. "Why not? Of course it's time to bring it up! You go home and tell him I'll come over this noon; otherwise tonight for sure."

At noontime Chen Jiaci came to the Zhou home and another conversation written on notes took place. "When your case was first handled, what was the verdict?" "Alien class element. Exaggeration of production figures leading to rural starvation. Misusing over seventy dollars of public money. Embezzling twenty dollars." Chen Jiaci took a brush and painted lines through "alien class element" and "exaggeration . . ." These two lines were like two crowbars prying up a large heavy stone that had been weighing down Zhou Jiajie's heart for twenty years. Under "misusing . . ." Chen Jiaci wrote, "returned year by year; no longer counts." Under "embezzling . . ." he wrote, "Even if it were true, it's not serious enough for such a verdict."

The next day Chen Jiaci returned, bringing with him Yang Shuncheng, who had been the deputy secretary of Fangxing Commune and was now the deputy director of its grain office. Zhou Jiajie set out some wine and they carried on another paper conversation as they drank. Chen Jiaci wrote, "Unjust cases are currently being reversed all over the country; your case can probably be cleared up. Can you speak or not? If you've been pretending, you can just give us a sign and we can, if you like, keep your secret until after your case is resolved."

That was the longest question Zhou Jiajie had ever been asked in his eleven years of silent conversations, and it was the one that caused him the greatest hesitation. After some time, he finally took up the brush and wrote, "Thank you for your help. I'm afraid that I will not explain myself clearly."

Chen Jiaci looked at the note and stared at Zhou Jiajie for a long time, until the tears welled up in his eyes. The grave injustice suffered by this beloved childhood friend who stood before him, plus the almost indescribable pain that he himself had endured these past years, all pressed at once on his heavy heart. At the same time, he felt a great elation in finally proving that Zhou Jiajie was really pretending to be mute and that now he had a chance to start a new life in this world that had recently grown lovable again.

On the sixth of January, the County Committee called a meeting of third-level cadres. There Zhou Jiajie's note was delivered to the County Committee secretary, Comrade Zhong Guanglin. Zhong Guanglin had long ago heard about someone called Zhou Jiajie. From the words "I'm afraid that I will not explain myself clearly," he inferred that Zhou probably could speak. He ordered the Organization Department to check his case file. The Commune Cadre Committee and the Organization Department cadres examined the original verdict point by point and found that not one point could hold water. They determined that Zhou Jiajie's father was not a landlord; he had merely hired some temporary laborers and sold some wine at the county market. The so-called misuse of public money was only Zhou Jiajie's borrowing one or two dollars when he had to go to the district township for meetings, and he had paid it all back later out of his wages. But the embezzlement of twenty dollars was retained in the new adjudication.

County Secretary Zhong asked Fangxing Commune Secretary Li Shuquan to call Zhou Jiajie to the county seat. Zhou's son brought him to town on his bicycle, and Li Shuquan told him, "Your situation has been discussed several times and we've decided it is an unjust case." Zhou Jiajie's heart was pounding like storm-blown waves, but his facial muscles retained their by now habitual lack of expression. He did not speak either—this too was a years-old habit that did not require the least bit of control. "He can't hear," his son explained quite sincerely, and another written conversation ensued. Zhou Jiajie wrote, "Wait until I am cured and then we can talk." Li Shuquan wrote, "I'll give you three days to be cured." The two men looked at each other closely, each one contemplating his next move.

Zhang Qunfang, a female cadre from Fangxing Commune, was standing nearby witnessing this bizarre confrontation. This young, straightforward, and able comrade had already figured out Zhou Jiajie's true situation and felt great sympathy for him. Watching Zhou Jiajie's face blushing red and then turning pale again, she could no longer bear to see him go on suffering so; she walked over, shook his hand warmly, and spoke in a friendly voice, "Don't worry any more. It's a new day! You still think you can't speak clearly enough? None of us needs to be afraid any more." Zhou Jiajie seemed visibly moved, but he was still full of anxious reservations and stood there as speechless as before. Li Shuquan and Zhang Qunfang found it extremely difficult to wait there patiently for him to speak his first words. For a full ten minutes the only movement was that of large beads of sweat pouring down Zhou Jiajie's face. Finally he stood up; he had decided to speak, but his tongue was very heavy and sluggish. Tears choked his throat as he barely and haltingly forced out three rather indistinct syllables:

"I . . . can . . . speak!" This was the first thing he had said in eleven years.

The strange thing was that the apprehension he had felt for twenty long years still clung to him as if from inertia. At that moment Zhou Jiajie had already escaped from his many anxieties, but his mind and tongue were still not working in harmony, and he just kept repeating the refrain that had rung in his head so many hundreds of times: "I'm afraid . . . I will not explain myself clearly."

The room was completely silent except for the sound of his son weeping for joy and sadness.

"I was afraid . . ."—it was a historic echo. The sound of his son's weeping was a fitting end to twenty tragic years of his family history.

"I never thought I'd see this day!" Zhou Jiajie confided to his son on the way home. The sounds of rejoicing were interspersed with the sounds of sighs, and unprecedented happiness accompanied feelings about a past too painful to recall. In the spring of 1979, all over the length and breadth of China, innumerable people were repeating that same short but profoundly significant sentence, "I never thought I'd see this day!" It marked the end of an era for an individual and for an entire nation, and announced the beginning of a new historical epoch.

On the road home, there were the same long lines of people and vehicles, the same wheat fields, and the same rows of flowering rape and beans; but Zhou Jiajie felt differently about all of them. When he left he was a longtime stranger to all of those things; but now as he returned to this world after a long exile, he was once more an equal member of society, one of those people walking, driving, and working there. He was once more a human being living in the human world.

His son began to pedal faster in his excitement to carry the great good news to their family. The road was quite uneven and they bounced up and down terribly. "Running proudly in the spring wind, the horse's hooves fly . . ." It had been so long since Zhou Jiajie had sung, but now he truly felt like singing a song; yet when he recalled how difficult it was just to speak and how bad he sounded, he decided not to spoil his present mood.

An acquaintance they met on the road used his customary gestures to ask Zhou Jiajie where he had been. Zhou Jiajie jumped down off the bicycle and said, "We went into Xinjin County seat." The fellow stood there stunned for a moment before he finally asked, "Who cured you?" That question caused Zhou Jiajie some consternation. How should he put it? He should thank Party Central, but it was too large, so he finally answered, "Commune Secretary Li cured me."

The whole family was sitting in the front yard waiting and hoping that their wishes would be fulfilled when the head of the household went into the city to be exonerated. If that were to happen the whole family could breathe freely again and hold their heads high once more.

Zhou Jiajie's daughter ran through the gate. His granddaughter ran into his arms. Zhou Jiajie hugged her tightly and, mustering all the strength at his command, uttered the two words: "Good———granddaughter!" He could feel that his eyes were wet again.

Everyone was dumbfounded. Zhou Jiajie looked over at his wife; two long streaks of tears were streaming down her dry, bony cheeks.

VIII

Zhou Jiajie returned once again to his position of twenty years before as production brigade Party branch secretary. His current possession of power was due not to any empty slogan or falsely inflated production figures, but to his ability to work the brigade's land for the genuine and substantial benefit of the people living there. When he finally put plow to earth, however, he discovered that the land was not what it used to be. He had not only to plow the fields, but also to bend over constantly to pick up many stones and to pull up deep-rooted congo grass. Out of the twenty-one Party members in his production brigade, only five were the kind who could get things moving. The population had increased greatly, but the arable land had actually decreased.

Zhou Jiajie was not one to remain idle. Enough garbage had piled up on this piece of land since he had left the scene that he would have all he could do to clean it up.

Things wouldn't be easy for Zhou Jiajie, either. The first time he opened his mouth to speak, a most unhappy event occurred. A very well known person walked over from the far side of the room where Zhou's exoneration had been announced. Zhou Jiajie quickly smiled and held out his hand, but the man just turned his face and walked away. It was Ji Weishi.

Perhaps Ji Weishi was not yet accustomed to the new atmosphere of the times and imagined that he sensed something unpropitious in it. He and a few others like him had gotten so accustomed to hearing only the sound of their own voices that they could not enjoy a hubbub of many voices.

But old man history tells us that it's better to be a little more noisy. A silent era cannot be a good one.

NOTES

Originally published in *Liu Binyan baogaowenxue xuan* (Beijing: Beijing chubanshe, 1981).

1. The traditional Chinese Lunar New Year is celebrated from about the twenty-third of the twelfth month to the fifteenth of the first month of the new year. During the Cultural Revolution, the festival was greatly abbreviated or not held at all.

2. During the Cultural Revolution, the Chinese people were asked by the Communist Party to "draw a clear line" between themselves and any family member or friend suspected of political deviance.

3. Searching out "rightist elements" during the early years of the Cultural Revolution.

4. The term *jiaodai* is jargon for "explain" or "confess," depending on the immediate context; it frequently applies to persons accused of political crimes.

5. *Dou,* "struggle," is jargon for verbal political harassment.

6. The "Three Red Banners" were the General Line for Socialist Construction, the Great Leap Forward, and the People's Communes.

7. The pragmatic slogan associated with Deng Xiaoping and the present Chinese Communist Party leadership.

8. The phrase "new things" or "socialist new things" (*shehuizhuyi xinshi*) was jargon for all sorts of social and economic innovations pushed by the Party during the Great Leap Forward and the Cultural Revolution.

9. This system destroyed incentives by paying people the same wages regardless of what they achieved.

10. The straw that peasants mixed with mud in building walls could, after some decomposition, be used as fertilizer.

11. "Supervised labor" (*jiandu laodong*) is a euphemism for work in a "labor reform" (*laogai*) camp.

12. The Socialist Education Movement, also known as the Four Cleanups Movement, was a nationwide campaign of political, economic, organizational, and ideological reform led by Mao Zedong and Lin Biao; widely considered a failure, it was also a prelude to the Cultural Revolution.

13. The "household production contract system" (*baochan daohu*), now generally translated in *Beijing Review* as the "responsibility system," is the "pragmatic" farm policy in which individual households, the smallest units of rural organization, are responsible for contracts that they make with the state and are paid more money if they exceed their contracts. During the Cultural Revolution this form of "material incentive" to work was viewed as "taking the capitalist road."

14. Luo Changxiu is the protagonist of the story "The White-Haired Girl" ("Baimaonü").

15. This was an attack by the Gang of Four on Deng Xiaoping and others who were trying to exonerate many cadres wrongly accused or imprisoned as "rightists" during the Cultural Revolution.

16. Shi Yunfeng was a student at East China Normal University in Shanghai who became nationally famous in the late 1970s because of his arrest and trial for opposing the extremist ideology of the Cultural Revolution and, in particular, the cult of Party Chairman Mao Zedong. At the direction of Peng Chong, second secretary of the Municipal

Party Committee in Shanghai and member of the Central Politburo, Shi was executed for his "political crimes," even though, with the overthrow of the Gang of Four, the politics that Shi opposed were already well on their way to official repudiation. Shi's case became a cause célèbre among intellectuals and political moderates, but was discussed only "internally" (*neibu*) until 1981, when Shi was officially exonerated. To mention the case publicly in March 1980, as Liu Binyan does here, required courage.

17. Tiananmen is the Gate of Heavenly Peace in Beijing that stands before the vast Tiananmen Square, which is symbolic of the political center of China. The Tiananmen Incident refers to April 5, 1976, when hundreds of thousands of people gathered in the square in a spontaneous tribute to Premier Zhou Enlai. Zhou had died January 8, 1976, and April 5 was the occasion of the Qingming Festival, when Chinese sweep family gravesites and make obeisances to the departed. The crowd had gathered in an antitotalitarian spirit, but was forcibly driven away and the demonstration declared "counterrevolutionary." The "verdict was reversed" on the incident in December 1978, when the Beijing Municipal Party Committee declared the demonstration "revolutionary."

18. This slogan, together with that of "Liberate thinking," was put forth by the Third Plenum of December 1978 and is associated with the "pragmatic" approach of Deng Xiaoping.

19. During the Cultural Revolution, Party leaders forced the peasants against their better judgment to plant grain sprouts too close together and to plant land with grain even when it was not suitable. As a result, good land was harmed and production fell.

20. Dazhai, in Shanxi Province, was a model agricultural commune during the Cultural Revolution. Its work-point system gave peasants credit for "political behavior" and de-emphasized individual material incentives. After the Cultural Revolution it was revealed that Dazhai's vaunted accomplishments had been staged with state support.

The Second Kind of Loyalty

Translated by Richard W. Bodman

Publication of "The Second Kind of Loyalty" in March 1985 created a furor that contributed to Liu Binyan's eventual expulsion from the Chinese Communist Party. Like many of Liu's earlier works, it focuses on specific, real people and their work units and expresses moral indignation about the misuse of power and the abuse of individual rights. What earned it a special place in contemporary Chinese literature, however, was its challenge to a forbidden zone in Chinese politics: can the system allow a loyal citizen to criticize the authorities? The piece depicts two people who dared to question the worship of Chairman Mao and the inadequacies of China's legal system. Their experiences show the harshness of Chinese prison life, the high-handedness of work-unit leaders, and the treatment of dissenters within the system.

The controversy over "The Second Kind of Loyalty" had mixed results. On the one hand, it highlighted the injustice done to Li Zhirong, one of the piece's protagonists, and eventually led to Li's exoneration and to an investigation into his murder. But it also provoked leaders at the Shanghai Maritime Academy to charge

Liu Binyan with "slandering" their faculty. Liu answered this charge with another piece of reportage, called "An Unfinished Burial," that focused specifically on the Maritime Academy. These two pieces of Liu's reportage eventually became part of the justification for his second expulsion from the Communist Party in January 1987.

"The Second Kind of Loyalty" was a watershed in China's literary reportage of the 1980s. In 1986, 1988, and the first half of 1989, writers continued to enjoy a relatively liberal climate for expression, and Liu's work inspired a sub-genre known as "social problem reportage literature." But, because of the example of the attacks on Liu, other writers took pains to avoid libel charges and did not follow Liu in focusing on individual work units or in naming individual miscreants. They looked for ways to continue to engage readers on social questions without directly confronting authorities. Some turned to extensive use of scholarly studies, while others addressed social problems from a variety of points of view to create what was called a "full perspective style." Questions of individual responsibility were avoided; writers tended instead to suggest that ultimate responsibility for China's ills lay either in traditional Chinese culture or in Chinese national psychology.

The translator wishes to thank the author for clarifying certain passages; the research service of the Moscow State University Library for confirming details of the Novikov gear as well as Chen Shizhong's graduation from the Moscow Machine Tools Institute; and Tom Moran, for getting me started. —TRANS.

His Abundant Energy Overwhelms Others

Just as I was thinking about him these past few days, he turned up. When I first met Chen Shizhong half a year ago, his experiences and character left me with a deep impression. He was an extremely unusual person. After he had left that day, I wondered, "Why don't our novelists ever portray this kind of person?" Indeed, my files contain records on more than ten extremely distinctive people—but people who would never appear in contemporary fiction. (I select the most important of my visitors and the most important cases that arrive in the mail and file them away in thick manila folders.) Why is it that the invented characters of fiction are never as fresh as characters of flesh and blood? I don't know.

It is no wonder that I didn't remember how he looked on his first visit, for indeed his looks were hardly striking. He was the most commonly encountered type of intellectual: neither tall nor short. Thin. A pinched face, pasty white. Eyes: not large. A pair of reading glasses. And while he was a person who got easily stirred up, neither his facial expression nor his gestures revealed much of his feelings.

"I've come to Beijing for someone else, because of an unjust verdict." He passed me a file labeled "Human Blood Is Not Water: An Appeal to the Conscience of a Reporter for the People."

It had been in April 1969—his memory was still fresh—while he was serving a sentence at the Nenjiang Prison Farm in Heilongjiang Province. He had personally witnessed a killing.

> More than a hundred of us convicts were cutting grass under the supervision of team-leader Li, an educated youth, and three PLA soldiers. Our task was to cut more than three hundred pounds of grass per day. Prisoner Li Zhirong had always accepted his "remolding" enthusiastically and that very morning alone had already cut 455 pounds of grass. In the afternoon he just kept on going.
>
> Liu Deyuan, the leader of the convict brigade, was in charge of placing the red flags. We "sketched the walls of our prison in the dirt"—that is to say, we planted four red flags in a square to form a security perimeter. But by a strange chance that afternoon he planted five flags, forming an irregular five-sided figure. Li Zhirong, with his head bent down, concentrated on nothing but cutting hay, and walked to this place . . .

Chen Shizhong made a mark for me on the upper-left-hand corner of the figure:

A PLA soldier ordered him to halt, saying he had overstepped the perimeter. Li Zhirong said he had not. According to the normal arrangement of four red flags forming a square, he indeed had not stepped over the line. When the soldier heard that he dared to talk back, he ordered him to come forward. Li Zhirong obediently came forward, so that he was about five meters outside of the imaginary line. At this point, a soldier who was warming himself by the fire, possibly the squad leader, walked over and asked what had happened. After the two had murmured for a short while, the squad leader asked Li Zhirong,

"What are you in here for?"
"Counterrevolution."
"What did you do before?"
"I was a platoon leader in the 208th division of the GMD army youth corps."
"Ever kill anybody?"
"Yes."

At this point the squad leader told him to turn around. Li Zhirong once again obeyed. The squad leader took out a cartridge to load his gun but dropped it, and it fell to the ground. He crawled around on the ground searching for a while before finding it. Now Li Zhirong was a former soldier, so as soon as he heard the sound of the cartridge being loaded, he turned around quickly, but the bullet had already struck him in the small of the back. The gun sounded, and he fell over. Then the squad leader fired another shot into the air. Team leader Li raced to the scene, the squad leader spoke a few words to him, and then Li called together the entire group of convicts. "Prisoner Li Zhirong illegally overstepped the security perimeter," he announced. "He failed to obey a warning shot fired by one of our soldiers, and was summarily executed. Conclude your work for the day immediately!"

At this moment, Li Zhirong, though in great pain, suddenly rose to his knees, and then once again fell over.

After the convicts had been escorted back to prison, a soldier was left behind to guard the spot. The next day, prisoners Li Bohai and Zheng XX[1] from the motor pool were sent to collect the corpse.

On their return they quietly spread the word that the crime scene had been altered. The red flags had been moved, and the corpse was a few dozen meters outside the perimeter.

The last thing Chen Shizhong said to me was, "This was a crime of murder committed in broad daylight before the eyes of over a hundred convicts!" He quickly recited the names of fourteen people who had been present. No matter how good his memory was, I thought, he couldn't possibly remember both the nature of the site and the names of those witnesses if he hadn't been constantly thinking about this event. At this point, he seemed suddenly to remember something important. "The next day when they went to pick up the corpse," he said, "the body was still warm! This shows that Li Zhirong didn't die immediately, but could still have been saved at any time during the next twelve hours! And all the while a PLA soldier was standing guard!"

Chen was neither a relative nor a friend of Li Zhirong, nor did he know Li's wife and child, yet three days after his own mistaken verdict was reversed on April 15, 1981, he wrote to the Standing Committee of the Heilongjiang People's Congress to complain on behalf of Li Zhirong. He got no answer. In the three and a half years since then, he wrote a letter to An Zhendong, deputy governor of Heilongjiang Province, which was passed on to Zhang Li, chief justice of the Provincial Supreme Court. The letter that came in reply said that the case had been referred to the Supreme Procuratorate[2] of the province. Chen then wrote to Yu Jian, chief procurator of the Supreme Procuratorate, and shortly thereafter received a telephone call saying that the case had been turned over to the Nenjiang region and apparently had already been settled. When he asked, "What happened to the criminal?" and "Are the victim's family members aware of the true circumstances of the case?" his caller was unable to answer. When Chen expressed his dissatisfaction he was told he could appeal to the military courts. And so he wrote once more, this time to the Chinese People's Liberation Army Military Procuratorate, and before long received a response saying that his letter had been referred to the procuratorate of the Heilongjiang military district. One month later, he wrote again to the PLA Military Procuratorate, thanking them for passing the letter on quickly but expressing the hope that they would maintain responsibility for it till the end and not wash their hands of it by referring it elsewhere.

Every two or three months afterwards he pressed them about the outcome of their handling of the case. Eventually the responsible authorities informed him that the army unit in question had been reorganized as the Fifth Corps of the Baicheng garrison district of the Jilin provincial military district, and that his letter had been turned over to that unit. In August 1984, Chen Shizhong once again sent letters inquiring about the matter to the PLA Military Procuratorate, to the political department of the Shenyang military district, and to the security bureau of the Baicheng garrison district of the Jilin provincial military district. He got no response from anyone.

At this point in his talk with me, Chen hung his head and kept silent for a long while. Clearly, he was deeply disappointed. I glanced at the thick manila folders stacked on the floor and bookshelves of my room and thought to myself, "There are plenty of unsolved cases where we know the real name of the offender and in which more than one person was killed. You don't even know the name of that squad leader, fifteen years have already passed, and the victim was, after all, a convict—this won't be easy!"

Our conversation shifted to another topic. Chen Shizhong had certainly kept himself busy. He had mentioned other matters to me half a year earlier, but as yet not a single one had been resolved. He had accused the leadership of the Harbin Municipal Federation of Trade Unions and the leadership of the Worker's Part-time University of gaining personal advantage from their official power to assign housing, and for this had already suffered reprisals: the school had done everything it could to block the important technical innovation he had been pursuing in his spare time, and now the factory in Changchun had withdrawn its support and torn up its contract with him. Moreover, his wife continued to torment him. . . . So how could this Chen Shizhong still have the spare energy to agitate on behalf of an innocent person who had been victimized fifteen years ago?!

He answered my unspoken question: "That Li Zhirong was originally a physical education teacher. In 1957 he was arrested and called a 'counterrevolutionary.' He appealed his sentence, and as a result his sentence was lengthened from ten years to fifteen. This was definitely a mistaken verdict, and if he had lived, it would have been overturned. When he served his sentence he was utterly obedient and devoted to his work, and yet he was killed. Isn't that piling injustice upon injustice? The saddest thing is that his wife, Hu Fenglan, went to visit him at the Xingkaihu prison farm in 1961, stayed a while, and on returning home gave birth to a son named 'Early,' which I guess meant that she hoped the boy's father would be released early, wouldn't you say? This boy never even saw his father's face and by now must be twenty years old. Mother and son to this day believe that their husband and father was 'a counterrevolutionary element executed while attempting to escape from prison'!"

I started to understand him a little. "Human Blood is Not Water" concluded this way:

> Just think how the dead man's family—his young widow and orphan son—have passed these years! Just think how the reputation of our "great wall of steel" [the People's Liberation Army] has been tarnished by a murderer! Just think how these scum who gain credit for creating false crimes and for killing people still lurk within our Party and within our army and have become the inheritors of our cause! And just imagine that this sort of thing could well have happened to you or me. If the victim had been one of your family, what would you have thought? . . . And what's more, if this case is not pursued until the real facts are laid bare, and if the wrongdoing is not completely repudiated together with the Cultural Revolution, then how can we be sure it will not recur in future?

He had good reason to ask this question. Indeed, from 1957 to 1966, most people failed to understand the rules that govern historical tragedies: if you do nothing to stop them, they will recur, gradually expand in scope, and some day reach the point where you yourself will find it hard to escape.[3]

Yet what really set me to wondering were not these views of his but his feelings. They seemed simple, from one point of view—perhaps no more than the age-old sympathy of one human being for another. Yet in Chen Shizhong's case, how could these feelings be so strong and so persistent that his own twenty years of hard luck had not diluted them? Why had the huge catastrophe of the Cultural Revolution, affecting tens of millions of people, not made him numb? (For in those ten years, what did the death of one person amount to?)

I don't think most of us can attain this level of sympathy. It struck me as a key to Chen Shizhong—a key that might unlock the riddle of his life.

Sending Himself to His Own Funeral

Not only had fate never favored this man, it seems never even to have taken pity on him.

Chen Shizhong was born in 1937, the year the Anti-Japanese War broke out. He was the child of a young couple who were in rebellion against traditional culture. His father died of illness before he was a year old. When he was barely three, his mother was killed by enemy agents for having sheltered two patriots. His only remaining relative, his maternal grandmother, also left this world due to poverty and illness. The nine-year-old Chen Shizhong was thus orphaned twice. He was powerless to resist these workings of fate.

For what happened to him later, though, he has to take some responsibility. At least half of the seeds of his misfortune he planted himself.

In school Chen consistently received excellent marks for both learning and conduct, and there was no danger in that. But from middle school onwards, he showed a strong interest in politics and an ability to be active in society: he held positions in the Youth League and in student government, and was chosen as a delegate to Shanghai's sixth student congress. He went to study in the Soviet Union, where for a long time he headed the Moscow branch of the Chinese Students' Association. He worked enthusiastically to promote Sino-Soviet friendship.

In those years in the Soviet Union, the passion for politics that later drew him into the abyss showed itself fully. During vacations, he voluntarily participated with Soviet college students on a wasteland reclamation team that went to do physical labor in Kazakhstan. By no means was every Soviet college student rushing to leave the comfortable life of summer recess in Moscow in order to sleep out in the wind and dew of remote deserts. Chen Shizhong not only went, but won a prize; he clearly had put his heart and soul into the effort. On another occasion, while doing an internship in a factory, he won a prize and then donated all the prize money to the students' association.

Chen chose a particularly tough topic for his graduation thesis: "The Novikov gear and its cutting tools."[4] The Novikov gear was a world-class, highly sophisticated project that had won the USSR's Lenin Prize for Technology and was a topic of rather great difficulty. What was Chen Shizhong driving at? Use of these gears had allowed the Soviet Union to save five million tons of steel. Five million! At the time, China's entire annual steel production was only about ten million tons.[5] In taking on this research, Chen also made important discoveries of his own. In 1960 he ended his period of foreign study with perfect 5.0 marks in nearly every subject. He was the only foreign student to earn a diploma with high honors. He earned a prize certificate for technological research as well, and returned to China with the title of "mechanical engineer." With the three thousand rubles he had saved from his scholarship by scrimping on clothes and food he bought technical books to take back home. His own wristwatch and fountain pen, meanwhile, were of the cheapest kind.

The first obstacle he ran into was that no matter how often he introduced his Novikov project to the Chinese authorities, he was received coldly. Even more disappointing were the disastrous consequences created by a whole series of "leftist" theories and practices that he personally observed three years after his return home. These upset him immensely. He often thought of writing to the Central Committee to offer his views directly. By May 1963, he finally could no longer restrain himself. With an enormous courage that led him to overestimate his own abilities, he assumed the exalted position of writing a letter to Chairman Mao. He urged Mao to pursue both domestic and foreign policies carefully, so as to avoid hurting old friends or delighting enemies, and to refrain from causing irreparable losses.[6] Just who did Chen Shizhong think he was? The leader of the Communist Party of a country? Having sent off two registered letters, he even expected a reply! When he didn't get one, he was indignant.

It seemed that Chen was either a naïve enthusiast or a political careerist. It had to be one or the other.

He waited, in a state of intense agitation, for two months and then could no longer keep his feelings in check. Who knows what sort of demon possessed him? With a foolhardiness large enough to swallow heaven and earth, he composed "A Critique of the Chinese Communist Party's Suggestions about the International Communist Line" and headed for Beijing.[7] He had gone mad and crossed the line that no Chinese citizen under any circumstances was supposed to cross. Naturally he was identified as an "active counterrevolutionary" and arrested.

Thus his bright prospects were cut off by his own hand.

Thinking Too Highly of Himself, He Risks Death to Offer a Direct Criticism

He later admitted that he had committed the most serious political mistake of his entire life. But he meant that only his actions had been in error, not his beliefs. He covered the walls of his solitary confinement cell with scribbled slogans and mottos: "Long live Marxism-Leninism!" "Long live Communism!" "Long live the unity of fraternal parties!" This destined him for yet another mistake.

Chen was neither a Party member nor an official of any sort nor a social scientist, and yet without anyone either forcing him or enticing him to do so, he simultaneously assumed the burdens of all three roles. While in prison he continued to write essays several hundreds of thousands of characters in length, frankly, sincerely, and incisively criticizing and admonishing the Party Central Committee led by Chairman Mao. Of these, the essay entitled "Admonishing the Party," which he sent off in 1964, was most representative:

> To the Central Committee of the Chinese Communist Party and to Comrade Chairman Mao Zedong:
>
> I, Chen Shizhong, write this letter to all of you from prison with feelings of incomparable sincerity. At this critical point when my life hangs in the balance, I resolutely put aside thoughts of per-

sonal safety or advantage and offer all of you my most sincere words of loyal warning, one last time.

I am a person who has committed serious errors. It has now been eight months since, at a critical point during the Sino-Soviet dispute, I wrote an essay defending the Soviet Union. I attempted to force my way into the Soviet Embassy, thus breaking the criminal code and landing in prison. I regret this extremely. From prison I sincerely beg forgiveness from the Committee, and from you, sir, and pray that you will all treat my case with leniency.

In the end, I am a young intellectual whom the Party has brought up single-handedly; everything I have was given me by the Party. I have the deepest class feelings for the Party, and I have unwaveringly devoted my life to the Communist cause. Thus while humbly bowing my head to acknowledge my errors, I still want to put the cause of the Party first and offer you the criticism of a comrade and the warning of a family member, hoping that I may rouse all of you to pay the greatest attention.

In my view, while the Central Committee of the Chinese Communist Party has recently achieved important successes in its line, direction, and policies both at home and abroad, nevertheless at the same time it has committed a whole series of serious errors, amongst which are errors of principle and of basic direction. Now, in the long march of history it is hardly surprising that a particular political party or person should make this or that sort of mistake. But what is most dangerous and most frightening is that the Central Committee to this very day has failed to realize that it has committed any errors at all. This is what makes me apprehensive at heart, and like someone with a fish bone stuck in his throat, I will not be content until I spit it out. Otherwise I would not be a good member of the Party family.

The causes that have produced these errors are multi-faceted, but the most important is the worship of or superstitious belief in the person of Chairman Mao. . . .[8] You, sir, do not in fact permit others to criticize your shortcomings and mistakes. Faced with criticisms of principle that have any degree of sharpness, you immediately become hostile, unleashing a cruel struggle and attack. If you continue in this way, then who will dare to speak the truth? And in the long run, how will you ever be able to hear opposing views? . . . Your every statement, nay your every word, is absolute truth that can only be praised and never opposed. . . . Yugoslavia, the USSR, Poland, Hungary, France, Italy, the U.S.A., India—the communist parties of these nations can all make mistakes, while the Communist Party of China is the only exception and has locked itself inside a red safe where it absolutely cannot make mistakes! . . . Yet, of all possible errors, there is none more frightening than to believe that one can never commit errors. . . . You repeatedly state that Marxism is not afraid of criticism, but the actual facts are precisely the opposite. Without going further for examples, out of all those people who have "criticized" Mao Zedong Thought from 1957 to the present, who has come to a good end?[9]

Please for the moment hold back the thunder of your wrath. . . . My belief that the worship of you as an individual is the worst disaster for our Party and our country is a conclusion that I have reached entirely on my own by independent thinking, based on harsh, objective facts. Developments over these past few years have filled me with apprehension, and I have a strong feeling that sooner or later there will come a day when many leaders at the center—including Liu Shaoqi, Zhou Enlai, Zhu De, Chen Yun, Lin Biao, Deng Xiaoping, Dong Biwu, Peng Zhen, Liu Bocheng, Li Fuchun, Chen Yi, and others—will be branded anti-Party, counterrevolutionary, revisionist elements![10] Having read this far, perhaps you will explode in anger: "Isn't what you're saying equivalent to a 'clean sweep' of all the leaders of the Party and nation?" But hear me out patiently. Because they cannot maintain complete unity with you on every issue in the course of the revolution, when the revolution reaches a turning point there will always be some among them who will disagree with your proposals and support their own opinions, thus becoming obstacles to the pursuit of your own line and policy. This will make them "anti-Party elements." . . . It would be fortunate indeed for our country and people if my predictions were merely groundless, imaginary fears. I wish it were so.

Having written this far, I would like to help you to analyze the objective factors that have created the current situation. From the masses of the people to the inner core of the Party, there are just three types of people: the first are those who sincerely support your opinions based on genuine understanding. This type is a minority. The second are those who sing in chorus and echo what others say; these are the great majority. And then there are those who disagree with you in their hearts but who for various reasons—principally a concern for their personal safety—don't dare to raise a dissenting voice. These are also a minority. Within the last, third category, there are also a significant number of people with ulterior motives. It is precisely these people, I fear, who are the most dangerous.

. . . What is frightening is that when you have made a mistake, there will be no one who will help you correct it. Thus, as time goes on, the only people to get your favor will be a group of petty people who flatter you, toady up to you, and examine your every word and every change of facial expression in order to divine your wishes. Among these there will be some genuine opportunists and schemers. Having thought this far, I am extremely worried about the fate of the Party and the country. With the sincerity of a member of the family, I am willing to use my death to warn you, and hope that you can stay clear of petty people and associate with people of character. . . . Those who voice their support for you with every breath are not necessarily to be trusted, while those who oppose some of your mistaken proposals are not necessarily your enemies. By all means, please avoid following the path of Stalin.

Let me turn to my own case. You are quite right to have said, "There is absolutely no such thing in the world as love or hate without reason or cause."[11] Entirely correct! If the Communist Party together with you, Chairman Mao, had not liberated all of China, then I, Chen Shizhong, this orphan, would never have gone to college or studied abroad, but would have long since frozen or starved to death on the street! When I ask my conscience, I truly cannot think of any reason to oppose the Central Committee; what I oppose is merely, sir, your mistakes. I do this out of love for you, and I hope that you will truly be able to stop making mistakes, or make fewer serious mistakes. The Committee may call me "anti-Party," but I believe the question is not one of attaching epithets or labels. I have the courage to engage in self-criticism for the mistakes I have made, and I fully hope that the Central Committee of the CCP will also set me a good example of how to accept criticism. If what I am now doing is considered "anti-Party," then I must steel my heart and bravely admit that for the cause of the Party, I intend to remain "anti-Party," will be resolutely "anti-Party," and "anti-Party" with all my strength. I believe that my being "anti-Party" in this fashion shows precisely the most sincere and the deepest love for the Party. If this loyalty itself should be considered "anti-Party," then how greatly I hope that more and more selfless and fearless Communist Party members—like you, the readers of this essay—will recall your oaths upon entering the Party, will observe the realities of life within the Party today, and will join me in rising up to be "anti-Party."

. . . I have seen your inscription, "Learn from Comrade Lei Feng."[12] Right now everyone in the country is learning from Lei Feng. . . . I admit that Lei Feng had many valuable points in his character and that I naturally should learn from him. But I believe that Lei Feng is by no means a perfect model and that his character possessed serious or even fatal flaws. His flaw was his habit of total obedience to the orders of his superiors; he never learned how to resist the mistaken decisions of a superior. Lei Feng had a famous saying that circulated widely, "Whatever Chairman Mao tells me to do, I will do it just as he tells me."[13] I believe that this saying is incorrect and unscientific, and that it harbors a great danger that even you yourself have not realized. First, it equates you with the Party; and second, it assumes *a priori* that you are always entirely correct. Not only are your past and present statements absolutely correct, so that Lei Feng must carry them out to the letter, but also even the statements you have yet to make in the future have already been determined to be literally true, and so Lei Feng has long since prepared to act in accordance with them. If this isn't one hundred percent blind obedience, then what is it?

Just reflect: if the entire population of the country, and every Party and Youth League member, became a Lei Feng, what kind of situation might arise? While the general mood of society and its morality would no doubt be refreshed, as soon as you made a mistaken pronouncement or a mistaken decision on behalf of the Central Committee, then who could come forth to help all of you to correct it? If everyone were a Lei Feng, then no one would ever dare to think, let alone "discover mistakes and correct them." And yet all of you call on everyone else to do this! Obviously, the slogans that you often cite—"Open up broad channels of communication and be pleased to hear of your own faults," "Blame not the speaker but be warned by his words," etc.—in fact are empty phrases that cannot be put into practice! That is to say, if all of you continue in this fashion, you will be all right as long as you don't make a mistake, but as soon as you make one, you will be mistaken to the end, and the disastrous consequences will be endless . . .

This quotation is already rather long. But it is only a few hundredths of Chen Shizhong's petition to the Party Central Committee, which totaled several hundred thousand characters. It has definite value as an historical document. It was written at a time when China had just emerged from a great famine that arose primarily from human causes,[14] and its author had narrowly escaped death. Chen Shizhong was endowed with no special foresight. Many in the Party had much higher levels of vision than his. What sets him apart is that even in those circumstances he dared to state his political opinions boldly. As a young man of twenty-six, not a Party member, engaged only in technological work, and knowing very little about Chinese society or the political situation within the Party, his understanding could not have been absolutely correct. But under normal political conditions, the political opinions and doubts that he had gradually formed between 1960 and 1964 should have had a chance to be aired. There should have been an opportunity to correct his misunderstandings, and his extreme actions and their consequences could have been prevented, don't you think?

Chen Shizhong seems to have had too high an opinion of himself. But if he had not, then he also would not have had the courage to speak out so boldly, as in the following:

Now I ask you to consider another young person: Chen Shizhong. In your view, which of these two young people is the better, Lei Feng or Chen Shizhong? Whom do you prefer? You will certainly say, "Of course Lei Feng is the better one; how can you compare with him?!" True, Lei Feng is the model that people throughout the country emulate, while I am a criminal awaiting sentence in a people's prison. These two are as far apart as heaven above and earth below and cannot be compared. But if we can put this point aside for a moment, I beg you to look at another aspect of things. When I look inside myself, I know that I have always been a member of the Party family. Were this not so, then why would I worry so much about the fate of the Party and the nation? And what would I be trying to gain by writing you an open letter from prison, full of direct criticism and bitter words? When I look back on my life, I see that my hardships have been just as bitter as Lei Feng's, and my feelings for the Party have been just as deep. But precisely for this reason, I feel all the more strongly that I have no right to stand on the outside. I cannot permit myself to put my hands into my pockets and observe from the sidelines. Rather, as a son or daughter should, I must cast aside thoughts of personal gain or loss and criticize you face to face for your errors, frankly and without reserve. I am confident that I could accomplish all the good deeds Lei Feng has accomplished, but there is one difference: I do not believe that this world possesses a savior endowed with foreknowledge.[15]

My dear Chairman Mao, turn around quickly, before it is too late!

Having read this letter, there is a very large possibility that in your rage you will all order me to be executed. Are there not plenty of precedents for this in the forty-two-year history of the Chinese Communist Party? My interrogator repeatedly warns me, "Right up to this very moment, we still consider you as one of us and are trying to save you. . . . If you will just change your attitude, there could be an unexpectedly good result." I have wondered a thousand times: could I put aside my own opinions, join the chorus, and admit that I was thoroughly wrong? To do so would naturally have advantages in recovering my freedom, but would I not have abandoned my lofty duty as a communist?[16] No, when the matter concerns the fate of the nation or the Party, I cannot trade my principles for personal advantage. My fear is that there will come a day when, due to your stubborn adherence to your mistakes, you will be struck down to the ground. Then, in the midst of adversity and despair, you will once again leaf through this document, sigh, and realize you are too late: "How I regret I didn't listen to Chen Shizhong's good advice at the time!" No, I will not play the role of an after-the-fact strategist. I must avert disaster before it occurs and try to make you listen to and adopt my loyal advice, however unpleasant it may be to your ear.

Do you want to know where my great courage comes from? It comes from your example! It is you who have repeatedly taught us to have the courage to uphold the truth and to correct errors. You yourself have many times been the target of attack by rightist opportunists who call themselves "leftists," and you have even been shut out of the central leadership,[17] but you have never lost heart, and the facts prove that you were right. Thus, a great man such as yourself should have an even deeper understanding of the fact that when a mistaken line has occupied the leading position it is very difficult to uphold the truth! And this is very commendable! I am determined to follow your example and to be worthy of our times and of the cause of the Party!

I have always thought that what our Party lacks are "loyal ministers who are forthright with criticism" who can speak up and dare to be frank. We have no need for those who always say yes and who shift their rudders to suit the wind. I am now using your own methods—giving you a powerful shove from behind and shouting "You are sick!"[18] . . .

What surprises me is this: how could it be that no one else has discerned the problems that I have discovered? I don't believe it. At the present moment, the abnormal condition of life within the Party is obvious to all who have eyes to see. I have always felt that there are many who look without seeing and listen without hearing, not breathing a word to a soul. I alone say what I think and insist on speaking out.

I dream about avoiding disaster before it strikes, but I also have a premonition that bad fortune will outweigh good. I don't even dare to believe that you, sir, will really have the chance to read these loyal but unpleasant words, written with my heart's blood. Perhaps, after reading this document, your "dragon heart" will be stirred to anger, and then my life will be over. But even in the face of execution I still wish to tell you sincerely, my esteemed and beloved Chairman Mao:

"Jupiter, you are angry; this proves that you are wrong!"[19]

"I loved you all, friends. Be on guard."[20]

At the end of his document, Chen Shizhong wrote,

I have had the honor to meet you, sir, three times in my life, and have been happy to shake your hand. While in prison, writing this document, I have seen you four times in my dreams. I think of you with deep affection. I have deliberately chosen the last day of this leap month in this lunar leap year to present to you this document, which is written with my heart's blood.[21] I offer to you, and to my beloved Party, this sincere heart—which is all that I have left.

Long live Communism!

The whole document was over thirty thousand characters. Many pages were covered with the stains of the young man's tears.

Chen's interrogating officer formally told him: "In accordance with your repeated requests, we have already forwarded your papers to the Central Committee, even though we believe there is absolutely no necessity to do so."

Chen Shizhong waited for a reply. One month passed. Then another. He lost hope. He became extremely anxious. The interrogator scolded him: "Who do you think you are that Chairman Mao should reply to your letter?" This startled Chen. Why, he thought, couldn't Chairman Mao answer my letter? Aren't we a democratic people's country? The scolding also deepened his concerns: it would appear that Chairman Mao at best could hear the voices only of high officials of rank ten or better; wasn't this equivalent to locking himself inside the Forbidden City and cutting himself off from Chinese society? In his heart, Chen continued to cry out: "You yourselves do not write to Chairman Mao, and when someone else writes to him, you do not let him see the letter; doesn't this mean the Party once again loses a chance to hear opposing views and to correct its mistakes? How could this not fail to delay decisions on important matters?"

Chen Shizhong was sentenced to eight years in prison and deprived of his rights as a citizen for an additional two years. Shortly thereafter, the great political turmoil that he had so unluckily predicted [i.e., the Cultural Revolution, 1966–1976] got underway.

Another of his predictions, however, did not come to pass. That was one contained in a poem that he placed in the middle of his essay "Reproving the Party":[22]

> I don't care if you cut off my head, as long as I have been true
>   to my principles;
> Once you have killed Chen Shizhong, it will be hard to find
>   another to succeed him.

There were, indeed, few who could follow in Chen Shizhong's footsteps, yet some could still be found. A youth, Chen Shizhong's junior by eight years, had long since brought himself forward, just as Chen had done. When Chen was sent to prison and disappeared from the scene, this person in many ways replaced him, and, due to his equally distinctive charms, made his own mark on the stage of Chinese politics.

Another Madman

Right when Chen Shizhong was boarding the Moscow-to-Beijing express train to return to the native soil from which he had been separated so long, Ni Yuxian was entering the ranks of the Chinese People's Liberation Army.[23] Ni had been a high school student, and what set him apart from most soldiers was his special passion for the theories of Marxism and Leninism. Ni saved money from his living allowance to buy sets of the selected works of Marx, Engels, Lenin, Stalin, and Mao, and he also read every classical work of Marxism-Leninism that he could borrow, including *Capital, Anti-Dühring, The History of the Communist [Bolshevik] Party of the Soviet Union, The Development of the Monist View of History,* and others. Unlike certain theorists—but like many young intellectuals of the 1960s—Ni Yuxian came to the study of theory under a mountain of doubt that had derived from his life experience. The study of theory in turn led him to focus with increasing concern on actual problems in Chinese life. He discovered that the basic concepts of Marxism-Leninism that he had learned were now violently at odds with China's social practice. The two were locked in sharp, irreconcilable conflict.

More than half the soldiers in his company were from Anhui. Something about them aroused Ni Yuxian's curiosity: why, as soon as they got a letter from home, did they rush off to read it in private, or even cry in secret? When he asked, it turned out that nearly every one of his comrades-in-arms had a relative who had died of illness or starvation.[24] Ni was thunderstruck. Soldiers from the disaster areas kept coming to the army to "receive nutrition," and officials were unable to shoo them away. The soldiers' explanation was extremely simple, "If we go back, we'll starve."

Ni Yuxian decided to do a broad survey to collect firsthand data. It turned out that the cause of the famine was by no means what the newspapers were calling a "severe natural disaster"; it was the whole set of extreme-left reforms that were being practiced in the rural areas. Policies of "high production quotas," "high gov-

ernment purchasing quotas," "egalitarianism," and the "communist wind" had twisted a perfectly normal countryside into a barren landscape covered with the corpses of famine victims.[25]

Just like Chen Shizhong, this eighteen-year-old "private," a soldier of the lowest possible rank, made up his mind to write a letter
to the Central Committee and to Chairman Mao.

Ni wrote a petition of thirty pages. He pointed out that the basic cause of the difficulties in the national economy was not some
sort of natural disaster but was man-made: "Any method," he
wrote, "that departs from concrete, objective reality and seeks to
leap into a communist society in a single step must suffer the cruel
revenge of the law of dialectics." He implored the Central Committee "to immediately readjust the system of ownership in the
rural people's communes, to establish true distribution according
to a person's labor, and to undertake a large strategic retreat." He
boldly set forth a whole series of corrective actions: setting farm
production quotas per household; permitting commune members
to plant, harvest, produce, and sell crops on their own for a certain
period of time; expanding personal plots and opening up free
markets; and eliminating state restrictions on peasants developing
their own sideline production. He also suggested the adoption of
graduated tax reductions according to which the more the peasants produced, the lower the percentage in tax taken by the state
would be. These measures would stimulate peasants' enthusiasm
to produce more and help to head off disaster.

Here was a youth of only eighteen years who, right at the
height of the movement "to oppose right deviationism and arouse
enthusiasm,"[26] dared to ask the Central Committee of the Party to
reverse its policies. He well knew that the consequences of sending out his appeal would be hard to imagine, and that bad fortune
would likely outbalance good. The whole thing alarmed the army
Party committee. Zhao Benqing, political commissar of Ni's regiment, issued an order: "This letter may not be mailed by a private
person; it must be handed over to the regimental political department for examination and then dealt with by the authorities."
From the perspective of later events, this decision was very likely
taken in order to protect Ni Yuxian. But Ni refused to hand over
his letter on grounds that "the constitution prescribes that citizens

have the right to lay any complaints whatsoever before the leaders of the country."[27] Battalion headquarters then issued an order forbidding him to leave the camp. Once again Ni disobeyed. He went to the Dashitou post office in Jinshan County, where he sent off his petition to Beijing by registered mail, return receipt requested.

Two weeks later, Ni Yuxian received the return receipt from the Office of the Central Committee. Three months later, his petition was redirected to the Shanghai Garrison Command. Ni's political commissar, in his report at the divisional Party congress, said, "In the 68th Regiment there is a soldier named Ni Yuxian who wrote a letter to Chairman Mao expressing views that are entirely revisionist! This is the reflection within the army of the national and international class struggle." Ni's entire unit was shaken when this judgment was passed down. And Ni Yuxian's political fate was sealed.

For two consecutive years Ni had been rated an "all-round model soldier." His marks in construction work and in military training had been uniformly excellent, and the army leadership had many times made ready to train him as an officer for propaganda work. None of this counted any longer. In 1964 he was given an individual "honorable discharge" at the rank of "private first-class." He left the army with two soap crates full of Marxism-Leninism and a head full of questions. His final evaluation from the Party branch of his company said nothing of either Marxism-Leninism or revisionism, but only: "Said comrade is a person of integrity, devoted to study, and upright in his conduct."

He Fights on Alone, Refusing to Join Factions and Never "Integrating Himself" with the Masses

Yet the struggles between true and false Marxism-Leninism and between true and false revisionism never let him go. Ni Yuxian was not willing to be alone, either, and so constantly got caught up in the whirlpool of politics.

He passed the entrance examination for the "trans-oceanic department" of the Shanghai Maritime Academy,[28] and it was there that he ran headlong into the "Great Cultural Revolution." In

July of 1966, a group of students wanted to overthrow the Academy's president Xu Jian, claiming that he was pursuing a revisionist line. On August 3, when a work team from the Municipal Party Committee convened a meeting of all students and faculty, a student leapt onto the stage to plead for President Xu's innocence. This was Ni Yuxian. Ni's actions unexpectedly won him over two-thirds of the votes of the students and faculty, and he was elected a member of the Academy's Cultural Revolution committee. For two months he devoted all his energies to halting "revolutionary activities" such as raiding private homes, armed struggle, and beating, smashing and looting. It was only because of Ni's intervention that some of the teachers at the Maritime Academy managed to escape fatal bodily harm or defamation of character.

The Marxism-Leninism that Ni had learned was still of some use. He remained clear-headed. The more fanatical and excessive the students became, the more doubts Ni had. He refused to join any Red Guard organization whatsoever, and from September 1966 onward he remained completely aloof from the movement at school, dissociating himself from the Cultural Revolution.

But he was never able to be a "free and easy wanderer,"[29] either. Far from "wandering freely," he even joined several worker organizations to oppose the activities of political careerists. He helped the workers to draft a manifesto censuring Wang Hongwen, Zhang Chunqiao, and Yao Wenyuan[30] for manipulating the movement in Shanghai. In a famous incident on November 28, 1966, Zhang Chunqiao sent in the army to crack down on students at Fudan University.[31] When Ni heard the news, he raced to the site that very night in order to see the true state of affairs. At dawn the next day, he drafted a forceful appeal entitled "Strongly Resist the Crackdown by Zhang Chunqiao and Yao Wenyuan on the Student Movement" and distributed it throughout the city under the name of several city-wide organizations. He personally ran up and down the streets and alleys of Shanghai pasting up slogans condemning Zhang and Yao. And so Ni joined the so-called "counterrevolutionary tide" that was "attacking the headquarters of the proletariat." Wang Hongwen dispatched rebel Red Guards of the No. 17 Cotton Factory to rip down the offending posters. Ni, viewed as a principal instigator, was put on a "wanted" list for arrest. To avoid trouble, Ni once again separated himself from the movement at the outset of 1967.

But he had by no means given up the fight. He chose a new battlefront where he could wage a new struggle—all by himself.

He Comes Up with a New Way to Pull the Tiger's Whiskers

For half a year, the vilest forms of human conduct—armed combat, murder, torture, betrayal—unfolded before his eyes scene by scene. Many good people who had done no wrong either committed suicide or were killed by others. Ni couldn't stop pondering the question, "Is the guiding ideology of the Cultural Revolution correct after all? Are its leaders true Marxist-Leninists?" He concentrated his mind to analyze one important event after another. He began to have doubts about Lin Biao.[32] Why was it that in his public speeches this "deputy commander-in-chief" and "chosen successor" repeatedly fanned flames of a boundless, religious-type fervor, spared nothing to demean and attack Marxism-Leninism, and emasculated Mao Zedong Thought, reducing it to only the "Three Old Articles"?[33]

As Lin Biao's true nature gradually became clearer to Ni, he could no longer tolerate the docility and blind obedience that had spread throughout the country. When Lin Biao smiled hypocritically, waving that little red book in one hand, tens of millions of people cried out madly and waved back with their *Quotations from Chairman Mao.* A single sentence from this book could spark armed violence or legitimate mankind's ugliest, most barbaric tortures, making butchers into revolutionaries! Ni Yuxian searched long and hard for a mode of action that could most efficiently bring about his heartfelt wish. He now realized that *Quotations from Chairman Mao* had been the primary means by which Lin Biao spread his left-deviationist dogmatism, and that Lin's "Preface to the Second Edition" dismembered the whole system of Mao Zedong Thought and turned it into something that opposed Marxism-Leninism! What could he do? From among his tangled thoughts a surprising idea leapt out: "I'll fight fire with fire! I'll put together an opposing volume, *Quotations from Lenin,* that will permit people to discern the errors of that little red book that was compiled under Lin Biao."

Ni Yuxian borrowed the lone set of *The Complete Works of Lenin* from the Maritime Academy library and set to work finding excerpts. He piled up card after card. He put special emphasis on selecting passages in which Lenin criticized left-deviationist opportunism and dogmatism. For half a year he toiled at his desk, often forgetting to eat and sleep, until the collection was ready. To correspond to the "Preface to the Second Edition," he composed an "Editor's Foreword" that contained a clear provocation: "The publication of *Quotations from Lenin* is certain to cause fear and uneasiness among the enemies of Marxism-Leninism and Mao Zedong Thought. They will stamp with fury and oppose it with all their might. . . . But I say, let every damned argument that vainly presumes to put Mao Zedong Thought in opposition to Leninism go to hell!"

There was a small printing plant in the countryside that had printed some of his "Attack Zhang Chunqiao" leaflets. Ni Yuxian went to contact the managers, and they surprised him by assenting. The type had just been set when the Shanghai Municipal "Revolutionary Committee" got wind of Ni's plans. The committee issued urgent orders to destroy the type and sent people to confiscate the original manuscript. Ni Yuxian fled with the manuscript. Then, after much difficulty, he reached agreement with a printing plant in Huzhou. They had started the presses for a trial run when all of a sudden the army representative in charge of approving publications arrived and required Ni Yuxian to "highlight politics"[34] throughout the work by inserting manifestos criticizing Liu Shaoqi and Deng Xiaoping as well as a front-page inscription from "Vice-chairman" Lin. Ni Yuxian could not bring himself to compromise and so could only destroy the type once again. After many more twists and turns he finally succeeded in secretly printing ten thousand copies at a small printing plant along the Yangzi river. Ni gave his books bright red plastic jackets. On New Year's Eve, 1968, in the midst of a heavy snow but with feelings of unbounded excitement, Ni transported his odd cargo back to Shanghai. Ni's book was "odd" because in this country that claims Marxism-Leninism as its guiding ideology, Lenin's works had become contraband!

Ten thousand copies of *Quotations from Lenin* sold out in a single day. Many more people wanted to order copies. But the next day a big poster had been pasted up on the door of the big auditorium at the Maritime Academy: "Root out and expose *Quotations from Lenin,* the great poisonous weed that brazenly opposes Vice-chairman Lin!" One big-character poster after another denounced the crimes of *Quotations from Lenin,* charging that its editor was deliberately opposing *Quotations from Chairman Mao* and that its "Editor's Foreword" sought to "provoke a quarrel" with and to "launch a counterattack" on Lin's "Preface to the Second Edition." Some people even urged that this volume of Lenin's writings be confiscated and burned.

Ni Yuxian wandered back and forth with his hands folded behind his back, looking at the big-character posters with perfect contentment—for this was precisely the goal of his death-defying behavior and the political payback for his hard and bitter work. He expected to be surrounded, but maintained his reserve: "Let us coolly observe these crabs and see just how long they can continue to run amok!"[35]

In March, Xu Jingxian[36] approved an investigation into the political background of the editor of *Quotations from Lenin* and anyone else who was involved. Part of the investigation was to determine the source of the funds used to print the book. Ni Yuxian was immediately placed in solitary confinement and held for questioning. The case investigation team could not bring itself to believe that the editing, printing, and distribution of this book had been accomplished by a single student. Nor could it imagine that the funds had all been borrowed by Ni from individual students at several universities.

Every day Ni Yuxian was hauled before Lin Biao's "sacred photo" and forced to apologize and bend over ninety degrees at the waist. He secretly found this amusing and felt satisfied, for he had finally accomplished something meaningful. It had, moreover, been his own decision, and he had accomplished everything by himself, from start to finish! He once again could feel proud of himself.

How could Ni be so meek and humble in allowing others to trample on him like this? One day when his guards were not paying attention, he slipped over the wall in the middle of the night and escaped. Soon he had returned to Shanghai, where, together with comrades from Fudan and the Normal School, he joined a "Second Attack on Zhang Chunqiao."

How could a small fry like Ni Yuxian ever escape the tight net of the "dictatorship of the proletariat"? When worker propaganda teams[37] took over the universities, Ni once again was ferreted out, locked up in a study group, and forced to confess his crimes. During the "one-strike, three-antis" campaign,[38] he was among the first targets to be attacked. His attackers not only wanted to investigate his political problems, they also wanted to investigate questions of his finances and personal life. They discovered, predictably, that in printing the *Quotations from Lenin* he had "embezzled" over one hundred yuan of "public funds." They also concocted a charge that "he had passed himself off as a member of the worker propaganda team and had raped a young woman." With this, the case was finally "complete" enough to discredit Ni Yuxian, and they expelled him from the academy.

The Gang of Four Has Fallen, yet He Is Sentenced to Death

This world certainly does not lack for marvels. Ni Yuxian and Lin Biao fought with each other for a full ten years, and the more they fought, the braver and firmer Ni became. Although arrested and tortured several times, he also escaped ill fortune several times. Although the henchmen of Lin Biao and the Gang of Four hated him intensely, they could neither control nor destroy him. But in Shanghai, after the fall of the Gang of Four, Ni Yuxian was nearly executed by the very leading officials who claimed (truthfully) that they had been persecuted by the Gang of Four and who had by then returned to power! How peculiar is that? Don't you find it hard to believe?

These leading officials could hardly have been unaware of Ni Yuxian's brave struggle against Lin Biao and the Gang of Four, could they? Everyone knew that many previously persecuted gov-

ernment officials and political theorists had been restored to freedom in the spring of 1975. At that time Ni Yuxian was a worker
earning a bare thirty-three yuan per month, and yet he dared to
write a piece entitled "On Socialist Democracy and the Dictatorship of the Proletariat—How to Prevent People Like Lin Biao
from Returning to Power"; this was in direct opposition to Zhang
Chunqiao's essay, "On the Complete Dictatorship of the Proletariat." Ni even stated plainly that he was arguing against Zhang
Chunqiao! He pointed out that a dictatorship without democracy
is only a Lin Biao kind of social fascism; that Lin Biao had already
gone to his own death, but that there were still large numbers of
people like him waiting in the wings; and that if the Central
Committee did not do something quickly, it would be not only
possible but a foregone conclusion that people like Lin Biao
would take power again. What professional theorist at that time
had the courage and the vision to write this sort of article?

Ni took another step that was, if not more dangerous, at least
equally so. He couldn't forget the fearsome consequences of the
letter he wrote to the Central Committee in 1963 admonishing
the Party. Nor could he fail to realize that the current Central
Committee was an even more forbidding place than it had been
before. Yet he still wrote a letter to Chairman Mao and to the
Politburo of the Central Committee. His friends all wrung their
hands, saying that this would never do; as soon as the letter was
sent off, he would at best be put in prison and at worst put to
death! To this Ni Yuxian said, "China suffers from the fact that no
one dares to tell the truth. If everyone is afraid of death and no
one speaks out, then China will be in greater danger day by day,
and politics will become more reactionary day by day. So I'll lead
the way!" He sped off to the Post and Telegraph Office on Nanjing
East Road and sent his letter by registered mail. At that time many
people were writing letters to the Gang of Four declaring their loyalty, but I don't suppose there could have been many in China
writing this sort of letter, could there?

The reason Ni Yuxian was nearly executed in 1977 was that he
had been too enthusiastic in agitating for Comrade Deng Xiaoping's return to work.[39] But how could the leading comrades forget that in 1976, when the Gang of Four was still in power, the

Municipal Revolutionary Committee had sent instructions to Ni Yuxian's factory calling him a "henchman" in Deng Xiaoping's "rightist reversal of verdicts"?[40] Could they have forgotten their order that Ni be attacked, and that he had indeed become the target of struggle for a full day? The Gang of Four itself had not arrested him over the Deng Xiaoping matter, but now the Municipal Party Committee wanted to put him before a firing squad. Does that make sense?

Why is it that Ni Yuxian had such deep feelings for Comrade Deng Xiaoping? Here's how he explained it:

> In 1976 the Gang of Four was arrested, but its violent suppression of the revolutionary masses in the Tiananmen Incident was not addressed, and Comrade Deng Xiaoping, who had struggled with the Gang of Four and been slandered by them, was still unable to return to work.[41] At the time, I could see clearly that the questions of thoroughly reversing the verdict on the Tiananmen Incident and on restoring Comrade Deng Xiaoping's good name were basic, key questions that would determine whether or not we could eradicate the counterrevolutionary line of Lin Biao and the Gang of Four and whether or not we could make China move from the darkness out into the light of day. Yet, due to the obstruction of X XX[42] and others, there were repeated obstacles, and so I decided that I would once again use my only weapon—my pen—to leap into this struggle!

On January 8, 1977, Ni Yuxian posted two "big-character poems" on the great steel doors of the Donghu Hotel on Shanghai's Huaihai Road. The poems called for Comrade Deng Xiaoping's restoration to office and resolutely demanded a reversal of the verdict on the Tiananmen Incident. One of the poems about Comrade Xiaoping was the following:

A Ballad for Xiaoping[43]

A court full of scholars and soldiers, a sky full of stars;
How many of them ever won the Chairman's praise?
With good reason Mao entrusted him with "China's Great Wall"
    [the People's Liberation Army]
And praised Xiaoping as a "man of rare talent."
Deng's diplomacy made the five continents submit;

His vigorous policies startled all within the four seas.
He doesn't plot secretly, his plans are all public;
He has no wild ambition but only a loyal heart.
Despite many rounds of praise and blame, he has escaped the
    executioner's blade;
Despite three demotions, he has stayed loyal to our nation's leader.
His successes and failures over half a lifetime are known to the
    whole world;
The rights and wrongs of this past year are quite clear to the
    common people.
Slow to yield, he easily attracts slander from the gang of foxes;
Firm as steel, it's hard for him to be intimate with the dog pack.
His rise and fall in official rank is of small importance,
But if you don't make use of Xiaoping, the people will not be
    appeased.

Readers crowded around as soon as the two poems appeared. Soon a solid wall of people was copying them down. The intersection of Donghu Road and Huaihai Road became tied up in a traffic jam. Ni Yuxian stood in the crowd, again enjoying the pride of authorship. He could sense the shimmering of a sharp, cold sword that hung over his head, yet he felt the double satisfaction of having done something that suited both justice and the people's feelings. He had clearly voiced what was in people's hearts! That being so, what did his personal safety matter?

Then, having gained an inch, he tried to take a mile. He decided to burn his bridges behind him. Late at night on March 30, 1977, he once again pasted up a long poem, this time calling for the reversal of the verdict on the Tiananmen Incident. He chose, for a location, the wall of the Park Hotel, Shanghai's tallest building. He called the poem, "I Don't Believe!—Commemorating the Anniversary of the Massacre at Tiananmen Square."[44] In his accompanying remarks, Ni noted that the Tiananmen Incident had been a revolutionary movement in which the broad masses of the people opposed the Gang of Four, and he once again called for the restoration to office of his beloved Vice-chairman Deng. His ten-meter-long call to arms immediately alarmed the first Party secretary of the Shanghai Municipal Committee, who personally issued an order to arrest Ni Yuxian.

In prison Ni was unwilling to admit guilt and as a result suffered the sort of cruel treatment that he had never experienced when the Gang of Four was in power.

Remarkably, although Deng Xiaoping was restored to office in August 1977, Ni Yuxian was dragged back to his factory for a struggle session on September 1. There the head of the Public Security Bureau announced to everyone that "Ni Yuxian is a counterrevolutionary opposed to Chairman X [i.e., Hua] and guilty of the most heinous crimes!" During the meeting, he conveyed the eight-word judgment of the Municipal First Party secretary that Ni was "reactionary to the core and poisonous in the extreme!" The whole audience then chanted, "Execute him!" After the struggle meeting, Ni Yuxian was put into a cell on death row. At the time the leaders of the Shanghai Municipal Party Committee, at the behest of a certain person, were preparing to suppress a group of political prisoners who had called for a reversal of the verdict on the Tiananmen Incident.

In his cell Ni Yuxian had concluded, from a variety of signs, that his last hour was upon him. Yet somehow he remained unusually calm and looked back on his own short life as if he were looking at someone else's. He was only thirty-three years old. Ten years earlier he had had his first brush with death. Since then there had been several occasions on which he might have died under the butcher's knife of the Gang of Four, but he never had. How could it be that now, nearly half a year since the destruction of the Gang of Four, he was being sent for execution? The leading officials of Shanghai were no longer the likes of Ma Tianshui.[45] Had they not all suffered oppression under Lin Biao and the Gang of Four? Had not he, Ni Yuxian, struggled ceaselessly for ten years to struggle against this group of careerists? How then could it be that the Shanghai officials now regarded him as a deadly enemy? It was not easy to understand. Could it be that these people were still close to the Gang of Four in their thoughts and feelings, and that this was why they were distant from him? He felt sad. His impending execution meant that the dark clouds hanging over China had not yet dispersed.

Even so, he couldn't give in. He had to put up a final struggle. On the evening of September 15, he wrote a final appeal to Vice-chairman Ye Jianying[46] on some sheets of toilet paper. He denounced the Shanghai Party Committee for following in the steps of the Gang of Four and for their crimes in butchering revolutionaries. He expressed his confidence that the verdict on the Tiananmen Incident would one day be reversed and that the people would demand that those responsible for perpetrating these new acts of injustice be tracked down.

His strong words enraged the head of the criminal court, who reprimanded Ni Yuxian by saying "the proof of your counterrevolutionary acts is ironclad," and "your stubborn resistance deserves only death!" Delighting in Ni's misfortune, the chief prison guard said, "I'll see you soon in another place!" He was referring to the execution ground. Ni no longer dared to hold any hope.

Yet his appeal did ultimately cause the higher authorities to hesitate. The planned execution was put off. While his fellows on death row went off to the execution ground one by one, Ni Yuxian miraculously lived through both New Year's Day, 1978, and the Spring Festival that followed.[47]

This was the time when those other heroes who had opposed the vile acts of the Gang of Four and had upheld the principles of Marxism—Shi Yunfeng in Jilin Province, Shi Hongxia in Shandong Province, Wang Shenyou in Shanghai, and others—were murdered in cold blood one by one, by people opposed to the Gang of Four.

It was only on January 11, 1979, after the Third Plenum of the Eleventh Party Congress,[48] that Ni Yuxian was released and returned from hell to the world of the living.

A "Lei Feng" in Chains

Chen Shizhong and Ni Yuxian—one in the north, one in the south—had never met each other, and yet fate seems to have caused the two of them to make a secret division of labor. After writing warning letters to Chairman Mao at almost the same time, one of them ended up in prison while the other escaped through sheer luck. Ni Yuxian then used his freedom and during the ten years of the Cultural Revolution did things that Chen Shizhong might also have done. Chen Shizhong lost his opportunity for political activity but did things while serving his sentence that Ni Yuxian might also have done had he been in prison. They divided their labor one final time in 1977, when Chen Shizhong regained his freedom and Ni Yuxian entered prison.

In his "Admonishing the Party," Chen Shizhong had boasted that "I am confident that I could accomplish all the good deeds that Lei Feng has accomplished." He wrote this before his sentencing. But what happened after Chen felt the heavy blow of the iron fist of the proletariat—a sentence of eight years, followed by six more years of "forced job placement" in the labor camp,[49] and then designation as an enemy of the people?

In the summer of 1970, Chen's labor reform gang was given the task of digging a ditch five meters deep and two meters wide. The soil was loose and kept caving in. Camp officials, in order to finish quickly, disregarded basic operational rules and had the prisoners dig tunnels instead of removing the top layers of soil.

One day, just before the lunch break, a tunnel entrance collapsed. Four prisoners were buried, while the roof of the tunnel, which was several meters of loose earth, continued to collapse. Chen Shizhong had just emerged from working in another tunnel when he passed by the entrance to the collapsed tunnel. Some inmates were on top of it, but were digging only half-heartedly to save the buried men. Chen guessed that they were unwilling to risk their lives while at the labor camp; but digging this way, when would they ever get down to where the men were buried? If people can't breathe, dammit, they die within a few minutes! Chen leapt into the tunnel, grabbed an iron hoe from the hands of another prisoner, and started frantically to throw back shovel after shovel of dirt. He quickly found a vertical brace that the trapped prisoner Shi Youde was hugging with both arms. Chen saw that the man was still conscious, spoke to him, and kept on digging, looking for the last remaining person buried inside. Clumps of wet earth of all sizes kept falling from above his head, and he could have been buried himself at any moment, but he paid no attention. Suddenly, his hoe hit something soft, which turned out to be the back of prisoner Mou Chengjie. Chen dug ever more frantically, but also tried to make his movements gentler. Carefully he dug Mou out of the earth and grabbed him in his arms—but Mou already looked like a corpse, his eyes wide open, dim and lifeless. This was the first time in his life Chen had seen a dead person. He wiped the dirt from Mou's nose and mouth and carried him out of the tunnel in his arms.

With resuscitation and the use of oxygen, Mou Chengjie was revived. A number of days later, though, he died from accelerated pulmonary tuberculosis.

It wasn't until he returned to the scene that afternoon that Chen Shizhong had time to feel frightened. He now realized that as he had been digging to rescue people, some other inmates had found a sawhorse, bound a thick board to its top, and thus made a shield to cover him as he worked below to rescue people. But over the lunch hour, the board had been snapped in half by large chunks of falling earth.

Chen Shizhong risked his life three times in such rescues and twice more on a firefighting team. Whether on dry fields, irrigated fields, or construction jobs, he always did the hardest, dirtiest, and most tiring work. After several years of labor reform, Chen had become hard to recognize: a clean-shaven head, bare feet, a pair of shorts, and 163 pounds of rock-hard flesh and bone. He looked like someone prepared to brave fire or boiling water at any moment. Only his glasses preserved a hint of the man who had once graduated from college in the Soviet Union.

Life in the labor camp had transformed his body, but by 1971 the heavy burden on his spirit had given him chronic high blood pressure. At its highest, it reached 210 over 130, and it put him in the hospital twice, for over five months each time. "I'm only a little over thirty—do I have to spend the rest of my life lying in bed supported by the public?" he wondered. He read a newspaper report that long-distance running could prevent or cure coronary heart disease. He wanted to try this, so he got up very early, unknown to his doctors, and secretly went out to run. The first day he ran one thousand meters slowly. He felt fine. The second day he ran fifteen hundred meters; the third, three thousand meters. Now he was confident. From then on he both lengthened his distance and increased his speed. A highway originated at the front gate of the hospital. He started running at the "zero" kilometer mark and ran till he got to "five," then turned around and ran back to "zero"—exactly ten kilometers or ten thousand meters. He would then run another thousand meters, gradually decreasing his speed. On the ten-thousand-meter course his fastest time was forty-four minutes. In the depths of the Heilongjiang winter, Chen wore an unlined cap and unlined shoes, but when his long run was over, he could still wring perspiration from both his T-shirt and shorts. His pulse reached two hundred beats a minute. He thus combined medical treatment with exercise, and at his three-month check up his doctors pronounced him basically fit.

He continued his long distance running for more than ten years without a break. After his release from the camp he took part in the Harbin Marathon and won three times. Would you have ever thought it? He even used his long-distance running to do good deeds. More than once he ran down petty thieves who were younger and faster but who lacked his endurance. When he caught up with them and forced them to return the stolen goods, he introduced himself by saying, "Do you know who you're dealing with? I'm the winner of the three-thousand-meter race!"

This long-distance champion also frequently forced the conductors of public buses to be more careful. Sometimes when he ran to catch the bus, the conductor refused to open the door at the bus stop, no matter how hard Chen banged on the door. When this happened, Chen said to himself, "Okay, we'll see!" As the bus drove on Chen would run alongside it, get on at the next stop, and then criticize the conductor: "Why didn't you open the door for me the last time?" This would leave the conductor speechless.

Later, after he became a teacher, Chen always began class by giving the students a maxim to remember. Most were famous sayings of revolutionary leaders or scientists, but one saying came from a Czech Olympic champion named Emil Zátopek, winner of the five-thousand- and ten-thousand-meter races: "When you can no longer keep going, you just keep going."

Taking His Life Back

How could this maxim be useful only in long-distance running?

In 1977 Chen Shizhong was permitted to take an urban job and was assigned work in the technical services office of a collectively owned factory in Harbin, the No. 3 Enamel Factory. He took his three meals in the cafeteria, which was staffed almost entirely by women, and played the role of the gentleman. Nearly every day he helped out by carrying coal upstairs or dirty water downstairs.

At noon, when other workers took naps, Chen volunteered free lessons in English and chemistry for young people.

Chen was sent to study at the Shanghai Industrial Enamel Factory. Although Shanghai was his hometown, and he had been away for a long time, he had no time for the city sights or visits with friends or relatives. Instead he dove headfirst into "seeking holy writ." During the day he studied with his class at the factory and at night took technical documents back with him to copy out by hand. All together he copied out four thick books totaling three hundred thousand characters. These he brought back to Harbin, where they became the foundation of the No. 3 Enamel Factory's collection of technical documents.

He was also sent, with twelve young people, to the No. 2 Glass Factory to borrow their six crucible furnaces to bake enamel powder during the National Day holidays. He divided the young people into two shifts that rotated every twelve hours. But who could take turns with him, the team leader? The responsibilities were too great to pass off. No problem—he just wouldn't sleep for forty-eight hours. He spent the holidays working alongside his young charges, without a break, next to thousand-degree furnaces.

Chen received an award that most people could not hope for. When his time came to leave the factory, everyone at every rank in the factory was reluctant to see him go. The mid-level officials, the Communist Youth League, the cafeteria, and the technical services office and enamel powder group hosted him in turn at four separate farewell banquets. The factory gave him a new suit of clothes, a new quilt, and a bookcase. Twelve Youth League members and young people saw him off to his new work unit in grand style.

What kind of a person was Chen Shizhong? Several years after the reversal of his verdict, some people continued to think of him as an ex-convict.

One after another these very moving scenes, together with the unanimous praise of the factory's more than five hundred workers, summoned back the tears that Chen Shizhong had silently swallowed all those years. The tears then washed away the marks left on his heart by fourteen years of humiliation.

A Harder Lot than Lei Feng's

Hard use makes iron corrode, but makes gold shine all the brighter.

When Chen Shizhong came to teach at the Harbin Workers' Part-time University, the administration told him that he could take two years to prepare his courses before teaching them. He refused. When the new semester started, he did special classes for three groups of graduating students. This entailed responsibility for every aspect of teaching "The Theory and Tools of Metal Cutting"—lectures, tutorials, laboratory experiments, job-site instruction, and curriculum design—or the equivalent of more than three times the normal teaching load.

Chen taught as many as ten consecutive class periods in a single day, and this would happen at least once a week. At the same time he went to audit five different classes at the Institute of Technology, the Science University, and his own school. He also served as head teacher for two successive classes of students. As if memorizing vocabulary items in the study of a foreign language, he committed their names and student numbers to memory within two weeks. He also looked into their families and backgrounds.

Chen's dedication was truly rare. To prevent a student from dropping out, he would visit the student's home time and again. He spoke individually with students who had missed too many classes because of illness, injury, or leaves of absence, or who were in danger of dropping out of school entirely because of family problems or lack of support from their factories. He used every trick in the book to keep them in school.

He changed the practice of taking attendance once a day and took it three times a day instead. During the first class period he sat by the door to see who arrived late, thus creating a sort of "deterrence." In order to prevent students from cheating on examinations, he gave his seventy-six students seventy-six different problem sets. This naturally increased by many times the amount of time he had to spend grading papers. Because the students came to class after a full day at work, they often dozed off, but

Chen Shizhong couldn't bear to see them do this—even once. So he bought aromatic ointment to dab onto the tired students. In one year he used up four jars, but thought it quite worth the cost.

Chen was also active in the world outside. He was vice–secretary-general and a permanent member of the standing committee of the Harbin Machining Society, as well as head of its membership and advisory subcommittees. He was an advisor to the Heilongjiang Provincial Translation Company. For all this work, as well as for the lectures that he often gave to other work units, he took no compensation even if it were offered. He collaborated with others in translating technical books that totaled more than a million characters. In three years he published over six hundred articles in various publications around the country. In whatever he did, his unusual conscientiousness only doubled his burdens. For instance, after becoming head of the membership subcommittee of the Machining Society, he went one by one to individual factories and schools to recruit members, causing the membership to increase dramatically from under two hundred to fifteen hundred. The task of filling out six thick volumes of membership rosters, in duplicate, fell to him. He had his ways of handling the burden, though. On business trips he took rosters with him to copy while traveling, and when hospitalized kept them nearby to fill out from his sickbed.

This behavior might fall under the injunction "Learn from Lei Feng and Do Good Deeds," might it not? Here we can pass over the many other incidents in which Chen resembled Lei Feng—helping old people and children on buses, helping passengers on trains, assisting conductors, trying to save accident victims on the street, and so forth. But when Chen Shizhong acted as Lei Feng had, his circumstances were much more difficult than Lei Feng's had been. Chen carried the material and mental burdens of a middle-aged man, which Lei Feng had not. Moreover, Chen was twice as old as Lei Feng, and fourteen years of hard living had left his physical strength and energy no match for Lei Feng's. Their housing differed, too: both lived in bachelors' dormitories, but Chen Shizhong was by no means as carefree as Lei Feng. Chen could never rid himself of some disturbing thoughts: First, how many former students, twenty-three years after returning to China from study abroad, still lived in bachelors' dormitories? Second, another annoying fact: after seven years of marriage, his wife, children, and mother-in-law—five persons altogether—still had to crowd onto a single bed to sleep. The problem wasn't that he was unwilling to lower his sights to a minimum standard, but that lowering his sights added to his worries about China: even during the "Great Cultural Revolution" Chen Jingrun[50] was still getting six square meters of living space. On every early morning run through Harbin's streets, he saw many new high-rise apartments that had been built in the past few years. And so he could not help thinking, from time to time, of his own little cubbyhole where, together with four young men just out of college, he squeezed into a room nineteen square meters, leaving him not even enough space for a desk. The entryway was piled high with the neighbors' belongings, so there was nowhere to put books. They had to carry their drinking water a distance of about a mile, and to use a toilet they had to go down from the third floor to the first.

While Lei Feng had never married, Chen Shizhong had married twice, and both times with such bad luck! His first wife had been very loving, but they were forced apart. His daughter had been born on the very day he went to prison. Now nineteen years old, she very much wanted to come and keep her poor dad company, but for one thing, there was no place for her to live, and for another, her father's second wife would not permit it. And this second wife's relationship with Chen Shizhong? Even among the bosses of labor gangs, he had never met anyone as formidable as she was!

For a moment let's imagine Lei Feng in Chen Shizhong's present position: after staying up late to grade papers, to talk with students, or to pursue research, Lei at least wouldn't then have to deal with insomnia as well. When teaching six periods in a row, Lei wouldn't have to continually run off to the bathroom at the behest of his prolapsed rectum. And when time after time he turned down compensation for after-hours teaching, accepting not a penny, Lei at least would be able to relax more than Chen Shizhong, because Chen Shizhong had to give his entire salary to his wife. He had to think long and hard even about sending a little money to his daughter.

Chen Shizhong did many Lei Feng–style deeds, but was by no means a Lei Feng–style person. If Chen had restricted his activities to merely emulating Lei Feng, then he would never have offended a single person. At most he would only have angered his wife, who constantly got angry in any event. Yet Chen continually refused to toe the line, inevitably damaging both his own peace of mind and that of others.

When more than thirty students wrote a joint letter praising their teacher Chen Shizhong, newspapers could not print it because "the leaders of his own work unit" did not agree. The magazine *Adult Education* heard about his achievements and sent a reporter to interview him, but leaders at the Workers' Part-time University turned the reporter away. Their stated reason was "The person in question is fond of concerning himself with politics."

Returning to the Minefields

As soon as Chen Shizhong left the labor reform camp, and even before his own verdict was overturned, he busied himself working for the rehabilitation of others.

Li Zhirong, with whose story this article begins, was just one of them. Another was the returned student Wang Kunyuan, who had been foreman of a workshop at the Harbin Electrical Machinery Factory, and who was sentenced to ten years' imprisonment in 1960 for writing a letter opposing the "Three Red Banners."[51] His verdict was later overturned, but his Party membership was not restored. Because Wang was far from home, Chen Shizhong, although not a Party member, busied himself to restore Wang Kunyuan's Party membership. More than twenty times he visited the law courts and the offices of the Municipal Discipline Inspection Commission.[52]

Wang Ye, a friend of Chen's from the labor reform camp, was accused of verbally harassing female students (a charge found to be pure slander) and fired from his job as a high school teacher. After that Wang made a living cutting grass and boiling alkali.[53] At the time of the movement to "Cut off the Tail of Capitalism," he was driven out of the city. His family of nine had no way to support itself. Chen Shizhong sometimes stayed up all night writing petitions on Wang's behalf. Eventually the Nenjiang regional Party secretary restored his name and applied Party policy correctly so that Wang became the head of the language teaching division in a high school.

Liu Dengzhen had studied medicine in church schools and was extremely talented. Later he was sentenced to prison for financial irregularities. When he got out, he made his living by cutting grass and collecting dung. A heavy snowstorm destroyed his two-room house, crushing one of his donkeys to death. Then the other donkey and the donkey-cart were both stolen, upsetting Liu so much that he nearly lost his mind. On three occasions Chen Shizhong sent him more than two hundred yuan to help him out. He also repeatedly recommended this top-notch talent to appropriate departments of government, but to this day there has been no result.

Hence Chen was, yes, somewhat "concerned with politics," but not excessively.

Chen often went to the Harbin Institute of Technology on business. As one enters the main gate of this school, one sees a statue of Chairman Mao about two stories tall. Behind it on a stone tablet are inscribed the words, "Long Live the Victory of Chairman Mao's Proletarian Revolutionary Line!" Every day more than a thousand people pass by this slogan, but only Chen Shizhong ever expressed any doubts about it. Chen felt that this slogan—just like "Continue the Revolution Under the Dictatorship of the Proletariat"—had come about under special historical circumstances and was designed to oppose the "Liu-Deng capitalist counterrevolutionary revisionist line."[54] He felt that the inscription should be removed. But when he wrote to several newspapers with this suggestion, there was no reply. He also wrote a letter to the Party's leading theoretical journal *Red Flag,* but still no one paid attention. This, he felt, was strange. "Could it be that I am wrong? To insist on saying that there is such a thing as 'Chairman Mao's proletarian revolutionary line' is to uphold the mistaken line that led to the outbreak of the 'Great Proletarian Cultural Revolution'—which nearly destroyed the whole Party and state. Why should we permit these sixteen large characters etched in gold to continue to glitter there?"

While this sort of "concern" exceeded what a lecturer in the natural sciences was supposed to express, the authorities could still forgive it.

It was much more important to refrain from "concern" about matters bearing on the leaders of one's own work unit. Every week Chen Shizhong cleaned the toilets in his dormitory. This sort of behavior, even if he did it once a day, would never cause him any trouble. But Chen criticized the leadership of the Workers' Part-time University for its handling of the Party's policy towards intellectuals. He expressed opposition to the selfish use of political position in the assignment of housing. And he criticized the school's leadership for not supporting his pursuit of an important research project in his spare time. All of this put the leadership in a very difficult position. They had to make a response.

Their natural psychological reaction was that this fellow Chen Shizhong was "odd." He just wasn't normal. Thinking about it a little more deeply, they came to believe that Chen might have a mental illness or be motivated by selfish ambition. Why would he, otherwise, keep accusing the leadership and sounding off in the newspapers? Why was he unwilling to let go of certain issues—issues to which people with far cleaner records and far superior to him in rank paid no attention? Could Chen have failed to realize the personal consequences that all of this might have for him?

Chen Shizhong was by no means cut off from the real world. Four years previously, on the eve of his departure from the Harbin No. 3 Ceramics Factory, he had supplied the factory with twenty-five suggestions for rational management. The first one was political and was written in lines of five-syllable verse:

> I loved the factory as my own family, and
> Have never been ashamed to boast of it.
> Before departing, I have some sincere advice:
> I suggest a policy of "rationalization."
> Enjoy taking advice that grates on the ear;
> Never put faith in flowery words.
> If you listen to everyone's opinions,
> The enterprise will develop by leaps and bounds.

Chen obviously knew that Chinese have a tendency to enjoy "flowery words" and to reject "advice that grates on the ear." Who did Chen Shizhong think he was? He could not have been un-aware that he was a step below others in position. Why, otherwise, would the school have always withheld the thousand yuan in hardship allowance that was due to him? Why would the Machin-ists' Press in Beijing not hand over the manuscript fees that were withheld from him due to his imprisonment in the 1960s? An even more important signal was a conversation between one of his students and the vice-chairman of the municipal federation of trade unions:

> "As a student at the Part-time University, in your view, who is the best teacher?"
>
> "Teacher Chen, of course. He's serious, responsible, and the students all love and esteem him . . ."
>
> "I suppose you're a bit biased in favor of your own teacher?"
>
> "No. I have lots of other teachers, so why shouldn't I mention someone else? . . . Mr. Chairman, you at the union select this per-son today and that person tomorrow to be model workers; why can't you see the model worker right under your very noses?"
>
> "Who?"
>
> "Teacher Chen Shizhong, of course!"
>
> "We'll look into it. But he might very well be 'working under internal restrictions.'"[55]

Yet the reason why Chen Shizhong was Chen Shizhong was precisely that he could ignore all of this, do exactly as he saw fit, and put thorns under his feet with his own hands.

How We "Completely Repudiated the Cultural Revolution" Here

Yet in comparison with Ni Yuxian, who was many hundreds of miles away in Shanghai, Chen Shizhong should have been con-tent. Those sixteen characters that Chen Shizhong wanted to eradicate left scars on Ni Yuxian that were still deep. Ni's daily life showed little sign of that crucial dividing line in Chinese history: October 1976, when the Gang of Four was arrested. After his re-lease from prison, Ni Yuxian was not granted political "rehabilita-tion." After his appeal was signed by Comrade Peng Zhen, and at the urging of the police and judiciary, the Shanghai Maritime

Academy was finally obliged to "re-investigate his case." In September 1979, the school authorities drafted their "Conclusions upon Re-investigation," which contained the following points:

1. Ni Yuxian's activities during the Cultural Revolution are insufficient to constitute political misconduct.
2. As for the previously adjudicated issue of his personal conduct, because ten years have already passed, and because it would be inconvenient to locate the parties in question for reinvestigation, the original verdict is upheld.
3. Accordingly, the sentence of "expulsion" from the academy handed down during the Cultural Revolution is annulled and replaced by an administrative sanction of demerit.

In other words, Ni's inveterate opposition, during 1966 to 1976, to Lin Biao, the Gang of Four and "The Great Proletarian Cultural Revolution," and the struggles that twice put him in danger of death, were merely "insufficient to constitute political misconduct"!

What was the story behind the "question of his personal conduct" that had been "previously adjudicated"? In the second half of 1969, Ni had found a purse and returned it to its owner, who was a young woman. She thanked him profusely and invited him to stop off for a cup of tea at her work unit on his way home. They met for less than half an hour. Yet when the special investigative team that was watching Ni discovered this incident, it joined forces with several of the "rebel" Red Guard bosses of the young woman's work unit, isolated her for questioning, and tried to force her to confess that Ni had raped her. She emphatically denied it, so they took turns day and night trying to trap or trick her into a confession, as well as threatening her that "those who protect counterrevolutionaries must be punished." The young woman still refused to yield, so they dragged her off to the hospital, illegally subjected her to a physical examination, and then tried to trick her by saying: "The examination reveals that you have already had a man. If you don't confess that Ni raped you, then you must confess with whom you did it. We'll sentence you as a hooligan, shave your head, parade you through the streets, cancel your apprenticeship, and expel you from the factory!" How could a girl from the countryside stand up to this sort of pressure? One week later she signed her name to the accusation that the special investigative team had long ago drawn up. Ni Yuxian was declared a "rapist," locked up, and expelled from school. (Of the five counts against Ni, the first four concerned his activities in opposing Lin Biao and the Gang of Four.) Afterwards, Ni eventually found his way to the young woman's father and elder brother, from whom he learned the truth. These two deeply sympathized with him and frequently wrote statements or personally sought out the special investigative team at the Maritime Academy to plead for redress. What they got in return were threats: "It is not permitted to reverse verdicts on counterrevolutionaries!" When Ni Yuxian went to the investigators in person, they said, "If you come back to cause trouble again, we will send you to the police to be locked up!"

After Ni Yuxian was arrested, the special investigative team tied his hands behind his back, strung him up from the rafters of a warehouse, and beat him. When he refused to confess, they applied even harsher tortures. Today he still cannot put his arms behind his back; this is an incurable scar remaining from "The Great Cultural Revolution." But why is it that the libelous statements written down on paper still cannot be corrected, fifteen years later?

There are reasons. If Ni Yuxian were completely cleared of blame, then when he returned to work at the Maritime Academy library, would the library's Party branch secretary still be able to introduce his political status at meetings in the following fashion? "This Ni Yuxian is pure poison and has committed serious errors. We must keep him under surveillance and make a new man out of him. The Communist Party made a new man even out of Emperor Puyi of Manchukuo,[56] so we will not fail in transforming him!" Nor would the Party branch secretary be able to address Ni Yuxian as follows, "Our Party is now exercising a policy of tolerance and so has given you an opportunity to earn your living. Your coming to work at the library is of a trial nature; you must be sincere and begin your life anew. If you speak or act irresponsibly, then after half a year we'll send you back!"

Another reason, perhaps even more important, might be that if Ni were cleared, what could stop him from tracking down the political enemies who had repeatedly tried to destroy him? Might they really have to confess their guilt, give up their positions, and compliantly hand over their hard-won power and privileges? Their fears would hardly be exaggerated. People in such a position would have understood Ni Yuxian perfectly.

He, Too, Is Off to the Minefields

In addition to promoting the public perception of Ni Yuxian as a "released convict," authorities at the Maritime Academy employed a whole series of other techniques to force Ni to repent, reform, and accept remolding meekly. They froze his salary at two grades below that of his college classmates; they capped his family's living space at fewer square meters than the Shanghai average. Ni's persecution led to heavy debts amounting to the large sum of five thousand yuan, but the authorities refused to give him any supplement whatsoever. In the end they obliged him, a college student from before the Cultural Revolution, to do odd jobs—the dirtiest, heaviest, and most simpleminded kind of labor there was.

Yet it cannot be said that leaders at all levels were entirely unfeeling towards Ni Yuxian. They would frequently seek him out for little chats, "helping" him establish a correct attitude toward life. Their main point was: you, Ni Yuxian, must "draw the lesson" from your many setbacks; i.e., you must improve your relations with higher authorities and most particularly with your immediate superior.

How did Ni Yuxian take this lesson?

He was now twice as old as he had been when he was in the army and wrote his letter to Chairman Mao. Then he was a teenager, and now he was in his thirties. Then he had been a young person without a care in the world, and now he was head of a family. But from the point of view of someone wise in the ways of the world, he had not matured at all.

At the library Ni worked in the Acquisitions and Cataloguing Group. The group chief was a person with only an eighth-grade education, who understood neither classical Chinese nor any foreign language, indeed who lacked specialized knowledge of any kind. Yet he was in charge of acquisitions and cataloguing for the library of an institution of higher education. This constantly led to ridiculous errors, as when he ordered from overseas a whole set of original editions entirely on the subject of crows. What galled Ni Yuxian the most was his antagonism toward the Party's new line, direction, and policies after the Third Plenum of the Eleventh Party Congress. He was arrogant, and even dared, in meetings before the entire library staff, to denounce leaders of the Central Committee as "no match for the Gang of Four."

Such statements continued to be heard from time to time within the Maritime Academy. When they were, Ni Yuxian always opposed them publicly. He used the theories he had studied intensively for so many years to refute his opponents, sometimes leaving them speechless. Naturally his relations with the leaders grew ever more strained, and in the public eye he seemed ever more "stubborn" and "conceited."

How could a person short on both talent and virtue have ever been selected as chief of acquisitions and cataloguing? Ni Yuxian understood the reasons clearly. It was because this person had closely obeyed Zhou XX in the library during the Cultural Revolution and had been a core member of his rebel group. And why was it that when everyone in the library knew him to be unfit for his job, he could continue working even after the Cultural Revolution? Ni Yuxian, who had already thought long and hard about China's personnel system, understood this as well. Ni called it "a system of lifetime tenure": once higher authority had appointed someone, that person could work until retirement or death. Ni had seen many talented persons in the prime of life crushed underfoot, while a small number who did no work at all, or followed old ways of doing things, or were even entirely unfit for their jobs, now held secure positions of leadership merely because they had once rebelled together with such-and-such a leader and had endured thick and thin with him!

The staff in Ni's group had long desired to replace their chief through an election, and Ni Yuxian of course was one of the active proponents of this plan. When they heard that Comrade Deng Xiaoping had directed at the Ninth Labor Congress that "our personnel system for officials must be reformed" and that "workers have the right to elect their foreman or group chief democratically," they entrusted Ni Yuxian with writing a report to the Party branch requesting that their group be an experimental site for the democratic election of group chiefs. Half a year passed without a response. Meanwhile the group chief, in a fit of pique, abandoned his job and did not come to work for several weeks. The comrades in Acquisitions and Cataloguing adhered to their responsibilities. They used the time set aside for political study to conduct an election by secret ballot. All thirteen people in the group cast ballots—except for the group chief, who abstained. A young person who had graduated with a major in library science from the Fudan University branch campus, who had a strong sense of responsibility and was well acquainted with the job, was elected with twelve votes. The original group chief received one vote.

Zhou XX, the representative of the Party branch at the meeting, saw that his loyal comrade-in-arms was about to lose his office. Surely this couldn't be! He immediately stood up and declared, "This election is an unauthorized, illegal action, and its result is invalid. The leadership will refuse to recognize it!" The person who rose in rebuttal was, once again, Ni Yuxian. As a result, the Party branch regarded him as the chief culprit responsible for sabotaging the peaceful situation in the library and pressured him to write a self-criticism. He refused to write one, but the refusal was of no use, because in the end Ni could not escape the charges of "seizing power" and "bourgeois liberalization."[57] Shortly, this "unstable element" was transferred out of the Acquisitions and Cataloguing Group.

After that did Ni Yuxian become "sincere" and refrain from "irresponsible speech or acts"? He did not. When the Central Committee decided to clean out the "Three Types of People,"[58] Ni once again came forward and at a full meeting of the entire staff accused Zhou XX face-to-face and exposed his political affiliations. Before the Cultural Revolution, Zhou was an ordinary manager, but later became one of the first to rise in rebellion. He frequently took part in raiding houses and in vicious denunciations of intellectuals. During the campaign to "purify the class ranks"[59] and the "one-strike, three-antis" campaign,[60] he personally oversaw the work of special investigation teams both at home and in the field. He personally handled stack after stack of investigative files, passing them on to higher authorities and creating tragedies for count-less individuals and their families. Some whom he persecuted went insane, and for this he received the accolade of being a "res-olute leftist." He ran the entire library. During the "Campaign to Criticize Deng,"[61] because "his standpoint was firm and his ban-ners clear," he was quickly brought in as a Party member, given an unprecedented raise in salary, and formally promoted to section-level official. After the smashing of the Gang of Four, he contin-ued his factional activities, gave important jobs to core members of his rebel group, and attacked and crushed anyone who held differing opinions. He also connived with Kang XX to denounce in public the line of the Third Plenum and to vilify Comrade Deng Xiaoping for "restoring capitalism." No item of library busi-ness—from ordering a first edition to reimbursing someone for a bus ticket—could be accomplished without his signature. Ni Yu-xian, knowing what he did about Zhou's past, insisted that "in my view a person like Zhou XX should be a primary target in the campaign to remove the 'Three Types of People'; it is no longer appropriate for him to be in a position of leadership!" Ni's opinion immediately drew support from many people both inside and outside the library, but the few who held high position naturally wished to prop Zhou XX up and so just put the matter indefi-nitely on hold.

Ni's actions were not entirely without consequences, however. Not long after the meeting, he discovered that some people were keeping him under secret surveillance.

Challenging Tradition

For several years, Chen Shizhong had researched techniques for "enamel grinding and machining." Enamel vessels are resistant to acid and corrosion, but the old methods of manufacture made it very difficult to ensure that a vessel was perfectly sealed, and with traditional techniques of machining, it was also very hard to make enamel products round. This is why, when enamel vessels are used in the chemical or pharmaceutical industries, a dangerous situa-tion can occur: a colorless gas, odorless but poisonous, can escape undetected and cause serious bodily harm or even death.

Generally speaking, success or failure is visible in our economic life—but in the political sphere it is not. Might there, for instance, be an invisible, odorless, barely detectable and yet beneficial substance, whose sudden disappearance when we are not paying attention might cause us loss?[62]

Chen Shizhong and Ni Yuxian both encountered repeated setbacks in their political battles, both made enormous sacrifices, and both nearly lost their lives. But their setbacks never caused them to flinch, nor did the injustice they suffered or the discrimination and attacks that they continue to endure, even now, ever make them embittered. On the contrary, they "died nine deaths without regret" for their actions; they ignored personal advantage, steadfastly supported the line of the Third Plenum of the Eleventh Party Congress, and devoted themselves to the Four Modernizations and to reform.

Chen and Ni felt an instinctive aversion to illegality and injustice. Each rose in resistance, without ever being summoned or directed to do so. The housing question provides a good example. How many resolutions, directives, and announcements has the Central Committee issued since 1980, when it implemented new guidelines for political life inside the Party? Still, the Harbin Municipal Federation of Trade Unions and its subsidiary, the Workers' Part-time University, as well as the Maritime Academy in Shanghai—Party organizations all—had by no means abided by all those directives. It was two non-Party members, Chen Shizhong and Ni Yuxian, who rose up simultaneously to struggle against the mistakes that Party organizations were making in their own work units. Chen Shizhong opposed the leaders of the Part-time University when they grabbed the new and better apartments, while Ni Yuxian fought the Maritime Academy when it used rank and salary as criteria to assign housing that had been built for the express purpose of relieving the housing woes of intellectuals.

By criticizing the leadership of the Part-time University, and by presenting frequent indictments to the Municipal Party Committee, the Municipal Federation of Trade Unions, and the Party newspaper, Chen Shizhong finally succeeded in forcing leading officials at the Part-time University to relinquish the housing that they had seized. This was hardly a thoroughgoing victory, but it did ensure that the Central Committee's policy was implemented in a limited fashion within this one work unit. What if there had been no Chen Shizhong? The Municipal Federation of Trade Unions would never have interfered in the question of housing assignments at the Part-time University, and the consequences of their errors would have lasted forever.

Chen Shizhong's repeated indictments also prompted formation of an investigative team from the Municipal Party Committee led by the head of its Organization Department. This team looked into many problems at the Part-time University and determined that Chen Shizhong was neither mentally ill nor motivated by personal ambition. Yet when the story of his struggle against irregularities in housing assignments at the Part-time University appeared in *The Harbin Daily News,* it had turned into the following: "The leadership of the Workers' Part-time University, having deepened its understanding of the current situation, has implemented the Party's policy towards intellectuals and has positively resolved Lecturer Chen Shizhong's petition." This made it sound as if Chen Shizhong had petitioned on his own behalf, and as if the Workers' Part-time University deserved praise for "positively resolving" problems!

Don't comrades like Chen Shizhong and Ni Yuxian share some of the responsibility for their hard luck? Of course they do. They are unusual, different from ordinary people, and maybe even a bit odd. For example, in 1983 Chen Shizhong suddenly announced that he wanted to "run for election." Election to what? To the post of advanced worker, and for the previous year—1982.

Here is how it had happened: in late 1982, during the year-end personnel evaluations at the Workers' Part-time University, the comrades in the Department of Mechanical Engineering unanimously nominated Chen Shizhong to be their "advanced worker." But since the Mechanical Engineering Department had already been designated the school's "advanced collective," Chen Shizhong, as the advanced person within the advanced collective, might very well have been selected as the advanced worker for the whole workers' union system and the city of Harbin. This is how things had happened for many years.

But a snag occurred when the university president and the department chairs conducted their evaluation meeting. In describing Chen Shizhong's strengths, the chair of Mechanical Engineering said, "When his work is done, Chen pursues research enthusiastically. If the leadership does not provide support, he pays his own travel expenses and takes money out of his own pocket to pay laboratory workers for overtime. He persists in his research—this is an excellent spirit." He had barely finished speaking when one of the vice presidents objected, "When did this ever happen? When did he ever not get reimbursed for travel?" Chen Shizhong was not present at the meeting, and because the vice president was the ranking authority, his statement influenced other people's impressions of Chen Shizhong. Afterwards, Chen went to question this vice president, who admitted that there in fact had been approximately three hundred yuan in travel expenses that had not been reimbursed. And the problem had not been limited to travel expenses. The organization wasn't even willing to write letters of introduction for Chen.

A second reason for opposing Chen's selection as "advanced worker" was that he had been applying for divorce at the time. This indeed was a fact. But Chen Shizhong and his wife had already been separated for five years, and in the month prior to the meeting, the court's verdict had already clearly stated, "The wife has admitted her errors and expressed her determination to correct them. We hope that her husband will forgive her. The divorce is denied." So what responsibility did Chen Shizhong bear?

Chen Shizhong's announcement that he wanted to run for election as "advanced worker" was a challenge. The target of his challenge was not merely the rather backward method of selecting advanced workers, based not on a person's true worth but on the likes and dislikes of leaders.[63] Chen's declaration of candidacy read,

At this time, when competition and reform are vigorously promoted in every field, I have had the novel idea of running for election as "advanced worker" to represent the Part-time University within the workers' union of Harbin Municipality. I am ready to risk the judgment of public opinion and to have my readers analyze and determine whether in fact I am doing this for my own personal advantage.

At this time I cannot help recalling the impartial conduct of Qi Gongyang,[64] who in recommending worthy men did not shrink from nominating either his enemies or his relatives. I would like to use my own conduct to fill a gap in public opinion.[65] The question, of course, is not just whether I, Chen Shizhong, can be an "advanced worker." Moreover 1982 is long gone, but does it really matter for which year I run for election as "advanced worker"? For more than twenty years, not only have I never been named an "advanced worker," but for a long time have also borne the stigma of being "anti-Party" and "counterrevolutionary"—and have I not continued to do my utmost for the people anyway?

When people make mistakes or do something bad, they never want to speak of it. And according to our traditional ideas of virtue, when a person has done a good deed, it is also improper to speak of it. So I don't understand, in the end, what a person should speak of. To boast of course is no good, but what's wrong with speaking if you have indeed accomplished what you said you would?

To be afraid that others will say this or say that is only our own selfishness making mischief.

I'd like to recite to everyone the ballad of Chen Shizhong:

One instance of fighting injustice; two of fighting fire;
Thrice he saved a person's life; four times nabbed petty thieves;
A five-time winner of the marathon; six years of forced job
    placement;
Seven separate verdicts; eight years of sentence to labor reform;
Ten letters of remonstration; a million words of reproof to the
    Party;
Infinite feelings of love for the Party; a heart unchanging till death.

Looked at carefully, Chen Shizhong's announcement that he would "run for election" was only a kind of appeal: "Look, my country! Look squarely at this loyal son!"

Loyalty, like beauty, takes different forms. To be diligent and conscientious, hardworking and unafraid of criticism, to obey meekly and never have a contrary opinion—this is one sort of loyalty. This type of loyal person will have to make larger or smaller sacrifices of personal advantage, but the path is relatively safe and smooth, and generally does not incur disaster. Because such persons are likable, they always advance steadily in their official careers.

The second kind of loyalty, the one embodied by Chen Shizhong and Ni Yuxian, is not so easy for superiors to like. At least until a short time ago, people with this kind of loyalty had to pay enormous prices in their liberty, their happiness, and even their lives.

For many years now, the first kind of loyalty has grown sturdy and luxuriant because it has received exceptional care and cultivation, plus constant watering and fertilizing. This was the demand of the times, and there is no need for us to criticize it at length.

In contrast, the second kind of loyalty grows only weakly and sparsely in our political soil. That it has managed to escape extinction and survive in this dry and barren earth is already a near-miracle.

When this second kind of loyalty does not thrive, there is a danger that a third kind of loyalty will arise.[66] This kind steals the sunlight, rainfall and nutrients that feed the first and second kinds of loyalty. It appears tender and sweet, charming and enticing—even more alluring than the first kind of loyalty. The problem is that its fruits are always bitter, and under certain climatic conditions, even poisonous.

Now is the time for us to re-evaluate and make new choices. History has supplied us with ripe conditions and urgently demands that we act.

NOTES

Originally published in *Kaituo,* vol. 1, no. 1 (March 1985).

1. The author withholds the given name to preserve the person's anonymity.

2. The procuratorate is the office charged with prosecuting cases on behalf of the government.

3. Liu suggests here that the Anti-Rightist Movement and the Great Leap Forward, both beginning in 1957, were precursors that led inexorably to the chaos of the Cultural Revolution (1966–1976).

4. The Novikov gear, named for Mikhail Leontyevich Novikov (1915–1957), was said to endure heavier loads, incur less wear, and reduce friction loss.

5. In 1957, Mao Zedong's disastrous Great Leap Forward set a goal of doubling China's annual steel output from five to ten million tons. Chinese readers who remember this period would find Liu Binyan's comment ironic.

6. Chen was hinting that China should try to maintain good relations with the Soviet Union, despite obvious strains in Sino-Soviet relations, in order to avoid giving Western countries a propaganda advantage.

7. Chen's piece was a comment on an article published in *People's Daily* on June 16, 1963, called "A Proposal Concerning the General Line of the International Communist Movement." This article laid out the Chinese government's position on ideological differences with the Soviet Union. By daring to dissent on the topic, Chen set himself up to be seen as an agent or dupe of the Soviet Union.

8. Chen here suggests a comparison between the cult of Mao and the cult of Stalin.

9. In the "Anti-Rightist" movement of 1957, many intellectuals who had criticized the Party were designated "rightists" and sent to labor camps.

10. Chen Shizhong was prescient in anticipating that this list of top Party leaders, who had been named to the Party's Politburo at its Eighth Congress in 1956, would eventually fall victim to Mao Zedong's purges. Only Liu Bocheng emerged from the Cultural Revolution largely unscathed.

11. From Mao Zedong, "Talks at the Yan'an Forum on Literature and Art" (May 1942), in *Selected Works of Mao Zedong* (Peking: Foreign Languages Press, 1967), 3:90–91.

12. Lei Feng (1940–1962), a soldier in the People's Liberation Army, was held up in national campaigns to "learn from Lei Feng" as a model of "the new socialist man": selfless, hardworking, and unquestioningly obedient to the Party.

13. Chen Shizhong apparently misattributed this quotation to Lei Feng. It does not appear in Lei Feng's diary. It does appear on a poster from the Cultural Revolution honoring the soldier hero Wang Jie.

14. The Great Leap Forward famine of 1959–1961.

15. Here Chen invokes *The Internationale,* the anthem of the international Communist movement, that says in its Chinese version, "There has never been a savior, nor do we rely on gods or emperors." He means, of course, Mao.

16. Chen was not a Party member but here identifies with the ideal of being a communist.

17. Chen refers here to Mao's stepping down on April 27, 1959, from his position as head of state, a position he relinquished to Liu Shaoqi. Mao retained the position of Party chairman.

18. This is a reference to Mao's own published prescription for curing a sick person. You shock the person by shouting, "You are sick!" then proceed with advice about cures. See Mao Zedong, "Oppose Stereotyped Party Writing" (February 8, 1942), in *Selected Works of Mao Zedong,* 3:56.

19. A Russian proverb.

20. This is the last line of the prison diary of Julius Fučík (1903–1943), a well-known Czech Communist and martyr in the resistance to the Nazis.

21. From the mention here of leap months, we can infer that the date of this document must be May 19, 1966, and therefore must be from an essay different from "Reproving the Party," which was written in March 1964, eight months after his imprisonment.

22. The lines allude to a poem by the Communist martyr Xia Minghan (1900–1928), written shortly before his execution.

23. On Ni Yuxian's life, see Anne F. Thurston, *A Chinese Odyssey: The Life and Times of a Chinese Dissident* (New York: Charles Scribner's Sons, 1991).

24. The Great Leap Forward famine of 1959–1961 was especially severe in Anhui.

25. Liu Binyan later estimated that more than thirty million Chinese had died in the Great Leap Forward famine. See Liu Binyan, *China's Crisis, China's Hope: Essays from an Intellectual in Exile* (Cambridge: Harvard University Press, 1990), 97.

26. "Right deviationism" was the charge leveled against Peng Dehuai and other critics of Mao's agricultural policies. The campaign lasted from 1959 to 1962.

27. Article 97 of the 1954 constitution.

28. A training school for China's merchant marine.

29. A term for those who tried to remain uninvolved in the turmoil.

30. These three, together with Mao's wife Jiang Qing, subsequently made up the infamous "Gang of Four" who were blamed for Cultural Revolution excesses after the death of Mao in 1976.

31. Zhang sent in the army after a Red Guard group that opposed him kidnapped Xu Jingxian, one of his followers. Zhang may have feared that Xu would be tortured into making confessions unfavorable to him. Ye Yonglie gives the date for this incident as January 28, 1967.

32. Lin Biao, an army leader, became Mao's "closest comrade-in-arms" in the late 1960s after promoting the cult of Mao and writing a preface to the famous *Quotations from Chairman Mao*.

33. "In Memory of Norman Bethune" (1939), "Serve the People" (1944), and "The Foolish Old Man Who Removed the Mountains" (1945).

34. One of Lin Biao's favorite phrases.

35. This is a quotation from Yuan drama that expresses popular indignation against corrupt officials. The characteristic side-stepping movement of crabs carries the metaphoric meaning of acting illegally.

36. Xu Jingxian (b. 1933) was a member of the Central Committee and the third most powerful leader in Shanghai, after Zhang Chunqiao and Yao Wenyuan.

37. These were sent to take over universities in July 1968, in order to stop violence and armed conflict between competing Red Guard factions.

38. Launched in February 1970 and intended in "one strike" to attack counterrevolutionary saboteurs and in "three antis": to oppose (1) corruption and stealing; (2) speculation and profiteering; and (3) extravagance and waste.

39. Deng Xiaoping was stripped of all Party offices after the April 5, 1976, demonstrations at Tiananmen (see note 41). Although the Gang of Four who had insisted on his removal were themselves arrested in October 1976, Deng was not restored to his positions until the July 1977 meeting of the Central Committee.

40. In November 1975, Deng Xiaoping had come under attack from the Gang of Four for "trying to overturn verdicts" on persons who had been stripped of power early in the Cultural Revolution.

41. On April 5, 1976, large crowds of Beijing residents gathered in Tiananmen Square to mourn the death of Premier Zhou Enlai, who had died on January 8. In addition to putting up wreaths in Zhou's honor, the mourners wrote and displayed many poems expressing opposition to the Gang of Four. The government then ordered troops to dispel the protesters, the "Tiananmen Incident" was branded as counterrevolutionary, and Deng—who had been Zhou's protégé—was stripped of all his offices. He was not rehabilitated until July 1977, ten months after the arrest of the Gang of Four.

42. Hua Guofeng, Mao Zedong's designated successor.

43. January 8, when Ni posted his poem, was the anniversary of Zhou Enlai's death. He may have chosen this day in order to suggest that Deng be Zhou's successor and to draw toward Deng some of the

great popular sympathy that existed for Zhou. Through frequent allusions to statements or actions of Mao Zedong, the poem attempts to establish that Deng had earned Mao's support and that his being kept from office first by the Gang of Four and then by Mao's successor Hua Guofeng was unjustified. Lines 3 and 4 refer to Deng's return to power in March 1973, when Mao praised him as "a man of rare talent" before appointing him chief of the General Staff of the People's Liberation Army and member of the Central Military Commission. Lines 5 and 6 refer respectively to Deng's successes as a diplomat and as a domestic policy maker. He gave a famous speech to the UN General Assembly proclaiming Mao's theory of the "three worlds" and claiming for China the right to lead the third-world bloc. Line 7 repeats a comment that Mao made in March 1966, when he sought to deflect criticism of Liu Shaoqi and Deng Xiaoping by asserting that "they have always worked publicly, not secretively." In line 12, the "rights and wrongs of this past year" allude to Deng's most recent dismissal in 1976, when the Gang of Four blamed him for the demonstrations at Tiananmen Square.

44. "I do not believe!" is a famous line from "The Answer," a poem by Bei Dao written shortly after the 1976 Tiananmen Incident.

45. Ma Tianshui had been vice-chair of Shanghai's Revolutionary Committee under the Gang of Four. Shortly after the Gang's arrest on October 6, 1976, Ma was arrested.

46. Ye Jianying (1897–1986), vice-chair of the Party, had been involved in planning the arrest of the Gang of Four.

47. Public holidays are customary dates for executions.

48. At which Deng Xiaoping gained full command of the Party and Hua Guofeng, Mao's designated successor, was sidelined.

49. Camp inmates who have completed their sentences often are unable to return home because they are given "forced job placements" at their labor camps.

50. Chen Jingrun (1933–1996), a famous mathematician, in the late 1970s became a well-known symbol for the mistreatment of intellectuals during the Cultural Revolution; but even he enjoyed better housing than Chen Shizhong.

51. The "Three Red Banners," which summed up Party policy during 1958–1961, were "The General Line for Socialist Construction," "The Great Leap Forward," and "The People's Communes."

52. The commission investigates misconduct by Party members.

53. China's northeast has surface deposits of alkaline soil. Poor people collect and process it to extract soda, which they can sell for a bit of cash.

54. As opposed to Mao Zedong's doctrine of "continuous revolution," which officially was the principal reason for launching the Cultural Revolution.

55. "Working under internal restrictions" meant one was not fully trusted by Party authorities for reasons of personal history, political associations, or former mistakes. The designation was not revealed to the person affected.

56. Aisin-Gioro Puyi reigned as the Qing dynasty's last emperor from 1908 to 1911. In 1932, the Japanese government created the puppet state of Manchukuo in northeast China and installed Puyi as emperor. With the arrival of the People's Republic, Puyi was imprisoned for war crimes and underwent thought reform. His ghostwritten autobiography ends on a note of fulsome thanks to the Party for having made him a new man.

57. "Bourgeois liberalization" was Deng Xiaoping's term, in the post-Mao period, for what he saw as the threat to China and the Communist Party in Western notions of freedom.

58. In the 1980s, when the Party was looking to promote new and younger talent, a guideline went out that there were "three types of people" (*san zhong ren,* i.e., rebels, factional partisans, and "beat-smash-burn elements") who should be avoided in this process because of their criminal actions during the Cultural Revolution.

59. The campaign to "purify the class ranks" was launched in late May 1968, as a way for Mao Zedong and Lin Biao to purge rivals and people who held dissenting views.

60. See note 38.

61. The campaign to criticize Deng Xiaoping started in late 1975, intensified after the Tiananmen Square incident of April 5, 1976, and came to an end in October 1976 with the arrest of the Gang of Four.

62. The author is hinting at the existence of a political substance. In response to an inquiry from the translator, the author wrote, "I believe there is such a substance. It is none other than the spirit of loyal criticism that Chen Shizhong and Ni Yuxian exemplify. This is a spirit born of love for the people and characterized by independent thinking, critical intellect, the courage to struggle against mistakes, and unswerving determination." Liu Binyan, personal communication, March 9, 1994.

63. The selection of "advanced workers" in theory is made by "the masses." Chen Shizhong and Liu Binyan make the point that selections are actually made in advance by leaders.

64. Qi Gongyang is an apparent error for Qi Huangyang (ca. 570 B.C.E.) a state minister known for his impartiality in recommending worthy men to the throne.

65. The "gap in public opinion" is people's lack of knowledge of the true value of candidates, a problem that results in part from traditional notions of modesty that prohibit a person from speaking of his or her own good points.

66. This "third kind" is presumably the kind demonstrated by Lin Biao, who flattered Mao and then apparently plotted secretly against him.

Report on a Void Investigation

Translated by Perry Link

This is the last piece that Liu Binyan published in China's official media. He wrote it in fall 1988 while a Nieman Fellow at Harvard University, and it appeared in the December 1988 issue of *People's Literature*. After that he never returned to China or was able to publish there.

The piece tells of a "petitioner" from Harbin, Heilongjiang Province, who comes to Beijing to seek redress of grievances. He approaches Liu Binyan, who at the time was a reporter for *People's Daily* and already well known as a champion of the downtrodden. The petitioner is arrested, tried on specious charges, and sent to an insane asylum. This kind of abuse of psychiatry, although familiar in the Soviet Union, had been successfully covered up in China before Liu's piece appeared. By now it has been much better exposed, thanks primarily to Robin Munro's book *Dangerous Minds: Political Psychiatry in China Today and Its Origins in the Mao Era* (New York: Human Rights Watch, 2002).

Liu's investigation of this case brought him into confrontation with Communist Party leaders in Heilongjiang Province. These people were afraid not just that Liu might expose their abuse of a petitioner, but also that Liu was working on behalf of Hu Yaobang, who was general secretary of the Party at the time and a strong advocate of political reform. Most provincial leaders in Heilongjiang, on the other hand, were allied with China's President, Li Xiannian, who was a leader of the conservative faction in the central leadership. During the Cultural Revolution, Li had been close to the radical Maoists; while many other leaders came under attack, Li somehow managed to remain continuously as vice-premier of the State Council. In the mid-1980s Li was locked in a behind-the-scenes struggle with Hu Yaobang and eventually played a major role in Hu's sacking in 1987. Two years later it was Li who originated the nomination of Jiang Zemin to replace Zhao Ziyang after Zhao had been forced from office in the wake of the June Fourth massacre.

Hu Yaobang's fall from power and Liu Binyan's second expulsion from the Party, events that both occurred in January 1987, represented a triumph for the Li Xiannian group and other conservatives. It led to conservative reaction not only in Heilongjiang but around the country as well. Sun Weiben, the new Party secretary in Heilongjiang, had been sympathetic to Liu Binyan's investigations and ready to cooperate with Liu and with Hu Yaobang in cleaning things up. So had been the Party secretary in Fujian Province, where Liu had done a similar investigation. Everyone was stymied, though, after January 1987. —ED.

A reporter's investigations, even if "voided," still have value. It is a fact of the journalist's life that no road taken is ever a total loss; any path yields at least something. As my career as a reporter now draws to a close for the second time,[1] I have to thank fate for the good fortune of a rich and unforgettable experience—my trip in September 1986 to Yichun, in Heilongjiang Province.

I want to share with you, my readers, the impressions that that experience left with me, even though what I can now tell you is less than a tenth of what is in my interview notes.

It was a visit that might well have never happened. The first time I met Wang Fumian was in Beijing in winter 1983. I had just returned from a trip to Shuangyashan in Heilongjiang, where I had collected a lot of material on people's struggles with a corrupt leadership.[2] In the atmosphere of the time, it was unlikely that my reporting on Shuangyashan could get into print; so why would I be interested in hearing another, similar story? Had it not been for the startling twists of fate that later befell Wang Fumian, my notes on the things that he told me that day, and on the documents that he showed me, would probably have remained peacefully inside my file cabinet (along with several other volumes of interview notes and letters from a dozen or more different provinces), turning into historical materials that would only "hibernate" for the time being.

This fellow Wang Fumian was forty or more years old, and he had a spirit and bearing that set him clearly apart from other petitioners.[3] He did not seem weak or supplicatory, but approached me with confidence, as if looking to dig something out of me that he wanted. He sat down to talk—but just as soon got up again, spoke vehemently, and paced back and forth in front of me, gesturing all the while, seeming even to forget my existence and to be delivering a speech to an audience of thousands. His eyes became piercing and his manner imposing; there was no trace in him of the meek attitude or tortured faces of most petitioners—who, whether intentionally or not, elicit responses of sympathy in their listeners by highlighting their own misfortunes. He seemed on the contrary to refuse pity from his listener and actually to distance himself somewhat from the listener so that he could appeal more directly to the listener's conscience and sense of justice. He was also supremely confident—as if the listener of course would have no reason not to listen to his speech to the end, and no reason not to take his side.

He seemed oblivious of my responses. I did not particularly doubt anything that he was saying—although would not have wanted to vouch for it, either. My mind kept wandering, as a jumble of thoughts kept hovering there and wouldn't go away: he was talking about the town of Xiaoxing'anling, where events could hardly have been more shocking than in nearby Daxing'anling—a place I had been meaning for six years to go investigate, but could not. Even if I had, and had written something, what newspaper would have published it? "Any report containing criticism or ma-jor revelations," it had been announced, "needs to be reviewed by the Party committee at the next highest level and can be published only after agreement comes."

I saw him again in March of the following year, and he hadn't changed. The more voluble his attacks on Wang Fei and others in the Yichun area became, the heavier became my own feelings of exhaustion and futility.

Only four or five years later did I finally appreciate that this man Wang Fumian embodied something that had already become rare in China. This was the *qi*, or spirit, referred to in traditional Chinese philosophy, literature, and medicine. Is a nation's *qi* as "robust as a long rainbow" or as "fragile as a thread"? This is no minor matter.

We agreed on the afternoon of March 13 that we would talk again. He had made an appointment to go the next day to the lo-cal "Letters and Visits Bureau"[4] for a face-to-face discussion of Yi-chun's problems. But early the next morning his wife, Li Huasheng (who, as usual, was leading her son by the hand and carrying her daughter, who had a leg that had been crippled by tuberculosis, on her back) came running to me in a panic. "They came for Fumian and took him away! In the middle of the night!" She burst into tears and could not stop.

In the deep of the night four police cars from Yichun had stopped in front of the hotel on New Central Street in Beijing and forced Wang Fumian into a jeep. When he insisted on reasoning with his captors, one of the policeman threatened him: "Wise up, guy—or we'll drive you nuts before we ever get back to Yichun!" The arrest warrant read: "The perpetrator is guilty of insult and li-bel."

This news stunned me—and then filled me with sorrow. I had been born in the era of the Northern Warlords,[5] had lived through fourteen years of Japanese imperialist rule, and had spent several years under the constant threat of arrest by the Japanese and the Nationalists. I was, in other words, no stranger to arrests. I stopped for a moment to analyze my own psychology. Why should this particular arrest make me feel so sad? Because, I believe, it hap-pened during a time when Chinese people were already supposed to have human rights; because it had happened right in front of me; and because it happened to a fearless man who had refused to submit to force for nearly twenty years. His flashing eyes and piercing voice still seemed palpable, as if right in front of me, but no: in a flash he had lost his freedom. His image in my mind turned immediately into a symbol. I sighed, but only to myself: how many people, in today's socialist China, live like little chicks, helpless to protect themselves?

The verbal threat from that policeman jolted me into another thought: they could do anything to him. On the long road from Beijing back to Yichun, more than one thousand miles away, they could torment him any way they wanted, as a way to unload their years of pent-up grievances against him.

I went straight to the *People's Daily* reception desk to place a phone call, thinking that the criminal escort party may not yet have left the city. I called the local police station—then another one, then the Eastern City Sub-bureau of Public Security—but couldn't get through to anyone. Finally I did get through, but was told that this kind of matter could be discussed only on a secure phone line. A state secret!

I asked someone to go in person to the Beijing Public Security Bureau, and from that enquiry learned that the convoy had set out for Heilongjiang the very night of the arrest. Now there's efficiency.

The next day I telephoned to Yichun to the Municipal Party Committee and the Municipal Public Security Bureau. It was Sunday and no one was on duty. I decided to place a call to the home of Wang Fei, who was on the Standing Committee of the Party Committee of Heilongjiang Province and chief of its Organization Department. (He was also a former secretary of the Party Committee for Yichun City.) He was in. His voice was mellow, full, and pleasing to the ear. It exuded an air of good intentions. I told him about the arrest of Wang Fumian and then said, "the arrest warrant said 'guilty of insult and libel,' but he came to Beijing to complain mainly about you, so I hope you can do something to stop the police from harming him." Wang Fei said he didn't know about the matter. Then he said that during the Cultural Revolution he, too, had suffered a lot of persecution, and had not come to work in Yichun until 1975. "This man Wang Fumian," he continued, "was victimized during the Cultural Revolution, arrested many times, and tortured. Later he was exonerated, paid workers' compensation, and given more than four thousand yuan in back pay. Things are very complicated here in Yichun City. There are people opposing the Party Committee, and it's possible that some senior officials are using him as a front man."

At least Wang Fei confirmed that Wang Fumian was a good person and had earlier been a victim. That assured me somewhat. I had learned in recent years—several times—that one person's power is limited; you can't do everything. So it had occurred to me that I might set the Wang Fumian matter aside and not pursue it—provided, of course, that it settled down and did not keep harassing me.

Li Huasheng and her two children moved into the guesthouse of the *People's Daily*. One day, upon returning to her room, she found that her things had been ransacked. Even the letter of introduction that I had written for her to the Party secretary at the Heilongjiang provincial hospital—asking for help in getting treatment for her crippled daughter—had been confiscated. (The letter was later put into a file at the Provincial Party Committee, where the Party secretary added a note saying that I should not have written it.) Plainclothes police from Heilongjiang had also moved in and were staying on the same floor.

When they arrested Wang Fumian they seized and sealed all of his wife's and children's possessions, including even fruit, medicines, and clothing. Hence it happened that, as the season arrived when all of the young women in Beijing switch to wearing skirts, Li Huasheng and her children still traipsed around Beijing in their padded winter trousers—living evidence for Chinese and foreigners alike of the place of legality and humanitarianism in China.

China's law on criminal procedure says that detention must not exceed twenty-four hours, and custody following arrest is limited to two months and in no circumstances can exceed three months. But in Wang Fumian's case two months passed, and then three, and he still got no hearing before a judge. Then on July 10 *People's Daily* suddenly carried a story at the top of page four, under the headline "Continuing to Rebel, the Three Types[6] are Savage in

Stirring up Trouble; Conquering Laxity, Yichun City is Determined to Investigate and Prosecute without Mercy." The story began, "Yichun City in Heilongjiang Province has recently investigated and prosecuted a troublemaking factional clique headed by the rebel faction boss Wang Fumian . . ."

I rushed to go find how this story had come about. An editor in the domestic politics section of the newspaper was acquainted with the article's author, who was an official in the Organization Department of the Heilongjiang Party Committee. In submitting the article he had made it clear that it represented "the responsible comrades on the Provincial Party Committee," who also had recommended that it be published in *People's Daily*. With backing like that, of course *People's Daily* had published it verbatim.

But I was puzzled. Hadn't they said Wang Fumian's crime was "insult and libel"? Why had it now turned into a political crime? The term "Three Types" in the headline, it turned out, had been a mistake of the night editor. But it was a mistake that made sense, because all of the crimes mentioned in the report were "Three Types" sorts of things.

The next day *Heilongjiang Daily*, the official newspaper of the Heilongjiang Provincial Party Committee, reprinted the *People's Daily* article in a featured position on its front page. It kept the mistaken headline. When the city-level newspaper *Yichun Daily* reprinted the article, it covered the front page with a lengthy commentary that denounced Wang Fumian as a "Three Types" case. Heilongjiang officials had used the technique known as "export for internal consumption": get the central newspaper to speak out first, and that will multiply the power of the threat, escalate the level of the accused's problem, and shift primary responsibility for it out of the province and to the center.

The Intermediate Court of Yichun City selected this choice moment for holding Wang Fumian's hearing. He was pronounced guilty on September 14, 1984. I was startled again to read the verdict, because the charges against him had shifted once more. Now it was "disturbing social order, libel, and cover-up." The sentence was five years.

That did not end the matter, however. Although he was allowed only four days in which to file an appeal to the Provincial High

Court, Wang Fumian did appeal, on grounds of "violation of legal procedure, unclear findings of fact, insufficient evidence, and inappropriate application of law." It was not a terribly complicated case, but the High Court sat on the appeal for nearly ten months, neither rejecting it nor calling a new hearing. Then, on June 27, 1985, it suddenly announced: "In the process of its deliberations the court has learned that the appellant Wang Fumian suffers a thought disorder. The results of expert psychological testimony indicate 'paranoia' that leaves him incapable of responsibility for his actions. Accordingly a meeting of the Judicial Committee of this Court has decided . . . on the following judgment: 1) Criminal verdict no. 29 (1984) of the Intermediate People's Court of Yichun is nullified; 2) Wang Fumian does not bear criminal responsibility."

There was a third provision as well. It was not written down, but was the most important: Wang Fumian was to be sent to the Psychiatric Prison Hospital of the Public Security Department of Heilongjiang Province. For life.

In 1985 Li Huasheng came again to Beijing. The effect that the *People's Daily* article had had on Wang Fumian's case was obvious, and she was now asking the newspaper to acknowledge its responsibility (at the very least it should not have labeled Wang Fumian a "Three Types" person) and to investigate the case. It was not a very strong demand—did not ask *People's Daily* for any damages, for example—but still got nowhere.

What possible hope remained? Yichun City was under a municipal Party committee, and Heilongjiang Province under a provincial Party committee, of the same Communist Party of China. So were all of the courts. It was an impregnable fortress of a system. Because everyone was obliged to submit to "Party leadership," no citizen or official could oppose a decision by the Party Committee in his or her city or province. Only a person at higher levels could do anything to change Wang Fumian's fate.

In August 1986, *People's Daily* held a staff meeting at which the manager, chief editor, and deputy chief editor were all present, and at which I decided to raise the question of Wang Fumian explicitly. I drew upon the several kinds of evidence that I had gathered for more than two years to show how extremely likely it was that the Wang Fumian case was false and had been driven by political revenge. I said that a mistake in our own paper's headline had had a crucial effect in the matter. We should take responsibility for that mistake and also try to get to the bottom of the case. The group approved my proposal unanimously and decided to send a team to Heilongjiang to investigate.

Treading Hostile Terrain, Every Step a Struggle

On September 7 three reporters from *People's Daily*—Zeng Xiangping, Liu Guosheng, and I—arrived in Harbin to begin our investigation of the Wang Fumian case.

We explained the purpose of our visit to the managing secretary of the Provincial Party Committee. This comrade was also Party secretary for Jiamusi City, and he was cooperative. He had only one attitude—a big smiling face of welcome. Our first request, of course, was to see Wang Fumian's court file, and then we wanted to meet with Wang Fumian personally. We also wanted to hear from people at the High Court about how they had handled the case. He smiled and said sure, sure, we can do that!

After two days, nothing had happened. Then a reply came saying that there was a new regulation that judicial files could be seen only by higher courts, higher-level Party committees, or the Standing Committee of the National People's Congress. I pointed out to them that we were bringing no ordinary journalistic request: *People's Daily* was the official newspaper of the Party Committee that was directly superior to the Heilongjiang Party Committee and we had come on orders to investigate our newspaper's responsibility in the issue at hand. Moreover the Wang case had already been nullified on grounds of insanity and absence of responsibility, and certainly had nothing to do with state secrets. So why couldn't we read the file? The answer was "we will study the matter."

As for meeting with Wang Fumian, that was no problem, they said, but we don't know which asylum he is staying in and will have to go find out. I had a hard time suppressing my laughter. Such a famous criminal and they have to find out where they put him? And anyway, we already knew: he was in the Psychiatric Prison Hospital of the Public Security Department of Heilongjiang Province, on the outskirts of Harbin a dozen or so miles way. Their answer to this was no answer.

Instead, this: of course there was no problem about seeing the people from the High Court, but the people who had handled this particular case were currently out of town. We'd have to wait a bit.

And so it went—blah, blah, blah. To me it was obvious that they were stalling for time. Their real tricks were still up their sleeves, their major deployments still in preparation.

I received a tip that the phone lines between Harbin and Beijing were humming with activity—one side asking instructions, the other giving orders.[7] Two former Provincial Party secretaries had already moved to the capital to take up posts.

Eight days later the High Court people who had been "out of town" finally returned, and three of them suddenly came to see us. One was a specialist in note taking. As we talked I glanced at his notes and saw something amazing: he was concentrating on writing down *my questions,* not the answers.

We placed a call to our colleagues back at *People's Daily* and asked them to check with the Supreme Court in Beijing about the procedures that were required before court files for cases like this could be read. The answer came back that permission of the Provincial Party Committee was all that was needed.

I lost my temper on the telephone one evening when that same managing secretary started prevaricating again about how he had to get permission from the Center before letting us see the files. "That's utterly irrelevant," I stormed. "You people are just afraid. It's obvious that your views and ours on this Wang Fumian case are different. If yours is the correct view, then letting us have a look at the real facts would be the best way to clear things up, wouldn't it? The Wang case has nothing to do with any Party or state secrets. Unless you people have something to hide, why won't you let us see the records?!" But my words did not upset the managing secretary. "We're not preventing you from seeing anything," he continued in his soft drawl. "It's just a question of procedure."

On September 21, thirteen days after our arrival in Harbin, we were at last allowed to go see Wang Fumian.

The patients had just finished lunch when we arrived at the ward. They all stood up to welcome us. I felt puzzled that I couldn't tell right away which one was Wang Fumian. I only noticed that one man in the crowd was laughing—weirdly, like a naughty child —in my direction. I looked closely and saw that, yes, this was Wang Fumian. He had put on weight. Having heard that I was coming, he had also shaved his beard. No wonder I didn't recognize him.

The three of us reporters talked with Wang Fumian for nearly two hours, taping everything. His mind was sober, his thinking clear, his use of words precise. He gave us some new material, especially about the process that had led to his diagnosis of insanity.

I remembered that he had told me, when we met in Beijing, how he had done everything he could to exercise his body during periods when he was detained during the Cultural Revolution. He had done the same during this detention, so his physical health was better than ever.

None of the doctors who treated him or nurses who cared for his ward found any sign of abnormality in Wang Fumian's psychology.

We toured the hospital, and I must acknowledge that it was very well run. I even thought of writing an article praising it. China does have a lot of good people—loyal to their duties, working in a humanitarian spirit. So there was still light, and still hope, even in places where the poison hands of insidious, ruthless, vicious despots all but blocked the sky.

Fully half a month had now passed and the Heilongjiang Provincial Party Committee still did not dare to let us see Wang Fumian's file. Was this a sign of how big and powerful they were? Of course not. But the tactic did not even succeed in wasting our time, because we used it to interview other people who were familiar with the Yichun scene. Even more important, two comrades voluntarily came forward to reveal a lot of behind-the-scenes details about Wang Fumian's adversaries. This was immensely edifying to me—oh, so *that's* the story!

Some very interesting things happened during our last few days in Harbin, before we went to Yichun.

Shortly after our arrival in Harbin I had gone to see an old friend, a deputy editor at *Heilongjiang Daily*. He volunteered to assign an assistant to me, and by chance a young comrade, a reporter in Yichun with whom I was acquainted, was willing to take on this role, so we agreed.

But then something fishy occurred. Just as we were about to set out for Yichun, the arrangement collapsed. *Heilongjiang Daily* did not notify us of this, but we learned indirectly that the young comrade had been told he could not go.

Another man, an elderly editor of the literary page of the provincial newspaper, had been a friend of mine since 1979. He had suffered considerably after writing an article about how I had been treated unjustly in the "'People or Monsters' incident."[8] He knew a lot about Yichun and was willing to use his vacation time to come along and assist our on-site investigation. But when he went to his leadership with this plan, his boss said, "If you'd come two days ago I could have agreed; now, though, I can't." Then, with a genial smile, the boss added, "You don't need to ask why; it's pretty easy to guess."

In 1983, while working on a piece called "The Marvelous Man from East of the Pass,"[9] I had befriended a young reporter at Heilongjiang Provincial Television. He, too, now volunteered to join our mission to Yichun. But on the evening of September 23, when he came to the Harbin railroad station to meet us, people suddenly appeared and blocked his way, then dragged him away scuffling and struggling in protest. This happened right in front of our eyes. It shows how outlandish our whole visit had become!

Who, behind the scenes, was directing all this interference? The secretary and deputy secretary of the Provincial Party Committee were both new appointments. Wang Fei had already been transferred out of the Organization Department and was now the Provincial Party secretary. There were hardly any elderly officials left at the department head level. The list of people who would have been willing to take the lead in playing these tricks—except for those who had retired but were still pulling strings from behind the scenes—was not very long. If I had spent some time I think I could easily have figured out which one it was, and even without a personal interview, sooner or later could have exposed him. I was surprised that he was willing to take the risk of leaving so much evidence in plain view!

The train to Yichun started moving. "A just cause naturally attracts help," as the saying goes. Despite all the roadblocks, more and more people had come forward to help us. A poet, an amateur lawyer, and reporters and editors from three different publications had all decided to join us—even though they well knew the attitude of the Provincial Party Committee. China really had changed.

In Yichun another bag of tricks lay in waiting for us.

Who Really Was "Paranoiac"?

Before we left for Yichun I paid a visit to the psychiatric hospital in Beian City to inquire into Wang Fumian's diagnosis of insanity. I had read the paperwork on the legal basis for the diagnosis before I went.

The comrade who accompanied me was in charge of diagnosing mental illness according to the psychiatric criteria of the Public Security Department of Heilongjiang Province. His handbook contained the following description of paranoia: "Paranoia is a rare mental illness. Patients display excessive confidence, are subjective, arbitrary, headstrong, and opinionated. They often are educated, highly intelligent, astute, and capable, but they see things in lopsided ways and are resistant to criticism. Their views are subjective, preconceived, farfetched and strained. The content of their delusions conforms somewhat to reality and is not wholly absurd. In early stages they are often mistaken for normal people with extreme thinking. Willfulness grows stronger in people with the disease. They run around making appeals, approaching higher authorities, submitting long, tedious letters of accusation, not giving up until they get what they want. A minority among them have exaggerated delusions of grandeur, arrogating to themselves the destiny to do great things. The distinguishing marks of paranoia are that desires are limited, targets are fixed, organization is tight, memory is excessively detailed, power of logical inference is strong, and hallucination is absent. Integrity is intact, and there is no evidence of mental weakness. Except for the delusions, the person is normal."

Reading this paragraph almost made me break into a cold sweat. How I wished I could go warn those people with "excessive confidence," those "highly intelligent" people who are "resistant to criticism" and want "to do great things," that they had better hurry up and change their tunes!

We interviewed the three doctors who had diagnosed Wang Fumian. They had read five or six notebooks on Wang's case, including a lot of material on the "appeals cases" that Wang himself had written. One of the doctors said, "This man writes, speaks, and argues quite well. Some of the problems he writes about are realistic; elsewhere he loses touch with reality." Another doctor said, "My impression is that this man has considerable talent." They had interviewed him for more than an hour, and also had spoken with Wang Fumian's father. These two doctors initially thought that Wang was not a case of "paranoia" but only a person of "abnormal character"—not a mental illness, and a condition that left the subject in possession of responsibility. If they had made that determination, then Wang Fumian's five-year sentence would have been valid, his appeal would have to have been considered, and the whole point of the diagnosis of mental illness would have been lost. The third doctor was the one who held out for "paranoia." He was the least qualified of the three, having not long ago moved over from veterinary medicine, whereas the first two were experienced psychiatrists. Still, his view prevailed.

Paranoia differs from other mental illnesses because it has no cure. Entering the hospital thus becomes the same as beginning a sentence of lifetime detention. It meant Wang Fumian would never again be "bringing suit."

Another puzzle: the Public Security handbook plainly stated that "running around making appeals" and "approaching higher authorities" were criteria for diagnosing paranoia. These doctors had also reviewed Wang Fumian's pile of "appeals material." So why didn't they take this material as the basis for their diagnosis? Why, instead, did they list a lot of other things—like Wang Fumian's proposals and activities in stimulating the economy in mountain areas and in finding jobs for more than one hundred thousand unemployed young people? Why did they think that Wang Fumian's proposals to market a beverage made from the nectar of monkey peaches from Xiaoxing'anling, or to sell pills made from ground wood ears[10] as anticarcinogens—or his statement that he was cooperating with a doctor to do research on medicines when the same doctor had said "that's absolutely not so"—were better evidence of his "paranoia"?

The three doctors also overlooked the important line in the "criteria for diagnosis" that said, "desires are limited, targets are fixed." Wang Fumian had had two preoccupations: appealing cases and doing scientific research to stimulate the local economy. He also threw himself into the study of law and had become famous for volunteering to argue for ordinary people in court. (The court later cited this as evidence that he was "destroying social order.") He had, as well, been very concerned about public construction in Yichun. He called for the building of more public toilets, and the people of Yichun to this day remember his poster on the topic: "Many places to eat, no places to sh—!" He also proposed a systematic plan for fire prevention. He absolutely detested corruption, and to make this point posted the following couplet at the sides of his door: "Corrupt officials cover the earth; fetid air fills the skies." (This later became "proof" of his crime of "sullying the excellent situation that has followed after the Third Plenum.") After 1976 he had been even more assiduous in opposing efforts to shield or to give important positions to people who had committed serious crimes during the Cultural Revolution. So even by this rough count, Wang Fumian's "desires" were by no means "limited," and his "targets" hardly "fixed." They were spread in at least six different directions.

Listening between the Lines

At the Yichun railway station we were met by the Deputy Chief of Propaganda for the Yichun Municipal Party Committee. He had arranged for us to stay on the second floor of the Party Committee guesthouse. He accompanied us, chatting and laughing, during three meals a day. The Municipal Party secretary also came to the guesthouse to have a long chat with us. We requested that the Party Committee arrange interviews with other people, and most of them came. Everything seemed quite normal.

But Comrade Cao Futian, the municipal deputy Party secretary who for a long time had been in charge of handling the details on Wang Fumian policy, could not see us. He was ill and in the hospital. By remarkable coincidence Zhao Xianrong, chief of the Organization Department of the Municipal Party Committee—a man who had had more contact with the Wang Fumian group than any other, and who had been responsible for Wang Fumian's warrant, arrest, legal punishment, diagnosis of mental illness, and other questions—fell ill at the same time. He was also in the hospital, and also could not be seen.

The Municipal Party Committee had submitted many reports on the Wang Fumian case to the Provincial Party Committee. We should probably see these documents, no? No. No special reason, but no. Can't see them. The files of the District Court on the Wang Fumian case were also sealed. This was on instruction from the Province; it was also a set policy that had been decided at an emergency meeting of the Municipal Party Committee that had taken place right before we reporters had arrived.

That meeting had lasted fully five days. It began at the "little house"—that is, the Party Committee guesthouse at which we were now staying—and later moved to the guesthouse attached to the Bureau of Materiel. I was surprised that no one came to "introduce" the Wang Fumian case to us when we arrived. This was highly abnormal. After all, since 1983, when the Wang Fumian special-case unit was established, a lot of people had been doing all sorts of investigation; more than forty people had been made to "reflect upon" their connections with Wang Fumian; three "fellow criminals" of his had been pursued, captured, and brought to justice; two were sentenced to prison. (Later this was changed to labor reform for all three.) Why, when journalists from the Central Party leadership's newspaper came to town, would people choose to seal their lips about such an earth-shaking case?

Something was wrong in the atmosphere. A lot of people had been waiting a long time for people from Beijing to arrive, but now, when we were here, no one dared to make contact. A few did find us, but somehow could only mumble—as if an unseen third party were present.

A local writer came to talk to me about some of his writing. I casually asked him where he lived and jotted the address down on the cardboard cover for an audiotape. I asked his phone number at work, and jotted that down, too. Immediately the conversation didn't work any more. He grew uptight, preoccupied. His eyes just kept staring at that cardboard cover. "Would it be OK to erase that phone number?" he asked, very respectfully. I erased it, but he kept staring at that audiotape cover. "And those other words, too?" I erased them, too. Actually there were only three words—the name of an entire district, where tens of thousands of people lived. Still he was obviously frightened, as if he were tiptoeing at the edge of an abyss.

A court official who knew something of the Wang Fumian case, and who apparently had some sympathy for Wang, sat down on the sofa in my living room. I poured him a cup of tea and handed him a cigarette. He seemed nervous and inhibited. He took a long sip of tea, and a long drag on the cigarette, but remained silent. I naturally felt frustrated that he refused to talk, but, seeing his pained countenance, could not bear to press him, either. So he sat there. He smoked three cigarettes, drank five cups of tea, and left.

The poet who had come along with us had a friend in Yichun. When the friend came to the guesthouse to see us, someone who was standing around near the service desk blocked him and said, "the reporters upstairs have said they will not see guests." Later we learned that two people were regularly posted at the guesthouse door to monitor everyone who was coming to see us. At the evening meal we mentioned this to the deputy chief from the Party Committee, and he immediately denied it. Absolutely no surveillance or interference was happening, as could be seen from the fact that "thirty-one people have come to see you in the last two days, and they all did see you, right?"

Thirty-one people? We ourselves hadn't kept count. Obviously he had—or someone had. There must have been a name list as well as tabulations on the running total. The deputy chief had slipped up, and, without meaning to, had told us something important.

Still, despite everything, quite a few people got through to see us every day. In the evenings Guosheng and I would go out to see those people who didn't dare to meet us during daylight hours. It was like the underground work I had done in the 1940s during the Japanese occupation and in the Nationalist areas.

We were supposed to have been able to interview Wang Fumian's "fellow criminals" Liang Yuming, Wang Furen, and Zhang Daorong, all of whom had been captured shortly after Wang Fumian's arrest. The Intermediate Court in Yichun sentenced Liang Yuming and Wang Furen to prison, but the High Court in the Province overturned these convictions on grounds of insufficient evidence. This act should have set them free—and did, for a time. But someone felt the release to be inappropriate, so they were arrested again and this time sentenced to "re-education through labor," with Zhang Daorong now added to the group to make three. They were assigned to three different labor sites. Just as Wang Fumian's family received no notice when he was sent to the mental hospital, so the families of these three men for a long time did not know what had happened to them. The people who enforced the sentences did, of course, know; they were in serious violation of the law.

Despite the layers upon layers of barriers, we three reporters and our five voluntary assistants did complete a broad investigation in the Harbin, Beian, and Yichun areas and in some subordinate forest areas as well. We brought to light the truth of the Wang Fumian case from start to finish and confirmed that the problems that Wang had exposed were, on the whole, genuine problems. Every member of our investigation team had a profound eye-opening experience. But we by no means got to the bottom of the severe maladies of Yichun.

The three of us who were *People's Daily* reporters offered a detailed oral report to Sun Weiben, the provincial Party secretary, on the truth of the Wang Fumian case and on the terrible effects that had resulted from all of the vicious behavior of Wang Fei, the former municipal Party secretary in Yichun, and the group around him. Then we drafted a written report for the Communist Party Central Committee in which we recommended that a more high-powered investigation team be sent to Yichun for further investigation.

We also prepared three articles to run in the *People's Daily.* By then Wang Fei was head of the Discipline Inspection Committee for Heilongjiang Province, and our first article criticized him. On November 15, 1986, as soon as that piece appeared, the same Discipline Inspection Committee, headed by the very Wang Fei, charged that it contained "serious errors." This made the next two articles unpublishable.

Two months later, in January, I was expelled from the Communist Party for the second time, and for the second time my career as a journalist was cut off. All reports of the general nature of the present article were now out of step with the times, and the Wang Fumian case sank to the bottom of the ocean.

So Everyone's Feeling Just Fine?

The piece of literary reportage that I had been planning was, of course, also aborted. It was interesting, though, that in fall 1987, at the very same time when Comrade Wang Fei was gloriously striding into the Great Hall of the People as a delegate to the Thirteenth Party Congress, Wang Fumian also regained his freedom.

His "freedom" was subject to certain conditions, though. Reliable sources in Heilongjiang told me that the Psychiatric Prison Hospital had invited two authorities in psychiatry to join in a group consultation on the Wang Fumian case with all of the doctors in the hospital, and together they determined that Wang was not paranoid and therefore did bear legal responsibility. Yet the 1985 sentencing by the Intermediate Court in Yichun was not reinstated. Instead Wang Fumian's father was made to sign a guarantee that he would supervise his son and that the son would not appeal cases or lodge charges, would not kill people or set fires, would not consort with "fox friends and dog pals," and would not complain to anyone that he had ever been wrongly arrested. Failing any of this he could be sent back to the asylum at any time.

Wang Fumian also did not qualify for any monetary compensation because no mistake had been made: his arrest was correct, his sentencing was correct, and his diagnosis of mental illness was never formally reversed. Now his release, too, was correct. He was a few thousand yuan in debt and could not afford a bicycle, so every day he took his crippled daughter to school by carrying her on his back and then walking back home. In March 1984 he had been assigned the status of "negative exemplar" in Yichun City, but for more than four years people had had no idea what he was really like. Now everyone could watch this three-dimensional negative exemplar exhibit his characteristics in broad daylight on the city streets: his appearance was haggard, he perspired more than a healthy person should, he wore an old, tattered overcoat, and he paced the city streets with labored steps. He served as a living warning to everyone: this is what happens to you if you appeal cases and file charges, if you show your strength and refuse to bend.

But the people of Yichun also thought of certain other things. Twenty years earlier they had seen Wang Fumian walk down that same street once before. That was when he was being paraded in public under "rebel faction" and military control. It was the middle of winter, forty degrees below zero, but he trudged along bareheaded and barefooted through the piles of ice and snow, showing not the least sign of fear.

He had been among the first to be "knocked down" during the Cultural Revolution. From the start he was adamantly opposed to the attacks on Liu Shaoqi, Deng Xiaoping, Minister of Forests Luo Yuchuan, and Secretary of the Yichun Special Committee Qu Changchuan. For this audacity his arrest warrant was published nationwide. During the Cultural Revolution he was arrested a total of four times, was frequently tortured, and was sentenced to twenty years in prison. (Later this was changed to: "wear the label of 'active counterrevolutionary' and submit to the supervision of the masses"). After the Cultural Revolution he was assigned to a position in the Yichun office for investigating abuses. He advocated vigorous pursuit of the "Three Types" of people and of anyone who had been guilty of serious violent crimes. When it became clear that his suggestion would not be adopted, he resigned his post in protest. But he didn't give up the struggle. He continued to investigate, to offer suggestions to the Municipal Party Committee, and to expose people inside Party and government

organs about whom there were serious questions that needed investigation. He put up wall posters on these topics. (This was before wall posters by individuals had been declared illegal.) The
deputy chief of the Organization Department of the Municipal
Party Committee—the local official in charge of other local officials—was relieved of his post after Wang Fumian had exposed
him publicly.

Still, many people who had committed serious offenses during
the Cultural Revolution got job transfers or even promotions,
whereas the question of permanent positions for teachers who had
been in temporary status for many years, or for people like Wang
Fumian who had suffered long persecution during the Cultural
Revolution and were still only temporary "workers standing in for
officials,"[11] never got resolved. After these victims demanded that
the Municipal Party Committee "carry out policy" (i.e., set things
right), the municipal Party secretary, deputy secretary, and chief
of the Organization Department held an audience in the Party
Committee offices for Wang Fumian and others, including Zhang
Daorong, Wang Furen, and Liang Yuming, who had been victimized during the Cultural Revolution. Separately from this meeting
the officials asked Wang Fumian to find out what talents and am-
bitions the aggrieved group possessed and to make recommenda-
tions on how they might be appointed to positions. (Wang's efforts to comply later became evidence that he was plotting to
establish "a second Party Committee.")

In early 1984 the Yichun Party leadership used two retired senior officials to pass a message unofficially to Wang Fumian: "If
you will refrain from running to Beijing to expose Yichun's problems, we can arrange a section chief position for you, and can set
up Zhang Daorong with a factory manager position." But a year
later, on March 14, 1985—just one day before Yichun officials
sent their police to arrest Wang Fumian in Beijing where he was
busy making his appeals—every level of the Yichun city government received a bulletin announcing the decision on "the Wang
Fumian problem." It charged that Wang Fumian and his "political
clique" (in later versions a "small factional clique") were opposing
the Party Committee and plotting to form a "second Party Committee." They were a "new Three Types" and must be punished.

After that several dozen people who had had contact with Wang Fumian, or who maybe had met him only once, were viewed as members of a Wang Fumian "clique" (never mind that they were from different work units) and were ordered to halt their work, go into solitary or semi-solitary confinement, and "reflect."

This whole multi-leveled farce left a deep impression in the minds of the eight hundred thousand people of the Yichun area. Yichun had been spared the armed conflict that broke out in many other cities during the Cultural Revolution, and yet somehow more than six hundred people had been killed and more than thirty-seven hundred left crippled by injury. Ten years had passed and still not one murderer or seriously violent offender (the proper meaning of the "Three Types") had been identified. Living memory about Wang Fumian left a huge, indelible question mark in the minds of the people of Yichun: how could it be that someone who had gone to jail during the Cultural Revolution for trying to protect senior officials, and who after the Cultural Revolution had devoted himself to ferreting out wrongdoers, now himself, oddly, had turned into a "Three Types" offender? And how could a person whose label of "paranoid" was found to be wrong still not be entirely free?

For the last four and a half years, Wang Fumian has brought no charges. He watches in silence, and will continue to watch in silence, as life around him, which he once so vigorously sought to improve, continues on its merry way . . .

October 7, 1988, at Harvard

NOTES

1. The first time Liu Binyan was expelled from the Party and fired as a journalist was in 1957, during the Anti-Rightist Movement.

2. Later published in *Gaosu ni yige mimi* (I'll Tell You a Secret) (Beijing: Zuojia chubanshe, 1986). In 1980, a ruling called "Document no. 7" said that any reporting containing criticisms or major revelations must be approved by the next-highest level of leadership before it can be published. This meant that Liu's critical writing about Shuangyashan would have to be reviewed by the very people he was criticizing.

3. Refers to people who travel from local areas to bring grievances to higher authorities.

4. The Central Discipline Commission in Beijing maintains a nationwide network of such offices to hear grievances and complaints.

5. 1912–1927. Liu Binyan was born in 1925.

6. See "The Second Kind of Loyalty," p. 206, note 58.

7. For many years Heilongjiang had been sending officials to Beijing to serve in important positions in Party Central and the State Council. Former Heilongjiang Party Secretary Yang Yichen had recently been sent to Beijing as chief of the Supreme Procuratorate. Yang was an ally of State President Li Xiannian, and the other Heilongjiang officials in Beijing were underlings of Li's political faction. Here the "humming phone lines" refer to consultations between officials in Harbin and Yang Yichen and others in Beijing about how to handle Liu Binyan and about whether he had the backing of Hu Yaobang. The fact that the Heilongjiang Party Committee dared to deny Liu the access that any reporter ordinarily should have shows that it was riding on the power of Li Xiannian and therefore not afraid of offending Hu Yaobang.

8. Liu Binyan's famous piece of reportage "People or Monsters?" concerned life in Harbin, and many local people in Harbin, including the "elderly editor" mentioned here, wanted the local press to republish it. The provincial Party secretary resisted, however, and punished his adversaries in the matter.

9. "Guandong qiren zhuan" tells about an illiterate farmer who resisted authoritarian organization of agriculture in the 1950s and then, with reform of agriculture in the 1970s, helped many villages to restore a startling productivity. Published in *Gaosu ni yige mimi*, 123–242.

10. A black mushroom that grows from tree trunks.

11. A practice in the Cultural Revolution whereby workers were given the responsibilities and sometimes the pay of officials—but not official status, which was governed by quotas.

PART THREE

FICTION

Warning

Translated by Madelyn Ross

To attribute the catastrophe of the Cultural Revolution to one gang of only four people was a sophistry that worried many Chinese in the late 1970s. True, Lin Biao was eventually added to make five, and many people pointed discreetly to Mao Zedong as a sixth. After July 1980, Kang Sheng, a close advisor to the Gang of Four, could be named as a seventh. But the scale of such counting was still absurdly small. What about the tens of thousands of other "gang" followers? In the present story Liu Binyan addresses a "warning" to the Chinese people. Although the four departed souls in this story refer to specific people (the magnificent casket is apparently Kang Sheng's), they represent "spirits" that are very much alive. Yet, partly because Liu's message was a bit too bold, and partly because he had not been crystal clear about who the villains of his story were supposed to be, he and his publishers were themselves sternly warned, in spring 1980, for "Warning."
—ED.

I

This was perhaps the most solemn place in the world. No noise, no movement. It looked as if a row of clocks, each having stopped at a certain time, never to run again, had been put out on display. Each item looked alike: a collection of containers all more or less of equal size, most made of wood and a few of marble. If one looked inside they were even more similar—just one heap of ashes after another. These were the last traces of what had once been living creatures, born and brought up on this earth, active for a few dozen years, and now in their final resting places.

Once, all of them had experienced both joy and sorrow, good and bad fortune. But what their final thoughts, feelings, and recollections were at the moment they closed their eyes for the last time and left the world of the living, is something that the photographs attached to the front of each container will never reveal.

I want to tell a story about a few of them who made their departures from life with smiles on their lips. Three of the containers were brightly colored carved marble, showing that the status of their owners had been out of the ordinary. These three men had once had a fierce desire for longevity, and thus, while alive, had daily consumed huge doses of tonics and elixirs that more than made up for the life juices that they had spent in pursuit of sensual pleasures. Now that they were dead, the excess of these potions could still be found inside their ashes, another fact that differentiated them from the crowd. Perhaps their desire for longevity had elicited God's sympathy, or perhaps some leftover potion was still having its effect—in any case a small amount of body heat from life still existed within their ashes. Thus, although their flesh and bones had disappeared, they still had not completely lost the feelings and spiritual attributes that had been so deeply rooted during their lifetimes.

While alive, all three had been consumed by one particular thought. Out of self-love and curiosity, mixed with a touch of terror, they had greatly wished to know how people would judge them after their deaths.

Few people visited this spot, for stepping into this other world naturally held little attraction for the living. But every time the sound of footsteps rang through this grand modern-day temple, the occupants of the three marble cinerary caskets became as excited as live wires. They would strain to catch the implication of every move made by a visitor from the living world outside. Yet they were always disappointed in the end, because no one ever spoke or expressed any feelings. Sometimes a visitor could be heard stopping in front of one of the containers of ashes, yet it was always difficult to ascertain whether he was paying homage to the dead or merely admiring the delicately carved decorative patterns on the marble. The sound of sighing from a visitor was always a tremendous comfort to the dead. They would savor it in their minds for days and nights on end, right up until the next visitor appeared.

Necessity is an extremely powerful force. If, out of necessity, mankind was able to create language, then why couldn't human remains that still preserved some body heat devise a way in which to communicate their feelings?

"They've completely forgotten us," the former general said one day.

"Perhaps it's better to be forgotten," said he who once was director of propaganda in a certain province as well as chief editor of its newspaper. The comment exhibited his cleverness.

"They can't forget. As long as my mines and factories still exist, they won't forget me," proclaimed the one who had been in charge of guiding the economy.

At this, the general, housed in his red marble room, and the director of propaganda, housed in his green marble room, both fell into a gloomy silence, nursing their wounded senses of self-respect and pride. There was no doubt that, compared to that man's, their own outstanding achievements would be easily forgotten. But the former newspaper and propaganda boss, being more quick-witted than the general, still had a comeback:

"What you say is true. But if anybody should happen to dig into the heavy costs you inflicted on people, then, old chap, I'm afraid your situation won't be so rosy. My newspaper always reported your accomplishments and covered up your mistakes. Remember the time you started construction of a factory, and ordered equipment, before you bothered to investigate subterranean conditions? When the project was over you discovered there was no electricity supply, either, so a few hundred thousand tons of steel got chucked into the sea. . . . Ai, I still say it's best for us to be forgotten."

The economic leader lapsed into silence, and the three of them became lost in their own thoughts.

Time flowed on in the outside world, and changes took place. But the environment around the ash jars remained quiet and unchanging. The air around them seemed to have frozen into a solid mass similar to the marble vessels themselves.

One day, however, a puff of wind did blow into the vault. Judging from the sound of the footsteps, the visitors that day were different from any that had come before. They stopped in front of the three large marble jars, and even their breathing was audible. Then came a sound like an atom bomb, violently shaking these three unoffending souls in their tiny coffins.

"These scoundrels were all sworn followers of Lin Biao and the Gang of Four!"

The three souls had completely lost the last vestiges of their hearing ability. But their tactile sense told them that someone had spit on the pure and noble marble surfaces that sheltered them. Two days later they felt a heart-rending pain when someone used a knife to deface the photographs attached to the fronts of their jars. Soon they were each covered with a black cloth, which helped the three terrified souls to recover a modicum of calm. Then they began to ponder deeply and painstakingly on who this so-called Gang of Four might be, and what relationship they might have had with them. . . .

Before too long the black cloths were removed. The three suddenly felt themselves swaying, and at the same time sensed the warmth of the living as it penetrated their marble jars. The three containers of ashes had been picked up. "Where are we going?" wondered the three souls, terrified. They could sense being carried from the moist dim vault out into the bright sunlight. Compared to the careful way they had been handled when initially carried from their memorial services into the vault, something was very different this time. The people who carried them now were either utterly careless or else deliberately displaying hostility and scorn. Under this rough handling, their once-human cinders were shaken to and fro until the order they had lain in these past years had been completely disturbed. This was very discomfiting.

Before the sun had had time to warm their marble surfaces, the motion suddenly stopped. Someone opened a rusty lock. Then, for the last and most violent time, the three were shaken up as they were thrown to the ground. The sound of human voices gradually died away, mingling with the sound of satisfied laughter.

II

Their world had been terribly cold and dreary to begin with, but now their grandiose marble garb made the three souls feel even colder. Cast onto the damp, dark ground, in a room that had long been abandoned, where neither sun nor human warmth ever penetrated, their cold loneliness can well be imagined.

But even all this could be endured, and gradually accepted. What really worried the three souls most was the question of safety. The desecration of their photographs had, at worst, been an affront to their dignity; compared to the crisis facing them now, this small matter was hardly worth mentioning. The question now was: would their misfortune end here or become even more serious in the future? Could the very worst happen? Could their stone coffins be smashed and their remains trampled upon and cast to the winds? Another worrisome problem was the fate of their families. One of the goals for which they had struggled throughout life had been to bring wealth and glory to their families. Wives, children, various relatives, assorted friends—all had basked in the benefits of being associated with them. Higher education, Party membership, job transferrals, promotions, salary raises, new housing, marital matches, trips abroad, and all other privileges available to Chinese were theirs. In addition, an inexhaustible supply of luxury products and nonmaterial pleasures, including many that for the common people were not only unattainable but downright unimaginable, used to arrive in a constant stream at their doorsteps. All of this sprang from the two or three magic syllables of their august names. Truly these names had glittered and shone like gold, attracting admiration and envy, symbolizing the pinnacle of power, glory, and wealth. When the three had made their eternal partings from their families, all of these privileges seemed solid, yea indestructible—for their sons, grandsons, and future generations. Using a few "connections," they could automatically obtain anything they might need. But now, in an instant, as their ashes fell from a top-class resting place into the dust, all the fruits of their fame were in danger: what if all were to be lost? That thought was bad enough. But even more fearful was the thought that the living standard of their entire clan might fall as low as that of ordinary people. No one was more familiar with the horrors of this possibility than the three souls. Tearful scenes of atrocious humiliations, scenes that they had not only witnessed personally but had taken an active hand in creating, were still fresh in their minds. Could this kind of fate now be awaiting their own families?

For many days the three souls remained completely quiet. Not long ago, they had found their greatest solace in those enchanting scenes and moods that they alone had once been privileged to enjoy. These recollections had helped them to forget temporarily the lonely and empty present. (Strangely enough, although they had long ago lost the flesh that is the seat of various desires, the memories of former satiations of their lust still brought them the most pleasant of sensations.) But ever since their fall into this place, these pleasant recollections had been countered by a simultaneous fear—that their families would be faced with wretched material conditions, be treated like dogs and pigs, constantly have insults hurled at them, and continually find the doors of opportunity now tightly closed against them. . . .

Yet this uneasy silence did not last very long. One day, the noise of windows shattering frightened the three souls so terribly that they nearly jumped out of their marble containers. Next there came the noise of an angry mob. To the accompaniment of sardonic laughter, some rocks came flying in the direction of those three poor little marble caskets. There seemed to be a competition to see who could throw most accurately and strike home most frequently. If our friends the souls had had the power to protest, they certainly would have cried in pain and begged for mercy.

"Why flog a corpse?" the general grumbled to his companions when he couldn't stand it any more.

"This is simply too barbaric," added the director of propaganda. "And furthermore, it violates our ancient Chinese custom of passing final judgment on a man as the lid is laid on his coffin." He failed to consider that when his own cronies were at the summit of power, their barbarism toward the living had far exceeded stone throwing. He also failed to consider that they themselves had long ago smashed the venerable tradition of leaving the deceased in peace.

Nevertheless, the stone-throwing episode actually brought the three souls a step closer to the world of the living, and thereby lessened somewhat their lonely isolation. It was now late autumn, when fierce autumn winds would sometimes howl through Beijing all night long. To the souls inside, this wind sounded like someone with a hard, thick broom mightily scraping away at all their marble surfaces. Sometimes they heard the sound of fallen leaves whipping at the window, and once in a while a few leaves would be blown through the broken glass to land on their marble covers. So in the midst of this cold loneliness they could take some comfort: they did after all have a few contacts with the outside world where they had once lived.

Fallen leaves and dust gradually built up a thin layer on the surfaces of their marble. It made the souls inside feel just a little warmer, just a little safer.

One of humanity's distinguishing features—hope—was something still not completely lost to the three souls. The economist based his hopes primarily on the case of an old leading cadre who, over twenty years, had gradually been restored from disfavor to a position of trust. His influence had grown steadily until he had reached the pinnacle of power. The economist recalled that this man's ashes had recently been delivered to the vault and had been set down not far from the three souls. But the fact that his cinerary casket had not later been thrown into this gloomy room with theirs seemed to show that this man hadn't been labeled a follower of the Gang of Four. Here, surely, was cause for hope. After so many years in the bureaucracy, the economist well knew that the greater a person's prestige, the more his "connections."

This old cadre must have had some powerful protectors who had kept him from the same fate that had befallen the other three. Didn't this fact clearly suggest that the luck of the three, who had once been under the wing of this great figure, might take a turn for the better?

This thought was a turning point and a source of inspiration. For some days each of the souls, prancing to the music of the wind, returned to the world of his memories. They retraced the paths of their lives, carefully sorting out enemies from friends, as well as analyzing the ups and downs of those who were close to them. They had, of course, next to no energy left in their ashes for pondering such things. The last tiny sparks of energy that they did have they cherished immensely, and they used them to concentrate on the last twenty or so years. The people who had been toppled during these years had long been practically forgotten and were of no great interest now; but those who had risen, quite a few of whom had clawed their own ways to the top, could still be intermittently called to mind. Yes, there were quite a few of them. Surely they were all still living, and still wielding considerable power. Although they were not all fellow conspirators, and some of them had even suffered extensively over the years, still they had all taken basically the same path as the three souls had, and everybody spoke a common language. Would they have changed easily—cast aside their hard-won gains and merrily altered their tune? Not very likely. . . .

The spark of hope began to glow brighter.

III

The sound of a faint but thoroughly familiar woman's voice came from beyond the door, breaking the silence of this nonhuman world. The sound of footsteps was followed by the wrenching of a rusty lock. The door opened.

The footsteps came closer. The woman sighed audibly, then spoke through tears.

"Can't you find a stool? You're not going to just put it on the ground like this, are you?"

The voice was terribly familiar, yet the souls couldn't quite remember who she was.

"You'll have to answer for this: I'm going to complain to the vice chairman!"

With this sentence she had resumed her normal tone of voice and the three spirits guessed who it was almost at the same instant. "Well, if it isn't Sister Ts——!"

Before they had time to think further, a heavy casket—several times larger and heavier than their own resting homes—was plopped down in front of them.

It was a large cinerary casket of tortoise-shell marble. It was the largest, most exquisite, and most magnificent cinerary casket to date in the People's Republic of China. If one were to put the caskets of the other noble founders of the state next to this one, there would be no comparison, for the others were made only of wood, and each bore a simple photograph on its front—a small copy of the photo chosen to hang at the memorial service. But the casket of this grand personage had on its front a stately bronze relief sculpture of the man it contained. In comparison to the others, the new casket was like an imposing mountain peak next to a pale dirt mound. Its magnificence was marred, however, by the human excrement that had been smeared all over it, and by the irreverent markings that had been scratched all over its embellishments. Bronze is too soft a metal—the casket would surely have been made of alloyed steel had this day been foreseen.

The three souls, with the infallible political sense they had cultivated over many years, knew immediately who this person was. Great waves of emotion rolled through the stagnant pools of their remaining feelings. They were filled with shock and indignation, but at the same time a complex subconscious emotion was born in the bottoms of their jars. Here into their disgraced ranks had come a new member whose misfortune brought them the comfort of seeing others suffer. They were also grateful for the sense of cordiality and safety occasioned by the arrival of their superior and protector.

Over the years they had grown accustomed to being submissive and self-effacing before their superiors, and thus the three souls found themselves quite tongue-tied now, unable even to voice their greetings. Yet at the same time they feared seeming discourteous and thereby arousing the wrath of their superior, who had always been suspicious and cruel by nature. The rules of proper conduct in the living world would hold equally in the nether regions.

Their chief's perverse disposition had worsened after his death. This was due to the ceaseless pain that had spread to every cell of his body before he died. Every waking moment of his final years had been spent with violent headaches and horrifying hallucinations. Innumerable apparitions haunted him, attacking him one by one. They clutched at him and tore him to pieces, screaming of their unjust deaths. Among them were those who had died in the late 1920s and the 1930s because he had informed against them, betrayed them, or framed them. Then there were those who had died in the 1940s because of the forced confessions that he had planned and personally obtained, and those who were victims of the massive, nationwide witch hunts of the late 1950s. Even more numerous were those from the 1960s and 1970s—everyone from graying revolutionary veterans to young men and women in their prime, and even babies in their swaddling clothes. These unjustly persecuted spirits, smeared in blood, their hair in wild disarray, flew at him in droves before his wide-open eyes. If he closed his eyes they would still be there. He would almost explode from terror and the intense pain in his head, and of course sleep became utterly impossible. No sedative would work. Finally the doctor was driven to a last resort: he showed the leader movies, one after another, with no intermissions, from morning to night. The movie images helped somewhat to disperse the illusions before his eyes and in his mind, and succeeded in calming his nerves to the point where he could manage two or three hours of sleep per night. But upon waking he faced a new round of the interminable struggle. He resisted, he moaned, he screamed—sometimes for help, sometimes for mercy, sometimes madly bellowing like an insensible wild brute.

One who has held the power of executioner over the lives of a billion human beings, when finally faced with the phantoms of those who have died under his blade, finds himself trapped, and can only withdraw in helpless defeat. . . .

Death ought to offer a kind of release; pleasures and pains alike should terminate when life does. But this exceptional figure could not shake off his exceptional destiny. Flames may have transformed his flesh and bones to cinders, but his pain, amazingly, had survived. Because he did not have a head anymore, the pain had migrated into each little carbon cinder that had once been part of his body.

The four souls passed many days in deep silence. The only sounds that broke through the deadly stillness of that vault were intermittent moans from the largest marble vessel. This moaning forced the other three souls to suppress some burning desires: first, to pay respects to their former chief in a manner appropriate to his station and to theirs; second, to comfort that extremely tormented soul in the hope of further ingratiating themselves. (This used to be one of their most developed skills, but by now they were losing their old touch.) They also had an irrepressible curiosity about the fate of their families and their reputations, and hoped that their wise leader might be able to shed some light on the subject.

Finally, the general—who of the three souls had been closest to the chief—mustered the courage to speak. He had barely uttered two words when an angry roar issued from the largest marble vessel:

"Shut up!"

A moment later, that familiar voice with its heavy Shandong accent began to speak, ever so slowly, in phrases that were interlaced with groans of pain:

"We must be patient. . . . Let them forget, forget our existence. Now . . . there's only one, only one hope left . . . if those people . . . continue in the old ways . . . and move in our direction . . . that's our only . . . only hope."

His three companions knew his meaning perfectly, and the familiar image of his face floated before them: those gaunt cheeks, that cold, solemn glint in his eyes occasionally flashing out from behind his glasses.

From then on, the tomb was silent once again. Would history in the outside world move along according to the wishes of these ghosts? Or would more ash jars pile up in this forgotten place?

The autumn wind in Beijing was gusting fitfully, occasionally sending a withered yellow leaf through the broken glass and into the tomb, where in some small way it dispelled the deathly stillness. . . .

November 1979, at the Literature and Art Conference

NOTE

Originally published in *Zuopin* (Guangzhou), no. 1 (1980).

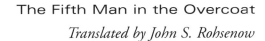

The Fifth Man in the Overcoat

Translated by John S. Rohsenow

The political relaxation of the late 1970s allowed the return to Chinese society of victims not only of the Cultural Revolution but of the 1957 Anti-Rightist Campaign as well. Intellectuals and former officials who had been in labor camps for as long as twenty years were reassigned to their original work units. Many literary works describe these "exonerations," but few penetrate beyond the happy appearances to explore the complexities that were inevitably involved. True to form, Liu Binyan stubbornly insists on penetrating, and in this thinly fictionalized account, refuses to whitewash what he finds. —ED.

I

Since the beginning of 1979, several hundred thousand people have come out into the sunshine from under the political shadows that have covered them for more than twenty years. Jin Daqing was one of these. But on his way out, he got caught in the shadowy twilight zone halfway between.

One day in March, this forty-five-year-old man, who wore a threadbare army surplus overcoat, walked up to a newly constructed office building beside the river. This building housed the newspaper on which he had worked for many years. As he noted the contrast between this elegant, eight-story building and the old one they had used twenty-three years ago, he smiled inwardly. It was a bitter smile. "The newspaper itself is still that one little sheet," he reflected. "But look how big the building has grown! The staff will be much bigger, too, of course . . ." His more than twenty years of abnormal life had turned his whole manner of thinking and feeling inward. His face wore a permanent expression of apathy.

He didn't seriously consider that walking across that threshold a few seconds later would mark a new start in his life, or rather the resumption of his life where it had been interrupted more than twenty years earlier. He seemed, rather than nervous, to be absorbed in his own thoughts. This attitude led directly to his first mistake.

He knew that, of the twenty-seven persons who had left the newspaper office in 1957, he was the only one who was being allowed to return to work here. This was because, having been stripped of official status, he could be accepted for work only back at his former job. He was puzzled that the other twenty-three people who survived were not also allowed to return to their jobs. In terms of professional ability, political credentials, health, and experience, nearly all of them were qualified to do newspaper work. Some in fact had been middle-level administrators when they left. The things that puzzled him were many indeed.

He was nearsighted, and this, added to his habitual absorption in his own thoughts—which came from too many years in a place where it was unnecessary to greet other human beings—caused him not to notice the man walking toward him in the dimly lit corridor. This man, smiling broadly, had extended his hand long before he had drawn near and seemed not to take offense at Jin Daqing's social blunder. Jin did not recognize the man until he had been ushered inside the office of the political affairs department. There he saw Ho Qixiong,[1] someone who had appeared countless times in his reflections on the past.

"Welcome back! Our old comrade-in-arms returns to the battle-front of the news industry!" Ho Qixiong's sallow face was all smiles, and his voice was full of warm feeling. At the same time, he never stopped scrutinizing Jin Daqing, who was seated at the opposite side of his desk.

Everything about the two men contrasted sharply. Ho Qixiong, who was short and small, wore a brand-new dark gray woolen suit. His face beamed. Jin Daqing—tall, strong, and serious—had by this time taken off his overcoat to reveal a plain cotton uniform that was faded blue in color and onto which patches had been sewn by the clumsy hand of a man. Ho Qixiong sat with his elbows on his desk, his fingers interlaced. He twirled his thumbs constantly as he spoke. Jin Daqing looked at Ho's hands, which were sallow and very soft. "He's never done physical labor," Jin silently observed. "I wonder if he's ever felt hunger pangs . . . probably hasn't."

At that moment Ho Qixiong was saying that, thanks to the Party Central Committee, under the leadership of Comrade Hua Guofeng, it appeared after initial reinvestigation that most of those on the newspaper staff who had been wrongly labeled "rightists" in 1957 could now be exonerated.[2] But we must be patient, as each person's case must be reverified and reconsidered on an item-by-item basis. And we may need to observe a nationwide quota policy. "Besides, we must of course review every individual's behavior over the last twenty years, mustn't we?" Jin Daqing glanced at Ho Qixiong. The weight of this last sentence was clear, even without reinforcement by the cold glitter of Ho's little eyes and the slant of his mouth. Who would do the "review" of everybody's "behavior" over the last twenty years? Ho Qixiong himself. Only the past twenty years and nothing else? Not likely. One's behavior now and in the future mattered more than the past. The crucial factor was how well one got along with Ho Qixiong.

As he waited for a response from Jin Daqing, Ho Qixiong kept weighing the case in his own mind: once this man is "exonerated," his Party membership will be restored, along with his grade-fourteen administrative rating—one grade higher than my own. With his years of seniority, plus his writing skill, he'll get an editorship at least. Ho Qixiong, of course, hadn't spent all these years doing nothing. He had built up a network of connections in every conceivable direction. The only trouble was that he just didn't have it with the pen. Besides, Ho wondered, who knows how this man will treat me? After so much bad blood between us, how generous can I expect him to be? He knew he faced an acute dilemma. It behooved him to be as friendly toward Jin as possible in order to nullify any antagonism Jin might bear him; on the other hand, he mustn't be too soft. He must make Jin understand that his fate still rested mostly in his, Ho Qixiong's, hands. Ho was also aware that Jin Daqing was no pushover. It was his own stiff-necked resistance in 1957 that got him stripped of office and sent way out to the sticks. Thus Ho Qixiong felt a need both to bury the hatchet and to prolong the burying process as much as possible. Judging from the general drift of national policy and from the respect that Jin Daqing commanded within the newspaper office, it was obvious that once Jin was exonerated he would be promoted. Ten to one he would go higher than Ho himself.

The topic shifted to Jin Daqing's work assignment. "I can be patient," Jin said. "I just want to get back to work, some regular nitty-gritty work, something like handling the letters in the public relations department." This took Ho Qixiong by surprise. He examined Jin's countenance for some sign of whether Jin was sincere or merely pretending modesty in expectation of a better offer. But Jin remained stony-faced, his skin tanned and leathery—a condition, thought Ho, that probably came from the ravages of so many years of wind and rain. (There was no way Ho could know that the social environment had been much more damaging than wind and rain.) A thought suddenly occurred to Ho: this guy has wised up. In the public relations department you don't have to write anything—it's a lot safer!

"We can handle that." Ho Qixiong's hands, which had been resting on the desk all along, now pressed together and knocked lightly on the glass-covered desktop. A happy thought warmed his heart: the public relations department was well removed from the center of things. Advancement would be much slower there.

Looking at Ho Qixiong's unusually small eyes, a thought occurred to Jin Daqing: some people's eyes are several times larger than Ho's. Could the amount perceived by the eyes be proportional to their size? Immediately he found this idea too frivolous. But no sooner had he dismissed it than another leaden thought began to weigh on his mind. In 1957, this man was the one who had handed out the "rightist" labels. Now the same man is in charge of the "exonerations"!

So actually there was nothing strange in that weirdly absurd situation everyone was talking about the other day: the leader of a memorial service for a man who had been "persecuted to death" turned out to be the very person who had done the persecuting. Again and again Jin Daqing's large hands clutched the overcoat that lay across his lap. As he recalled all the well-meaning and fine comrades who one by one had fallen, he became aware of the tears that welled in his eyes.

Ho Qixiong noted the surge of emotion in Jin Daqing and made an inference: now he's going to bring up the salary question. Hmmm? Too shy to talk about it? Is he waiting for me to bring it up? Well and good: this will be a fine chance to show sympathy, show kindness, and also show him who's boss. Ho proceeded to remove his set smile, and—gazing at the cigarette he was turning in four fingers of two hands—slowly began to explain.

"The Party Committee knows you've had it rough all these years." Glancing at Jin Daqing he continued, "Times are hard, very hard. And back pay is impossible, quite impossible. Yet . . . we are old comrades, and just out of personal affection, if nothing else, I can't ignore your need. I still have a bit of clout around here . . . there ought to be some way we can make things up to you a bit . . ." Once again he glanced at Jin Daqing, who continued to show no reaction.

"Me? My own losses?" Jin Daqing's thoughts had been running in an entirely different direction. Using both hands he had slowly, steadily, been rolling up the worn-out old overcoat that lay in his lap. Finally it was tight as a knot. Then, still clutching the taut overcoat in his ten stubby fingers, Jin saw the faces of four people once again flash before his mind's eye. He was the fifth person to wear this overcoat. . . .

At this point, if he followed the forms, he was supposed to say how grateful he was to the Party; how thankful for the concern of the local Party Committee; how the punishment he had received many years ago was at least partly deserved, and he himself hardly blameless; how he still today must strive diligently to reform his thoughts. He was also supposed to say something like this: Back in that year you, Comrade Ho Qixiong, selflessly and courageously stood up to defend the interests of the Party. Your denunciations and counterattacks all sprang from your love for the Party and for the socialist cause. Your denunciations of me at that time were just like your pardon of me today: both were entirely necessary, entirely correct. Who can say I've been thoroughly reformed, even today? I must beg you to give me more help and guidance in the future. . . .

But he didn't say a word of it. He appeared to be distracted, and as he took his leave, merely rolled his eyes in Ho Qixiong's direction and weakly shook Ho's hand. He was depressed: four people! They all should have survived, as he did, to see this day—even if they had died the next. . . . But I alone survived. Why me? Why? There were so many others better than me!

There was another person—a person he did not need consciously to think about at that moment, or any other moment, because every drop of blood that coursed through his veins was in constant mourning for her. This was his wife. After keeping him company through twenty-three long, dark years, that uncommon woman had died a few days ago after a long illness. . . .

Ho Qixiong interpreted Jin's sombre attitude quite incorrectly. Extinguishing his freshly lit cigarette in the ashtray, Ho mashed it fiercely and hardened his heart. "OK," he thought, "you want to fight, we'll fight. Just wait and see!"

II

The public relations department, which in the fifties had been called the readers' correspondence department, was an auxiliary branch of the newspaper's editorial department. In the past, when the paper's mission had been to propagandize the ideas and goals that had been handed down from above, this department had had practically no function whatsoever. All of the many letters sent in by readers would just pile up in a corner or be handed over to some other office. (As often as not, the letters would end up in the hands of the very people they were complaining about.)

Jin Daqing threw himself wholeheartedly into his work with the readers' letters. One day a familiar name caught his attention: Jiang Zhenfang. He remembered a small, delicate young woman —perhaps a bit too kindhearted—who in the second year of her marriage had seen her husband labeled a "rightist." She had refused to save herself by divorcing him or, as the political slogan expressed it, "drawing a clear line." The letter now before him was from her younger sister. It asked for exoneration from a charge that made Jin jump in disbelief when he read it: "Whore. Bad element."

At first he imagined the worst. Had heavy economic burdens crushed her? Or, under so many pressures, had she abandoned herself in a fit of depression when her husband died? But after consulting the newspaper's personnel files, Jin began to doubt this line of reasoning. The other principal in this case of illicit relations was a notorious hatchet man at the newspaper, known popularly as "Fat Hands Dong." He was a Party member and had recently been promoted to chief of the automobile pool. Why had he chosen to confess his affair, without anyone informing on him, and without any pressure to confess? And why, after explaining everything, did he go around bragging as if this were something to be proud of? On top of all this, several of his witnesses seemed dubious.

It is perhaps normal that a case of "relations between the sexes" should arouse some interest. But why such a tumultuous uproar? Jiang Zhenfang had been paraded through the streets countless times, with a string of worn-out shoes, signifying adultery, hung around her neck.[3] Her own students cursed her, spat on her, beat her, smashed her windows, abused her children. This doubtlessly was all part of her being the wife of a rightist whom she refused to divorce. But even so it seemed like gross overkill.

In the end this woman went insane and entered an asylum. Her children had to be adopted by her younger sister.

One night when Fat Hands Dong was on duty at the automobile pool, Jin Daqing went to see him. Even before he knew why

Jin had come, Dong was busy rattling off his "exploits" a mile a minute. Jin listened to him in silence, all the while gazing at Dong's ceaselessly gesticulating right hand.

"That palm isn't so big after all," mused Jin. "Amazing that it's been used to slap more than two hundred and forty people . . ."

Dong's account of things was so filled with crude language that he was hard to listen to, but some of the unspoken assumptions of his narrative were worth attending to. He repeatedly stressed details, as if afraid that people would not believe his confession. Two points he stressed in particular were that Jiang Zhenfang had a dark mole on her right breast and a scar from an operation on her abdomen. These two points of information were what he had been spreading around for several years, and were what everyone considered to be the ironclad proof of Jiang Zhenfang's guilt.

Jin Daqing could not devote all his energies to this one case. In the daytime he would read and reply to incoming letters, as well as receive official visitors to the newspaper. At night his ninety-five square feet of living space was usually packed with visitors. Most of these were people who had repeatedly appealed to the provincial authorities, or even the national authorities, for redress of various grievances. Most of their appeals had already been approved —some even by the provincial Party secretary himself—with orders that local authorities resolve the problems as soon as possible. But all this was to no avail. The last recourse was to descend upon Jin Daqing. With him there was no limit on time, as there was with the officials. He always listened attentively and tried to help each one find a way to solve his problem. Sometimes he even took care of their room and board. Where else could they find this kind of treatment?

Activities such as this could not escape notice for very long, however. Not only had Jin's "exoneration" not yet come through, but even if it had, a so-called exonerated rightist still had to be tested and observed. Even if he rejoined the Party he would be viewed as a borderline member, half in and half out, who could be kicked all the way out at any time. That's what some people meant by "letting the masses be judge of the labels."

When the first draft of Jin's "exoneration" document had been completed and was waiting only to be approved, it contained

some favorable comments: "Some of Comrade Jin Daqing's suggestions in the fifties were worthy of adoption; the motives behind
his suggestions were also benign," etc. But as luck would have it,
the winds of orthodoxy were blowing hard this April,[4] calling into
question the very basis of any and all "exoneration." The political
department, moreover, had discovered that Jin's room was becoming a "rendezvous for malcontents." Hence all the favorable comments in Jin's document were expunged and replaced by sentences
like: "He may be reformable, but this is not to say he has not committed mistakes, some of which were severe," etc. His exoneration
was shelved.

III

Jin Daqing made an appointment to go with Jiang Jinfang to see
her sister in the insane asylum. He knew that one could not rely
on information supplied by a mentally disturbed person. But he
had to go just the same. Every night for weeks the image of his
close friend Gu Tiancheng, who had died in his arms, kept ap-
pearing in his mind. He remembered what Gu's dying words had
been.

This Gu Tiancheng, five years his junior, had been a mild-man-
nered and timid person. How could he ever have been labeled a
rightist? The question still preyed on Jin's mind. He knew only
that Gu had been accused in 1958 during the "supplementary"
phase of the Anti-Rightist campaign, and therefore his offense
must have been minor. But he seemed from that time on to be
stricken with paranoia. He seldom said anything in public. When
he had to come out with even a single word, he would peer fear-
fully in every direction lest he bring more trouble upon himself.

He worked hard and conscientiously at the labor camp, but
was naturally clumsy and often injured himself. When this happened he was fearful of being criticized for the injury, so he just
endured the pain and pretended all was well. But his bed was
right next to Jin Daqing's, and there were some things he couldn't
hide from Jin. Once when he was stealing a glance at a photograph of his wife and children and suddenly discovered that Jin
was looking at him, Gu laughed pathetically and buried his face

in his bed quilt. Jin could hear his sighing beneath the quilt and could only heave a long sigh himself. Jin Daqing did not care for this kind of temperament but had to sympathize with Gu, and pity him.

Gu Tiancheng would occasionally ask him, very cautiously, "How long do you think it'll be before we're sent home?"

Who could say? But Jin Daqing could not bear to disappoint Gu, so he had to lie, saying things like, "I'd say pretty soon now," or "I don't see why they wouldn't send us home for a family reunion at Spring Festival." Gu was only too ready to believe such lies. When Jin Daqing saw Gu's face light up at his comforting words, he was upset to the verge of tears.

Autumn harvest at the camp took a long time. Even after it had turned bitterly cold, they had not finished gathering all the crops from the fields. Gu Tiancheng was approaching his third winter at camp, and his life had already become extremely difficult. During a rest period one afternoon he passed away. He was wearing that old army overcoat that had been passed on to him by the third person, and his hands clutched a steamed bun that had frozen hard as a rock. Jin Daqing embraced him and tried to warm him with his body and his breath. After what seemed like ages Gu barely opened his eyes, and called out his wife's name. . . .

The person walking slowly toward him, supported by a nurse, looked more like a shadow than a human being. Could this be the beloved wife for whom Gu Tiancheng had longed day and night? A shiver ran down Jin Daqing's spine as he looked into the eyes of this walking shadow. They were nothing but two empty hollows, two dry wells. Jiang Zhenfang simply sat down and stared blankly, first at her younger sister, then at Jin Daqing. The sister took her hand and wept. The tears fell upon that same hand. Staring at the yellowed parchment of her face, Jin realized that the only traces of life still left on it were those two black hollows that had once radiated love and borne joy and fulfillment. He could not help recalling Gu Tiancheng and the photograph that Gu had treasured as his own life. "If only the departed knew . . .," as they say. No! It was better that Gu Tiancheng had never known. The only question was, should Jin now show to her the picture of Gu that he had kept?

Jiang Zhenfang turned around and looked at him coldly and suspiciously. When she did so, her younger sister leaned forward and spoke directly into her ear, pronouncing each syllable with great care: "He—was—with—Gu—Tian—cheng, he—was—with —Gu . . ."

Jin Daqing could see the patient's expression soften, and decided to hand over his enlarged photo of Gu.

The patient took the picture and studied it from top to bottom. All of a sudden a heart-rending cry of anguish shook Jin Daqing to the depths of his being. With wide eyes fixed on him and both hands outstretched, Jiang Zhenfang shouted at the top of her voice, "I want him! I want him! Give him back to me! . . ." Jin Daqing retreated across the room as Jiang Jinfang came forward to restrain her sister. Some nurses rushed over as well. Pushing the patient back and holding her up at the same time, they took her away.

As they walked back from the hospital, both Jin Daqing and Jiang Jinfang were so upset that neither spoke for a long time. When they reached Jiang's house, Jin stopped and said to her: "You must try to recall your sister's habits. . . . Did she go to a public bathhouse? Could anyone, male or female, have ever seen her body? . . . Also try to find out if she ever wrote anything during her lucid intervals."

He seemed to detect in Jiang Jinfang's eyes an element of bewilderment and fear. Then, as they shook hands to say good-bye, he looked at her solemnly: "This whole thing may get messy, and you and I may get dragged into it. But times are better now, don't forget. Besides, you can rest assured that I will take the responsibility—all of it. But it'll still take some courage from you, of course." As he began to leave, he turned back to drive his point home. "Remember," he said, "This isn't just for your sister. There are so many others like her!"

IV

Jiang Zhenfang's mournful cry echoed in Jin Daqing's ears for a long time. It rang as an urgent appeal as well as a wordless accusation. It also seemed to pose a mammoth question: Why?

He had long felt the injustice done to women in China. When a man was purged there always had to be some evidence, at least. And regardless of whether this evidence was true or false, the most it could bring would be political downfall. Furthermore, if the truth came out some day, a man could still look forward to a comeback. But women were different. All you needed was some rumor to spread, based on straws in the wind, or on plainly nothing at all, that Ms. Comrade So-and-so was you-know-what with you-know-whom, and that was curtains for the woman. At best, there would be a big brouhaha on the rumor mill; at worst, conjugal strife and divorce. It could even mean public scorn *for life.* Try to explain? How could you begin? Even if you could prove your innocence, the rumors had the case on record differently. Your reputation was shot. Would you be able to go explain yourself in person to each and every individual who knew you?

Jin felt there had to be a connection between the cruel fate of Gu Tiancheng and that of his wife, Jiang Zhenfang. Gu himself had said that in 1957 he never uttered or wrote so much as one politically incorrect word. Yet the so-called Party leadership decided that he was an anti-Party anti-socialist right-wing element. At first he had resisted this charge, but later he saw that resistance was futile. He and his wife wept for two nights before he signed a confession. This signing also came about as a result of persuasion by the "leadership," who advised that a perfunctory admission of guilt would allow the matter to blow over. How could he have known that he would still have to bear the "rightist" label, still have to be banished, still have to . . . ?

Jin Daqing sent Jiang Jinfang to the Bureau of Education to request, in her capacity as family of the deceased, a record of the official verdict on Gu Tiancheng that had been delivered in 1957. He was shocked to discover that no such verdict had ever existed, still less been approved by any level of district or municipal authority. This meant that Gu Tiancheng had never been a "rightist" at all! Heaven only knows whether fate has ever treated any person, or any family, as flippantly as this. The man at the Bureau of Education was impeccably polite as he informed Jiang Jinfang that, because Gu had never been a "rightist," therefore he could not be "exonerated." Jiang Jinfang protested, detailing the tragedy of this couple over more than twenty years. . . . But the man only threw his hands in the air in helplessness. "What do you want *us* to do? You shouldn't have come here. You should have gone to . . . ah . . ." Indeed. Whom to ask? Where to appeal?

Yet Jiang Jinfang's visit to the Education Bureau was not a total loss. Out of sympathy, the people there went to Gu Tiancheng's file and found for her the incomplete record of a meeting that contained the sole piece of evidence against Gu Tiancheng. When he saw this Jin Daqing was beside himself with rage. The messy handwriting was barely legible. But there was no doubt about it: Gu Tiancheng's fate had been sealed by the convener of the meeting, Ho Qixiong. Ho had been schoolmaster and Party secretary of the high school where Gu Tiancheng and Jiang Zhenfang were teaching. The record read as follows:

> Schoolmaster Ho: You may have *done* nothing wrong, but we still can look at what you say. If you don't say anything we can consider your thoughts. And how do we know your thoughts, if you don't say anything? This can be judged from outward appearances. In all these meetings we have held since 1956, you have said less than anyone. And with a background like yours, you almost *have* to have certain dissatisfactions with the Party and with socialism. How could we expect you to be pure? You can't possibly be. Yet you keep quiet, you won't come clean.
>
> OK, everybody, just take a look at what the problem is here. This is even worse, even more dangerous, than those who are willing to expose their erroneous ideas, and who are courageous enough to unburden their hearts to the Party. This man is set against the Party in the deepest recesses of his mind. If this isn't the most dangerous, most vicious form of anti-Party anti-socialist behavior, then what is it?

Reading this record seemed to bring a flash of light to Jin Daqing's mind, clarifying for him several things he had previously been unable to piece together.

V

It was now early May. Those political winds which blew counter to the liberal spirit of the Third Party Plenum were at their height.[5]

No one, probably, was more alert to this shift than people at the newspaper. Editors rushed around to revise plans, rearrange layouts, solicit new manuscripts. Writers tried to recall manuscripts they had already submitted, or—badgered by panic-stricken families—to submit quick recantations of those articles. Readers, on the other hand, were bewildered. They wondered what kind of major upset had suddenly befallen this country of theirs. All the slogans like "Liberate your thought," "Break down the closed doors," etc., which only yesterday had been parroted all up and down the hierarchy, had in the twinkling of an eye become flagrant heterodoxy. The remnants of the Gang of Four popped up with new truculence: "What's this about false charges and wrong verdicts? *We* are more wrongly accused than anybody! How about some fair treatment for *us?*"

The political cold wind happened to come at the same time as Jin Daqing's investigations. He felt doubly chilled all over. He could even smell the poisonous vapors that were brewing inside the editorial department especially for him. Any little thing he might do or say was observed, noted down, and sent in secret to the hands of Ho Qixiong. The number of times he had visited Jiang Jinfang's house; whom he had received in that ninety-five-square-foot room of his; what he had said there—all of this and more was reported in due course. Every time he thought of this he smiled inwardly: They are on the decline. Covert activity is all that is left to them.

It was common for Jin to encounter unnatural, menacing smiles in the corridors of the editorial department. Sometimes he could hardly restrain himself from stopping people to ask what they were laughing at.

But when lying alone in bed in the dead of night, he again found repose. What did it all matter? The worst that could come of it would be a forced return to his same old life of the past twenty-three years. Now that his wife had gone to rest, he felt even less concerned about this possibility.

When he looked at the worn-out overcoat hanging on the wall—that old overcoat that had borne witness to so many tragedies—he cared even less about himself. He could stand above those brewing troubles that threatened his own safety and simply smile at them. For he was the fifth. He could well have been snuffed out long ago, in which case that yellowed overcoat would have changed hands once again. If he could now work to avert more such disasters, of what consequence was his own fate?

At times like this he would lose himself in reminiscences. He would remember those long winter nights, so cold and lonely, and be filled with complex emotions. Starting with the artist who was first to fall, he recalled their voices and expressions one by one, three men and one woman. When he got to the third, who was a woman comrade named Li Tao, his reminiscing suddenly broke off and his mind shot back to the present. A burst of inspiration had nearly made him sit up in bed. Li Tao had been Ho Qixiong's wife! That's right, back in 1957, when Ho had been transferred to the newspaper office, he and Li Tao had shared a correspondent's post. So how did Li Tao turn out to be a "rightist"? And who could have been her accuser?

VI

There was a regular meeting of the newspaper's editorial department on May 27. But this meeting was unusual in that everyone was required to attend, even the chronically ill and the retired. The atmosphere could not have been more solemn, and was quite tense as well. Everyone knew something big was going to break.

The deputy secretary of the Party Committee, Mr. Ho Qixiong, was to chair the meeting. You could see in his expression a burning excitement beneath the solemn exterior. Little beads of sweat dotted his sallow brow. The eyes are the most candid part of the human body, and they betrayed his real mood: for him the meeting would be like celebrating a major holiday.

After the customary opening clichés, he got right to the point. He was lecturing in his own words, which is something he rarely did and which shows that on this occasion he was speaking straight from his own true feelings and political attitude:

> It is the same with the exoneration of rightists—we must not overdo it. We have recently seen a certain person who, though still not pardoned, has been sticking his tail in the air like something high and mighty, and again feeding us all that junk from

1957. What does this tell us? It tells us he has not reformed himself, and that we have also carried "the reversal of mistaken verdicts" too far. This person—flaunting both witnesses and material evidence—is attempting to help people reverse their verdicts. And what's the problem with that? It's just like 1957, when the rightists attacked the liquidation of counterrevolutionaries that had taken place in the early fifties. They said the liquidation was all a mistake, remember? Now we have just one more case of anti-Party, anti-socialist behavior. People are using the slogan "Liberate thought" to attack the very foundations of the state.[6]

The speech stirred up a warm response from the audience. Several people were falling over themselves to express their agreement with Ho Qixiong, and even demanded the immediate launching of a new Anti-Rightist movement.

"I want to say a few words," came a voice from the back, as a lanky figure slowly unfolded himself into a standing position. The people in the front all peered backward curiously. It was none other than Jin Daqing, the main person under discussion.

"Of more than twenty rightists," Jin began, "I am the only one who has come back. And I haven't been exonerated, so it looks like the person we're talking about here is me. I want to address something very specific. As everyone knows, the high school teacher Jiang Zhenfang was once labeled a 'bad element.' Her family appealed, and asked for a reinvestigation. I did my own investigation, and I'd like to tell you what I found. Since our chairman has already raised this question, we must be sure to get to the bottom of it. First I'd like to ask Dong . . . I'm sorry, I can't remember his full name, everybody calls him Fat Hands Dong . . ."

"I object!" Fat Hands leapt to his feet, flailing his famous palms in the air. "This is a personal insult!" The room rocked with laughter.

"I'm sorry, I apologize," said Jin Daqing very earnestly, not imagining that this comment would only elicit new gales of laughter from the listeners. "I should call you Comrade Dong, and I'd like to ask Comrade Dong . . . no, first I have to explain to everybody why I am asking this question. The original evidence upon which Jiang Zhenfang was labeled a 'bad element' was supplied by . . . uh . . . *Comrade* Dong, and this evidence is what I'd like to ask about. Comrade Dong, you say you had illicit sexual relations with Jiang Zhenfang and cite two pieces of evidence to substantiate your claim. I want to ask you, since you say you have seen a black mole on her breast: just how big was that black mole? And was there one, or more than one?"

Fat Hands Dong was stunned. Struggling to maintain his composure, he tried to lead the discussion back to the agenda. "It seems to me inappropriate to discuss a subject of this nature at a meeting as serious as today's."

The crowd buzzed. One voice rose above the hubbub to shout out, "What's more serious than whether somebody is a 'bad element' or whether somebody has been wronged? Answer!"

A sudden hush, as everyone listened in intense curiosity to hear what Fat Hands Dong would say.

The chairman intervened in an attempt to break the siege. "Couldn't we postpone details such as this until . . ."

"No!" said Jin Daqing with firm bluntness. "You yourself raised this question just a moment ago. It was the question of whether or not I was trying to help bad elements reverse their verdicts. Remember? If we're going to do that we have to determine whether or not Jiang Zhenfang has indeed been a bad element. Comrade Dong was the primary witness, and the most important one, so of course we must listen to what he has to say."

He turned to face Fat Hands Dong. "I've given you my first question," he said. "My second question is this: you have said more than once that you've seen the scar on Jiang Zhenfang's abdomen. May we please know whether this scar was horizontal or vertical?"

A dead silence descended on the whole room. Three seconds passed. Five. The audience was growing restive. After approximately fifty seconds Fat Hands Dong finally mustered a reply: "As I recall, there was only one mole. As to its size . . . gee, how can I describe it? . . ." Again laughter from the listeners. Perspiration streamed from Fat Hands' face. On the question of the scar, he came out with another evasion and again incurred derisive laughter.

Stern and confident, Jin Daqing continued, "Wrong, Fat Hands Dong! You can't get off that easily. There are two moles on the breast of comrade Jiang Zhenfang. Look! Her sister recently did this sketch." He held up a piece of paper that showed two moles rather close together. The one on top covered about one square inch. The one below was smaller, about the size of a dime.

"As for that scar," Jin continued, "if you'd really seen it you'd have no trouble describing it. I respectfully request that the Party Committee look into Fat Hands Dong's crime of false accusation—and further, ascertain who was behind it . . ."

"Only the Party can decide such things," a voice interrupted. Then a tall man who had a few days' growth of beard stood up. This man was an important factional leader, and was currently in charge of a department. So his words had weight. "Today's meeting was originally a regular meeting of the Party, with non-Party members from the masses invited to participate. Recently Party Central has stressed the slogan 'The inner circle must come before the outer circle.' We must have no blurring of this borderline. I move that all non-Party people leave the room and all Party members stay behind to continue the meeting."

This put the listeners in some disarray. Rising to his feet, Ho Qixiong had already opened his mouth to proclaim the adoption of the suggestion to limit the meeting to Party members. But he was silenced as one more sonorous voice rang out: "How can you do *that?* You summoned these people here. Now, before the meeting's over, how can you say they don't belong here? Besides, *are* these issues purely internal Party matters? . . ."

VII

The meeting had stirred up the whole newspaper staff from top to bottom, some two to three hundred people in all. Beginning in early June, the political winds in China once again shifted a bit, and people regained some of their boldness. Someone came forward with important news for Jin Daqing: Li Tao had been labeled a "rightist" in 1958 because of a few letters from Ho Qixiong informing on her. Li Tao had of course been kept in the dark about this. Ho Qixiong had even tried to persuade her to sign a guilty plea, promising that he would not divorce her. But Li Tao had consistently refused to sign. What good would it do?

As soon as the verdict on Li Tao had been handed down, and she was stripped of her Party membership, Ho Qixiong had divorced her. By that time such things were so common as to be taken for granted, and so this event did not arouse anyone's curiosity. Next Ho Qixiong tried to force Jiang Zhenfang to divorce her husband. . . .

The reinvestigation of Jiang Zhenfang's case could have led to her exoneration and an alleviation of her illness. This hope was dashed when her younger sister Jiang Jinfang had another piece of very bad luck: her husband allowed himself to believe the vicious slander of some anonymous letters and came home quarreling a few times. He suspected her of infidelity, of hanky-panky with Jin Daqing. While Jin Daqing could shrug this off with a laugh, nothing so easy was possible for Jiang Jinfang. For her it was a new catastrophe on the coattails of the last. And there was no way Jin Daqing could try to explain to the husband—it just meant he couldn't see Jiang Jinfang anymore.

But Jin Daqing did learn a lesson from this. He came to realize that Ho Qixiong was not alone, and hence that he must expand the scope of his observations. . . .

We cannot end without an epilogue on Jin Daqing's "exoneration" question. Ho Qixiong was adamant that the facts of each charge be carefully verified one by one; at the same time the political department, in charge of the investigation, became bitten with wanderlust. In early June two of their number were assigned to "outside investigations," which brought them first to Beijing, then to Sichuan, Yunnan, and Guangxi, and finally to Anhui via Shanghai. They had a great time at all the famous sights and didn't get back until mid-September. Jin Daqing, by some stroke of luck, finally did get exonerated—though not without qualification. A long "tail" would always drag behind him.

Meanwhile Ho Qixiong did fine. Since both Li Tao and Gu Tiancheng were posthumously exonerated, and their cases thereby closed, the bloodstains on Ho's hands were permanently whitewashed. Fat Hands Dong, who had benefited greatly from Ho Qixiong in matters of Party membership, promotion, and housing allocation, insisted that his framing of Jiang Zhenfang had been due solely to a personal grudge and had had nothing to do with anyone else. Hence Ho Qixiong to this day is pure as the driven snow. One hears now that he has even been nominated as a candidate for the Municipal Party Congress. His only worry is whether he can get enough votes, because—according to his highly developed sense of smell—the winds in China, not only in the province but in the whole country, are becoming less and less fragrant.

NOTES

Originally published in *Beijing wenyi,* no. 11 (1979).

1. The personal names in this story suggest the characters of the people to whom they are attached. The surname of the central figure, Jin, means "Gold," while his personal name, Daqing, means "Great Clarity" or "Great Justness." The full name of Ho Qixiong, on the other hand, can be understood literally as "Where's His Heroism?" (Incidentally, we here use "Ho" to romanize the surname that actually should be "He" according to the Pinyin romanization system. This is necessary to avoid confusion with the pronoun "he" at the beginnings of sentences.) The name Gu Tiancheng suggests one who relies on whatever Heaven deals him. The names of the women characters in the story all have positive connotations.

2. In 1957 millions of Chinese were labeled "rightist" in a national campaign in which work units were required by a quota system to identify 5 percent of their personnel as rightists. After 1978 many of these arbitrary labels were finally removed.

3. "Old Shoe" is a euphemism for "adulteress."

4. The oscillations between tightness and relaxation in Chinese social control had reached a relatively tight point in April 1979.

5. The Third Plenary Session of the Eleventh Congress of the Communist Party of China was held in December 1978. It marked the advent of many of Deng Xiaoping's Western-leaning reforms, including "liberated thought" for writers and artists.

6. Literally, "to attack the four unmovables," (1) Party leadership, (2) the dictatorship of the proletariat, (3) Marxism-Leninism-Mao-Zedong-Thought, and (4) the socialist road.

PART FOUR
REVIEW ESSAYS

An Unnatural Disaster

Translated by Perry Link

Zheng Yi is a distinguished writer of fiction and reportage whose most famous work is probably *Lao Jing* (Old Well, 1984), which is a novel, later made into a prizewinning film, about love and the quest for water in the barren hills of Shanxi Province. Long an admirer and friend of Liu Binyan, Zheng Yi has followed and even amplified Liu's tradition of writing down unpleasant truths in defiance of political and social prohibitions. His story "Feng" (Maple, 1979) was the first work in post-Mao "scar literature" to dare to show armed combat among Red Guard groups and to associate the violence directly with Mao. Zheng Yi's *tour de force* of this kind of writing was *Hongse jinianbei* (Red Memorial, 1993), a book that resulted from careful investigations he conducted during the late 1980s into the politically inspired cannibalism that occurred in parts of the Guangxi Autonomous Region in 1968. Liu Binyan read the manuscript of *Hongse jinianbei,* and, even before it was published, wrote the following review for *The New York Review of Books,* vol. 40, no. 7 (April 8, 1993). It is reprinted here by permission. —ED.

It took twenty-four years for the news of the shocking facts about cannibalism in China's Guangxi Autonomous Region in southern China to reach the ears of the world. Most of the Chinese people know nothing of the truth even today. Similarly the grim truth about China's great famine of the early 1960s, which snuffed out more than 30 million lives, has continued to be sealed off from the Chinese people. The remarkable success of the Communist government's propaganda can be seen in the fact that nearly all Chinese people continue to refer to that huge famine as "the three years of natural disaster" or "the three-year period of difficulty." These are euphemisms for man-made catastrophe on a scale seldom seen in world history. But what does the ordinary Chinese citizen know of it? At most, only the tiny part that he or she experienced personally.

When the Chinese writer Zheng Yi's first accounts of the cannibalism in the Guangxi region appeared, many of the Chinese who saw them were reluctant to face the evidence squarely. Frustrated at this reluctance, Zheng Yi eventually decided, after living and writing underground in China for three years, to leave the country. If Chinese people have trouble dealing with these facts, Zheng reasoned, then I'll have to begin by presenting my evidence abroad. At the end of March 1992, he escaped to Hong Kong in a small wooden boat. He now lives in the U.S.

He carried with him a documented story of Mao Zedong's Cultural Revolution at its worst. In Guangxi, as elsewhere in China, the Cultural Revolution began in 1966 when Mao declared that "rebellion is justified" and sought to mobilize student rebels in "Red Guard" organizations to attack Liu Shaoqi, then president of the People's Republic, and others of Mao's own political rivals. Young people responded enthusiastically, taking the "right to rebel" as permission to express pent-up popular resentment against corrupt and repressive Party bureaucrats at local levels.

The first rebel groups were composed mostly of students and intellectuals. When they began threatening local power, more conservative groups, consisting largely of workers and government officials, emerged to oppose them. In a great many places two or three factions, each claiming to be the most steadfast in its loyalty to Mao, struggled for dominance in an increasingly lawless environment. Mao fanned the flames of the strife by promoting ambiguous slogans that convinced each side more than ever of its own righteousness: *Dictatorship means the masses' dictatorship; If we don't finish them, they will finish us;* and so on. As the factional strife worsened during 1967, garrison troops sometimes became involved. Rifles and other arms—in some places even machine guns and tanks—were employed. By 1968 there were pitched battles, sieges, makeshift prisons, and executions.

In most places, "revolutionary committees" controlled by the dominant faction (usually the one that had repressed the original student rebels) became a de facto local government. These regimes sought to create an atmosphere of terror in order to enforce their rule. One way they did this was to make examples of people who had been, or whose relatives had been, "class enemies" before the revolution—former landlords, rich peasants, "bourgeois" intellectuals, and others. It did not matter if one had been an infant in 1949 and a docile citizen ever since; in 1968 such a person could be forcibly taken from home and subjected to "struggle" (*douzheng*).

This term, which arose during China's land reform movement in the late 1940s, refers to collective accusation and taunting of an accused person at a public meeting. During land reform in the later 1940s, peasants would take turns relating their cases of suffering at the hands of a landlord, pressing their accusations until the landlord confessed. After 1949, "struggle" became a standard tactic in other kinds of political campaigns. Party leaders would identify a victim and direct the events. The presumption of guilt hung over the victim as soon as the accusation was made. The victim was not allowed to answer charges, and bystanders, even if inclined to offer a word of defense, could not possibly take such a risk because of the certainty that the taint would spread to themselves. At the end of each struggle session a sentence was pronounced. It was based not on evidence but on a "confession" that the struggle itself had elicited.

During the Cultural Revolution struggle sessions could end in beatings, torture, forced denunciations of family members, and killings. Many people resorted to suicide, divorce, or internal exile in order to avoid being "struggled." No one has been able to count the number of killings and suicides that took place throughout China. The government says one-tenth of the population "suffered political persecution."

Nor has anyone been able to describe all the local variations of the violence. (In Dao County, Hunan, for example, activists lured family members of class enemies back to their home villages for traditional holidays, then beheaded them in public using a large grain cleaver.) But there is wide consensus that the brutality was worst in Guangxi, where "unnatural deaths" during the Cultural Revolution are officially estimated at 90,000, but said among the populace to be at least twice that number. The original Red Guard "rebels" in Guangxi were students who called themselves the "April 22 Group" after the day of the group's founding in 1967. They were opposed by "The United Headquarters of Proletarian Revolutionary Factions," who had the backing of local Party bureaucrats, who were, in turn, backed by Wei Guoqing, governor of Guangxi. Wei secured from Central Cultural Revolution officials in Beijing an order to suppress the April 22 group, then lent his army in support of this effort. Thus, while "unnatural deaths" elsewhere in China meant primarily suicides or street-side killings, in Guangxi the term included the slaughter of April 22 members both in battle and in mass executions after their surrender or capture.

A person could claim credit for delivering blows against the opposing side. This was true everywhere in China during the Cultural Revolution, but again Guangxi defined an extreme. Zheng Yi documents a case in one town where teen-age girls formed a shock-force that would descend on "class enemies" and beat them to death. A girl who had killed six people was called "Sister Six"; another who had killed nine was "Sister Nine"; and so on. In Bobai County, an activist attempted to rape the daughter of a class enemy, but she resisted. He then killed her and reported to the Party branch with a request that he be made a Party member because of his demonstrated resolve in opposing class enemies. The officials told him that the demonstration must be made not just to them but to the village at large. The man returned to the girl's corpse, severed its head, carried it to the school basketball court, and used it to shoot baskets as a crowd gathered and watched.

Shortly thereafter a big meeting was held to induct the man into the Party.

In Qinzhou District, with a population around 300,000, Zheng Yi found official Party surveys, done in 1983, of the grisly phenomenon of promotion as a reward for murder: 10,420 people were killed in Cultural Revolution violence; 1,153 people were admitted to the Communist Party after demonstrating credit for a killing; 458 officials received promotions; and 637 people were given urban work permits, on the same basis.[1]

Zheng Yi was not the first to expose the violence in Guangxi. In 1968, a few conscience-stricken local Party officials sent off urgent reports about it to the central authorities in Beijing. The only concrete results of these reports were reprisals against those who had issued them. Sixteen years later, shortly before Beijing's famous "Democracy Wall" was suppressed, I personally read on the Wall about a hundred posters written by petitioners from Guangxi. They called upon the Deng Xiaoping leadership to deal severely with the primary offenders—the military and political strongmen in Guangxi. But the leader of those strongmen, Wei Guoqing, had been one of Deng Xiaoping's favorite followers during revolutionary struggles decades earlier. Wei was, at least for the time being, untouchable.

But Wei continued to insist on the "correctness" of the Cultural Revolution while Deng Xiaoping, beginning in the late 1970s, sought increasingly to discredit the Cultural Revolution in order to win popular support for his own rule. This difference led to a split between Wei and Deng, and to Wei's fall from power in 1983. Wei's dismissal then cleared the way, at long last, for central authorities to send people to Guangxi to investigate the shocking reports. By the time Zheng Yi and his bride-to-be, Bei Ming, went to Guangxi to do their own investigation, in 1986, all of the most flagrant offenders among the officials had already been transferred elsewhere. Yet many who had been part of the murderous "United Headquarters" group were still in power. The families of the victims, as well as everyone who had been active in the ill-fated "April 22" group, continued to live under the threat of repression.

Zheng Yi was particularly concerned to investigate reports that victims of the Cultural Revolution had actually been eaten. The people who had been involved in such acts of cannibalism put him under tight surveillance and tried however they could to prevent him from gathering hard evidence. They tried to block access to Party archives. They tried to prevent him from traveling to outlying villages to interview accused murderers and the families of victims. An atmosphere reminiscent of the White Terror[2] intimidated many from telling him what they knew. Those who sympathized with Zheng Yi were obliged to take elaborate precautions when helping him, as if doing underground work. In the end, thanks to assistance from a few Party officials and from the families of victims, Zheng Yi was able to get the evidence he needed.

Zheng's book *Hongse jinianbei* begins with detailed accounts of some selected cases of cannibalism. One tells of Deng Jifang, reportedly murdered by a man named Yi Wansheng. Deng's father had been a landlord in the 1940s. In the early 1950s, when the Land Reform Campaign arrived, the father and his three sons fled into the nearby hills. When they were captured, the father and the two older sons were executed, but the youngest son, Deng Jifang, because he was a minor, was let off with a two-year sentence at a labor reform camp. After his release he went back to his village to find that his mother had hanged herself and that no one in the village welcomed him. He then made his way to a neighboring village where a childless peasant family was willing to adopt him and later arrange a marriage for him so that they might continue their family line. The official file on Deng Jifang's murder states that "after his marriage he always stayed at home honestly and straightforwardly growing rice and planting crops."[3]

On June 5, 1986, Zheng Yi went to Sixiao village in Qingtang township, Zhongshan County, accompanied by two local officials. Sixiao was Deng Jifang's native village and the place where Yi Wansheng, the man accused of murdering Deng, still lived. In *Hongse jinianbei* Zheng Yi writes:

> During the Cultural Revolution leaders in Sixiao village, dutybound to uncover "class enemies," found themselves with no convenient scapegoats. Suddenly remembering that the youngest son of a former landlord of theirs was now living in the neighboring village, Sixiao Party Secretary Huang Paoci ordered his armed militia to go make the arrest. When Deng Jifang saw the approach

of the militia from the window of his home, he knew that his time had come and decided to hang himself immediately rather than to endure the torture that inevitably would follow. But the militia leaders stormed inside, cut Deng down before he died, and dispatched him under escort back to Sixiao village.

At one point on the way, Deng abruptly refused to take another step. He was then packed into a bamboo cage used for carrying pigs and marched forcibly back to Sixiao village. There the villagers tied him to an electric pole and beat him into semi-consciousness, but apparently still were not satisfied. The official file on the case says they then "seared his chest and back with a red-hot stir-frying spatula."[4] As the torture continued the zest of the crowd escalated, until some in the group—including senior Party members, officials, labor-reform activists, and "poor peasants"[5]—raised the demand that Deng be killed and, moreover, that this be done by disembowelment. While Deng was still barely alive, they dragged him onto the stones of a river bed where five or six people "used pine branches to hold down his arms and legs while the poor peasant Yi Wansheng sliced open Deng Jifang's abdomen with a vegetable cleaver . . ."[6]

We found Yi Wansheng, who in the meantime had become famous in the area as a "murderer," inside his shabby, cramped hut. He readily admitted every detail of his case, and indeed seemed almost cocky about it. "Right! I admit everything! Anyway I'm eighty-five years old, haven't long to live anyway. You think I'm afraid of jail?" The old man glared at me defiantly. I averted his challenge, and instead invited him to discuss his reasons for killing.[7]

"Why did I kill him? They ran into the hills to be bandits . . . upset the whole village. I was in the militia back then, spent all day on sentry duty. In a few weeks the rifle butt wore holes right through my clothes! . . . What was so evil about his father? We had a famine one spring, and he wouldn't lend grain to us villagers; he up and lent it to other villages! When he ran to the mountains to be a bandit, he led the other bandits back to attack the village. . . . He had them burn up a huge pile of straw that we were going to use for fuel in our limekilns. They burned it! No lime!

. . . Yes, I killed him. I give the same answer no matter who asks. . . . Why should I be afraid? So many of the masses were behind me,

and the man I killed was a bad man, so what am I afraid of? . . .
Am I supposed to be afraid his ghost will get me? Ha, ha! I'm a
revolutionary, my heart is red! Didn't Chairman Mao teach us, 'If
we don't kill them, they'll kill us!'? It's life and death! It's class
struggle! . . . Yeah, I was wrong. The government shoulda killed
him, shouldn't have left it to us. . . . I just did the handiwork. The
first knife didn't work, so I threw it away. I got him open with the
second knife. But I wasn't the one who pulled out the heart and
liver."

On this last crucial detail, the official document on the case does
not square with Yi Wansheng's account. It says: "After opening
Deng Jifang's abdominal cavity, Yi Wansheng proceeded to remove the internal organs. Because the abdominal cavity was un-
comfortably hot in comparison to the river water, Yi Wansheng
splashed water inside to bring the temperature down. Then Yi
Wansheng reached his hands inside Deng Jifang's abdomen and
pulled out the heart, liver, gall bladder, and kidneys. After slicing
them up with his cleaver, he laid them out on a wooden plank."[8]

Yi Wansheng continued: "When the heart and liver were out, and
sliced into strips about the size of your fingers, the masses rushed
up to grab them. There was such a crowd that I didn't even get
any." But the official document says: "Huang Paoqiu [apparently
a mistake for the aforementioned Huang Paoci—ZY] stepped forward to take away more than half the pieces for himself. He went
home and [two characters are unclear here—seem to be *youzha,*
"fried in oil"—ZY] on a wok lid outside his door, then ate them,
sharing some with the masses. . . . Yi Wansheng took three strips
of finger-sized liver, each about three inches long, home to eat.[9]

Zheng Yi describes a number of such incidents. After investigations in several counties, he was able to make some general conclusions about the cannibalism in Guangxi. It was, first, unprecedented since it was cannibalism based on hatred. At earlier times
in China, because of the folk belief in some places that human
blood has medicinal powers, small amounts of blood were sometimes gathered from the bodies of executed criminals. During the
great famine of the early 1960s, there were also instances of the
consumption of human flesh, but these were the result of life-
or-death hunger and regarded as horrifying aberrations. But in
Guangxi in 1968, hunger was not the issue. What happened was

that "revolutionary masses"—meaning supporters of the dominant United Headquarters—killed "class enemies," who were either family members of landlords and others with inherited bad backgrounds, or members of "rebel groups" such as April 22. After killing the enemy grew fairly common, eating the enemy became the way to demonstrate an even higher level of "class awakening."

Zheng Yi found that many people, while afraid to resist the cannibalism openly, privately found it abhorrent. He tells of one village where political fervor and human conscience arrived at a subtle balance. Village leaders cut human flesh and pork into equal-sized pieces and boiled them together in a large pot in the village square. They suspended the pot above eye-level while villagers passed by to receive one piece of meat each. All villagers could then say, "I have shown a firm class standpoint," but also say, perhaps only to themselves, "It is possible I have not eaten human flesh."

Zheng Yi concludes that the cannibalism took place in three stages: In the "beginning stage," the flesh-eaters were motivated by personal hatred but still felt strong inhibitions. They would steal away, usually in the still of night, to the execution ground where a class enemy had been shot some hours earlier. There they would slit the abdomen and remove the heart and liver. Because they trembled, and moreover lacked experience, they sometimes punctured a bowel, or cut out the lungs by mistake, obliging them to go back for a second try. After boiling the organs, they would gather around a stove and hurriedly consume them. No one would say a word.

In the "mature stage," the victims were disemboweled right after they were executed, in broad daylight, in village squares or marketplaces with red flags flying and political slogans pasted on walls. Inhibitions were weaker now, because "eating class enemies" had become recognized as a revolutionary act and a sign of personal mettle. After the killings, the leaders would begin by taking away the best parts—heart, liver, and genitals. The rest was left for "the masses" to slice off at will.

In the "hysterical stage," the eating of human flesh turned into unpredictable street-side terror. At any time, putative "class enemies" could be dragged out to undergo "criticism and struggle."

Struggle led to death, and death to cannibalism. As soon as a victim fell to the ground, and even if he were still breathing, a crowd would rush forward, drawing the knives and cleavers they had come equipped with, and slice off parts in a free-for-all fashion. At worst, collective banquets of human flesh would follow.

How many people had their flesh eaten, in all, and how many participated in the eating? The numbers can only be estimated, because government records on the matter remain tightly guarded secrets to the present day. Zheng Yi was able to get full access to the records of only one county in Guangxi, Wuxuan County. There he copied lists that gave the full names of sixty-four people who were eaten in 1968, together with the locations of the murders and a compilation of grisly details: heart and liver eaten, fifty-six people; genitals, thirteen people; entire body, including soles of the feet, eighteen people; disemboweled while living, seven people.[10] Zheng Yi estimates that if sixty-four victims could be fully identified in Wuxuan, the total number for that county, including undocumented or undiscovered cases, may be near one hundred. Since Wuxuan has only 5 percent of Guangxi's population, and since Zheng Yi found cannibalism in all five of the five counties he personally visited, the total number of people eaten, he reasons, must be at least several hundred.

Another document from Wuxuan County shows that 130 people there were punished after 1983 for having taken leading roles in the cannibalism.[11] From this fact, and considering that victims in the later stages of the movement were cut into small pieces and shared among many, Zheng Yi estimates the number of people who participated in eating human flesh to be in the high thousands for Wuxuan County, and many times that for Guangxi as a whole.

With cold irony, Zheng notes the "punishments" for cannibalism levied after 1983: dismissal from the Communist Party; political demerit noted on the records; reduction in salary. No one faced criminal charges. Some were made to apologize to the victim's surviving family members. Zheng tells of a mother whose preschool son was killed, because his father had been a "class enemy," by three men who tied the boy by a rope to the tailgate of a truck and dragged him until he was dead. Fifteen years later the three entered the mother's house, accompanied by a Communist Party official. They sat down to "sincerely apologize." The mother was obliged to pour tea for the four men.

Zheng Yi's original intention had been to write a novel based on what he could learn about Guangxi during the Cultural Revolution. But the appalling facts that he and Bei Ming discovered caused him to change his mind in favor of writing a factual account. Then, just as he was setting pen to paper, the Tiananmen movement of 1989 erupted.

Zheng Yi and Bei Ming were drawn into the movement at the outset and stayed involved until the very end. After the June 4 massacre they began a life of internal exile. Zheng Yi was on the government's nationwide most-wanted list and the object of a search by police forces who were mobilized to highest alert in every province and city. Nevertheless he was able, somehow, to travel across half of China. How he could remain undiscovered for three years, and even be able to write during that time, might seem impossible to imagine. It might seem equally impossible that Bei Ming, who was jailed for ten months and then released, but who remained under the close scrutiny of secret police afterward, could find her way far to the south of China to rejoin her husband, with whom she had lost contact for many months, and even deliver safely to him the entire collection of his forbidden research materials.

The basic explanation for these apparent mysteries is fairly simple. A Chinese proverb says, "a just cause attracts abundant support." Among those who helped Zheng Yi and Bei Ming were not only scholars, writers, teachers, students, and editors, perhaps as one might expect, but also a large number of government officials, office workers, private entrepreneurs, militiamen, policemen, and unemployed "floating" peasants.[12] They were also helped by a monk, a sing-song girl, and an ex-convict. Not one of these people betrayed the fugitives, and not one refused to help. They provided food, shelter, transportation, and secure communications. Before seeing them off to their destinations, they often gave them money as well.

During the three years Zheng Yi lived underground, he seldom had to go without funds. He relied almost entirely on the support of strangers who not only helped him but were willing to take personal risks to do so. Those who today are so effusive in their praise of Deng Xiaoping's economic policies and of social stability in China somehow overlook the important fact that there are people all across China—including many officials, military police, and even state security police—who have shielded hundreds of dissidents and have helped them make their ways safely out of the country. All these people are among the regime's latent opponents.

In addition to *Hongse jinianbei,* Zheng Yi wrote another book called *Lishi de yibufen* (*A Part of History*) during his three years as fugitive after June 1989. Both manuscripts begin with an unflinching look at the evidence of the Guangxi cannibalism that is briefly summarized above. They then put these events into the larger setting of the Cultural Revolution and attempt to explain—historically, psychologically, and politically—how such egregious excess could possibly occur. When Zheng Yi finished writing *Hongse jinianbei,* he said to have heaved a sigh, tossed down his pen, and said, "All right, now they can come for me." The book had become, for both Bei Ming and him, the whole reason for their struggle to carry on. They looked for ways to hide photocopies of the text and supporting documents in several different locations inside China. Still not feeling secure, they eventually took miniature photographs of the pages and passed them to an Australian couple, who were in China as tourists, to carry out of the country.

Zheng Yi wrote *Lishi de yibufen* during the last half of 1989. Its form is a series of long letters addressed to his wife, even though he knew he could not send them to her at the time, since he was in hiding and she in prison. One of the letters discusses the Guangxi cannibalism, but read together the letters are much broader, adding up to an intellectual autobiography.

Zheng Yi belongs to the generation of Chinese who became adults during the Cultural Revolution. Although his family had a rough time under the Communists, his natural idealism led him to become a loyal follower of Mao Zedong. During the Cultural Revolution he expected that a Paris Commune style of democracy that Mao was advocating would take root in China. Then, in

1968, when he and millions of other young people answered Mao's call to "settle and work in the countryside," they learned that the "socialist" countryside was usually nothing but a place of miserable destitution in which peasants had no rights whatever. Feeling that they had been deceived and manipulated, these former Red Guards began to have fundamental doubts about the Maoist line. They sought desperately for any books they could find on Western philosophy and politics, hoping to find a better formula for China. When Zheng Yi could find such books he read them compulsively. Because they were precious contraband, the books were rationed on a tight schedule among young people stationed in several villages. Zheng Yi would skip sleep to read all night.

When he began writing his own criticisms of Mao-style socialism, he inadvertently allowed one of his letters to a friend to be intercepted by the authorities. This event forced him to flee, and he spent some time living in the forests and plains in China's northeast, where he gained an even deeper appreciation of the true nature and scale of China's suffering. Next he went to work as a laborer in a coal mine, and at the same time began writing underground literature aimed at exposing the despotic rule of Chinese communism. By this route a young man who began with a sincere faith in Marxism-Leninism turned finally into an all-out rebel, and now into one of China's most powerful writers, whose works deserve to be translated and widely read.

NOTES

1. Leadership Group for Party Rectification in the Qinzhou District of the Communist Party of China in Guangxi, *Qinzhou diqu 'Wenhua da geming' da shijian* (Major events of the "Cultural Revolution" in Qinzhou District), 1987, p. 52.

2. Referring to Kuomintang repression of Communists and others during the 1920s to 1940s.

3. Zhongshan County Public Security Bureau, preliminary investigation file on the murder of Deng Jifang by Yi Wansheng, "Report on the Disembowelment of Deng Jifang," p. 2.

4. "Report on the Disembowelment of Deng Jifang," p. 4. (Note is from Zheng Yi's text.)

5. "Poor peasant" is a technical term. During land reform in the early 1950s everyone in Chinese villages was given a label designating socio-economic status. "Poor peasant," the lowest class status, was politically one of the best.

6. "Report on the Disembowelment of Deng Jifang," p. 5. (Note is from Zheng Yi's text.)

7. On the first page of Yi Wansheng's file (note 3), a political authority had written the following instruction: "Yi Wansheng's means of murder were cruel and barbaric. He should be held accountable and punished appropriately." But nothing was ever done. When I asked why, the answer was. "He's too old. Arresting him wouldn't mean anything. If we took him in he'd probably just die in jail." (Note is from Zheng Yi's text.)

8. "Report on the Disembowelment of Deng Jifang," p. 6. (Note is from Zheng Yi's text.)

9. "Report on the Disembowelment of Deng Jifang," pp. 6–7. (Note is from Zheng Yi's text.)

10. Wuxuan County Office for Handling Problems Left Over From the Great Cultural Revolution, "*Wuxuan xian bei chi renrouzhe mingdan*" (Name list of people whose flesh was eaten in Wuxuan County), July 4, 1983.

11. *Wuxuan xian wuchanjieji wenhua da geming da shijian* (Major events of the Great Proletarian Cultural Revolution in Wuxuan County), pp. 29, 30.

12. In recent years a large number of rural Chinese have flocked to the cities in search of urban employment. Because they lack legal registry in the cities (and thus access to publicly subsidized housing, education, medical care, and other things) they are called a "floating population." Their numbers as of early 1993 are estimated between 50 and 70 million nationwide.

A Great Leap Backward?

Translated by Perry Link

China's urban economic boom in the 1990s was startling to many observers in the West, where it drew extraordinary praise in both popular and scholarly publications. Meanwhile people inside China saw less rosy aspects of the boom: diversion of public property to private profit by people who held political power, the enrichment of a new communist-capitalist class, a growing gap between rich and poor, and the consequent rise of cynicism within the public. But these observations were confined to private oral comment. Publication was forbidden.

He Qinglian's 1998 book *Zhongguo de xianjing* (China's quagmire) challenged the prohibition on public exposure of the problems. In the fine tradition of Liu Binyan, it spelled out in public, with great detail and sharp analysis, complaints that had long been simmering in the public mind. Publication was difficult, but once the book was out, reader response was overwhelming.

The following essay was first published in *The New York Review of Books,* vol. 45, no. 15 (October 8, 1998),[1] and is reprinted here by permission. —ED.

Most of the good news from China during the Deng Xiaoping era concerned the country's economy. It grew at an average annual rate of 10 percent from 1981 to 1991, and 12 percent from then until 1995. Average personal income more than tripled in the 1980s, and doubled again in the first half of the 1990s.[2] Some Westerners were dazzled. In November 1992, *The Economist* referred to "one of the biggest improvements in human welfare anywhere at any time,"[3] and six months later *Business Week* told of "breathtaking changes . . . sweeping through the giant nation."[4] Foreign corporations, eager to be part of the China boom, poured investment in at record rates. China's foreign currency holdings soared.

Yet during the same two decades, especially the 1990s, there was much bad news as well. People died from drinking phony liquor; fake fertilizers killed crops; there were growing markets for illicit drugs, for sweatshop labor, and even for the sale of young women for wives and male infants for sons. Corruption was rampant. Industrial pollution was serious and growing fast. State enterprises were failing, unpaid workers were striking, and banks were mired in bad debt. The gap between rich and poor became much wider. During 1997 and 1998 average personal income growth has fallen off sharply, and for large portions of both urban and rural poor it has reversed.[5]

No one during the Deng years produced a systematic account of how these two aspects of China's economy were related. The regime and its defenders argued that so long as the economy surged forward, other problems would eventually take care of themselves. In the US, many business leaders, followed by the Clinton administration, argued that Western commercial engagement with China creates not only more wealth but progress toward democracy as well. Skeptics countered that more wealth, by itself, does not necessarily cure social problems or lead to democracy.

China's Quagmire, the first systematic study of the social consequences of China's economic boom, vindicates the skeptics so resoundingly as to force us to reconceive what "reform" has meant. In her book, which was published in Beijing early this year, He Qinglian, an economist trained at Fudan University in Shanghai, shows how Deng's reforms between 1979 and 1997 did indeed lead China out of the stifling agricultural communes and urban work units of the Mao era. But what resulted, she argues, was not "civil society," or even a market economy in the normal sense, but a strange way of life that the Chinese people had hardly imagined when they first embraced reform. She compares the Chinese people to the mythical She Gong, who felt a strong attraction to dragons in paintings, only to be terrified when confronted by a real dragon.

The first spurt of growth in the Chinese economy resulted from the release of farmers from the commune system beginning in the late 1970s. Besides growing and marketing their own crops much more efficiently than they had under state planning, farmers created "village enterprises" that were quickly successful in light industries such as foodstuffs (soy sauce, noodles, etc.) and clothing. By the late 1980s, however, the rural economy slowed and in some places even contracted. This happened because the immediate gains from freeing agriculture could not be continued, and because many village enterprises fell victim to extortion, overtaxation, and embezzlement by local officials. During the late 1980s and early 1990s a "floating population" of 120 million rural people migrated to Chinese cities in search of work.

The boom in the 1990s took place mainly in urban China. He Qinglian writes that from the outset the urban "reform" amounted to:

> a process in which power-holders and their hangers-on plundered public wealth. The primary target of their plunder was state property that had been accumulated from forty years of the people's sweat, and their primary means of plunder was political power.

He Qinglian shows how this "plunder"—a process that involves only transfer, not production, of wealth—is primarily responsible for the rapid rise in average personal income in Chinese cities. Even the newly produced wealth, she demonstrates, is the result not just of new economic energy and efficiency, but of two additional factors. One is that China receives large foreign investment—in the mid-1990s this ranged between thirty and forty billion US dollars annually, or about one fifth of all investment in China. The other is that China's state banks support state enterprises with emergency transfusions of funds (called "loans," but unrecoverable) that are drawn from the personal savings of ordinary citizens. As of early 1997, almost half the money in personal savings accounts (two trillion yuan, or $240 billion) had been lost in this way. Because China's press is controlled, few ordinary savers are aware of this fact. The practice also represents a subsidy of the cities by the countryside, since many savers are rural.

Notwithstanding the widespread discussion of the effects of the private "market" on China, China's state enterprises, although they were never very efficient, still dominate the urban economy.[6] Steel, cement, and all heavy industry—and all media and telecommunications—still, by law, must be state-owned.[7] With few exceptions, only state enterprises receive loans from China's banks (which themselves are exclusively state-owned) and only state enterprises can have access to foreign currency. Still the state sector's share of the economy has steadily declined. Twenty years ago it was the only sector, and today it produces about 30 percent of the gross domestic product. But the 70 percent of "non-state" GDP includes all of agriculture and rural industry, which together are 60 percent of GDP. Contrary to the impression given in the Western press, only about 10 percent of GDP comes from urban private enterprise.

The state sector of the economy also dominates the concerns of the Chinese leadership—concerns that are, as always, essentially political. The stability of the Chinese government depends on preventing urban unrest, especially in Beijing, Shanghai, and the other major cities. Farmers can protest (and indeed have protested, in the 1990s, much more than the Western press has generally reported), but such actions do not rock the regime as do urban demonstrations or strikes.

And who are the urban citizens whom the government needs to keep content? About 85 percent, in one way or another, work for the state. Workers in state industry make up between 45 and 47 percent of the urban work force; another 18 percent or so work in government offices; between 20 and 22 percent work either in government-sponsored "urban collectives" that were founded in the late 1950s (and do labor-intensive work like pasting together cardboard boxes) or, more recently, in profitable "tertiary"—i.e., service—industries such as retail stores. These are state-affiliated companies that exist within larger state enterprises (whose profits, as we shall see, can be skimmed by private executives).

The 15 percent of the urban population that works in the private economy started to emerge in the early 1980s when "individual entrepreneurs" were allowed to set up one-person enterprises such as bicycle repair shops or sewing services. In the mid-1980s, it became legal for families to run small enterprises such as restaurants, and then to hire as many as seven non-family employees. According to China's constitution, private enterprises with more than seven employees remain illegal today, but this provision, like the guarantee of free speech and several others, is ignored in practice. During the late 1980s and 1990s government-approved foreign enterprises (e.g., McDonald's) and Sino-foreign "joint enterprises" (e.g., Beijing Auto and Jeep-Cherokee) could hire larger numbers of employees, and later Chinese companies could do so as well, although very few Chinese private enterprises grew to rival state enterprises in size.

Private enterprises are taxed more heavily than state enterprises. Many have failed (up to one third within the last two years, in some provinces), while others (including Jeep-Cherokee) are only barely surviving. Still, enough have succeeded to produce a good economic record for the urban private sector, which employs 3 percent of the population and produces about 10 percent of GNP. Chinese, foreign, and "joint" enterprises that employ cheap labor to make shoes, toys, and other consumer goods for export have been the most profitable.

Much of He Qinglian's book describes how the Chinese economy got to where it is today through what Deng called "reform" and what He Qinglian calls "the marketization of power." During the first decade of reform between 1979 and 1989, Party officials enriched themselves mainly through manipulating the public funds and supplies that were under their control. China at the time had a two-track pricing system for raw materials and industrial commodities: a controlled price for state enterprises within the planned economy, and a much higher market price that applied to all "non-state-owned" enterprises: private, joint-venture, and foreign companies, as well as the village industries. In a process popularly called *guandao* ("official turnaround"), officials would arrange to procure raw materials or commodities at the fixed price and then "turn around" to reap large illicit profits by selling on the private market.

Popular protests against *guandao* had a modest effect in the late 1980s, at least until the suppression of the 1989 Tiananmen movement. In the three years after 1989, memories of the government's violence and a sag in the economy combined to present the regime with the specter of further unrest. During his famous "southern tour" of 1992, Deng gambled that this threat would vanish when he issued his call for everyone in the country to go into business and get rich—"even more boldly," he said, than in the 1980s, and "even faster."

His message led virtually every official, government office, and social group or organization in China to "jump into the sea" and try to make money. This was done in a variety of ways, and the most lucrative, He Qinglian shows, were usually exploitative or illicit.

Public funds were used for speculation in real estate or stocks, including foreign stocks. If such investments made a profit, the speculators would take it; if not, they would pass the losses on to state accounts. In "tertiary industries," the friends or children of powerful officials would take control of the most productive section of a state enterprise (such as a clothing factory's retail outlet) in order to run it as a semi-independent company. Profits went to the entrepreneurs; losses, if any, to the affiliated state enterprise.

In joint enterprises with foreigners or overseas Chinese, the Chinese partner could arrange for the business to use property and obtain materials and licenses at well below fair prices; in return the foreign partner would deposit foreign currency in overseas accounts, in the personal name of the Chinese partner. This maneuver had the added benefit of allowing the Chinese partner to export capital, which is illegal in China. He Qinglian calculates that in the 1980s the outflow of capital to private foreign accounts was nearly half as much as total foreign investment coming into China; after 1992, the outflow equaled the inflow.

He Qinglian also shows how the plunder of state resources in the 1990s was several times as frenzied as the *guandao* of the

1980s had been. In the 1980s a number of millionaires emerged in China; but in just one or two years after 1992, a considerable number of powerful Chinese piled up tens or even hundreds of millions. Deng had opened up vast new fields for speculation, and, writes He Qinglian, China saw "a new high tide in the carving up of state property by China's power elite." The net value of China's state enterprises has been steadily declining, and it is possible that sometime during 1998 or 1999 the aggregate value of such enterprises will reach zero.

Defenders of current policies in China have argued that such costs of reform are the inevitable results of dismantling an inefficient state system, and that China really has no choice but to swallow hard and suffer the pain until reform can work. But this analysis ignores the ways in which reform itself has fed corruption. He Qinglian's chapter "State Enterprises: The Bottlenecks of Reform" shows how the new flexibility given to managers of state enterprises has in many cases led them not toward market efficiency but instead toward sacrificing efficiency for their own selfish interests and those of the higher officials who protect them. The golden rule of the corrupt manager, in He Qinglian's analysis, is to have a relationship of utter loyalty and trust with one's superior. In addition to outright bribes and kickbacks, one can please this person by employing his friends or relatives, by offering him the use of cars, by providing goods that he can "try out," and in many other ways.

Once a manager can depend on a superior's loyalty, all else is possible. Since no one within a state enterprise can then effectively challenge a manager's decisions about allocation of resources, the manager can act with impunity. The manager becomes, in He's artful phrase, the "semi-owner" of an enterprise in the specific sense that he or she has all the powers of an owner while remaining free of all the responsibilities. He Qinglian argues that what China actually has is not a true market but only a kind of "simulated market" in which "the actual competition is political" and where "power determines the allocation of resources but has no need to see to their efficient use."

Late payment, partial payment, or nonpayment of wages have become common among state workers of all kinds, including officials and teachers. In spring of 1998 the number of laid-off state workers reached at least twelve million, and another ten million seem headed for layoff by the end of the year. A small city in Guangxi reported that it could pay only 2 percent of the salaries on its payroll. For several years demonstrations, slowdowns, and strikes have been common. The response of the state has been to ban protests where possible and to support state enterprises with emergency loans from the banking system.

Since state enterprises usually cannot repay these loans, they remain on the books as acknowledged or unacknowledged bad debt. China's banks announce only part of their bad debt publicly, so its full extent is not easy to measure. The official figure is that 20 percent of loans are "nonperforming," but the actual figure may be between 40 percent and 60 percent. (In the spring of 1998, the state banks in Guangdong announced bad debt of 200 billion yuan, but inspectors sent from Beijing found the actual figure four times that amount.) By international standards China's banks are bankrupt, and deeply so.[8]

Despite the country's financial crisis, opportunistic officials have, during the 1990s, been able to shake loose at least 500 billion yuan—about $60 billion—to use in speculation, especially in real estate. The money has been siphoned from state funds that had been intended for the purchase of state grain, for education, and for disaster relief, and has been supplemented by funds raised through usurious loans. Since 1992 speculation in land has driven housing prices in major Chinese cities to levels that are more appropriate to a modernized society than to a developing one. By World Bank standards, the cost of a family residence should fall somewhere between three and six times the average annual household income.[9] In China prices range between ten and thirty times household income. At present 70 percent of new construction, representing 100 billion yuan ($12 billion) in capital, remains empty. Because the construction was financed by overextended state banks, the government will not permit prices to fall.

The people in China's more modern cities who enjoy rising incomes have recently been spending less of their money on consumer goods like television sets and VCRs. In addition to saving for down payments on housing, they have been spending their money on medical care, children's schooling, and other expenses that the state once covered but now come out of family budgets. This shift in spending patterns, combined with the fact that buying power has been declining among farmers and state-sector urban workers, has created a serious oversupply in consumer goods. The value of the excessive national inventories has recently reached three trillion yuan—$360 billion—putting strong downward pressure on prices. But for the state there is no easy way out: cutting prices only puts state enterprises further in debt, while cutting production means more layoffs.

Future Chinese generations will have to reckon with another, even larger, debt that the economic boom has both incurred and postponed, and that is the debt to the environment. He Qinglian does not address this issue in detail, but other scholars have done so.[10] Air pollution in Chinese cities has been estimated to be five to ten times that of US cities, while new industries, in order to maximize profits, refuse to install pollution control equipment. In north China, where rainfall is scant, diversion of water to agriculture and industry has caused streams and small reservoirs to dry up. During the first six years of the 1990s the Yellow River, China's second largest river, was dry for a total of 333 days. In the 1950s the water table in Beijing was sixteen feet below the surface; today it is more than 150 feet down.

China supports the world's largest national population on only about 7 percent of the world's arable land, but it is losing that arable land at an annual rate of 0.5 percent to erosion, construction of buildings and roads, and the encroachment of deserts. China now has two thirds of the arable land it had four decades ago, and 2.3 times as many people. Specialists estimate that China's gross domestic product is reduced by about 15 percent annually because of losses caused by environmental damage, and this omits the effects that cannot be measured in money, such as the premature loss of life of people stricken with environmentally induced disease. Zheng Yi, an exiled Chinese writer who is completing a study of the environment in China, calculates that each year China's economic activity causes environmental damage whose reversal would cost at least eight trillion yuan, an amount that exceeds the country's annual gross product.

Such damage has been exacerbated by this year's floods. The Yangtze River has flooded periodically in China's history, but the record-breaking floods of 1998 are nature's retribution for decades of environmental devastation and neglect. Beginning with Mao Zedong's "Great Leap Forward" of 1958–1959, China's richest natural forests in Sichuan and Yunnan provinces, at the headwaters of the Yangtze, were cut "more, faster, better, and cheaper." Since 1958 those forests have shrunk by 45 to 70 percent, and, nationwide, about one third of China's topsoil has washed into the Pacific Ocean. Small dikes and dams have fallen out of repair because of shoddy work resulting from corruption, and, in recent years, because government spending on irrigation has been dominated by construction of the huge and controversial Three Gorges Dam.

More than 300 million people have been affected in this year's flooding, and deaths have reached into the tens of thousands (the government acknowledges just over three thousand). In earlier years the government handled floods by blowing up small dikes and dams, deliberately inundating parts of the countryside in order to protect cities. Rural people had no choice but to bear the sacrifice. But in 1998 there are signs of rebellion in the countryside. As of July 31, the Yangtze flooding had led to 130 incidents of violent uprising—attacking and occupying government offices, sacking state warehouses, and burning vehicles and buildings—in the four provinces of Anhui, Jiangxi, Hubei, and Hunan. The longer-term effects of flooding are likely to be grain shortages, another large increase in rural migration to the crowded cities, and, in the countryside, increasing incidence of armed revenge against the cities, the government, and the well-to-do. The great flood is exacerbating nearly all of China's social tensions, even as government resources for dealing with those tensions and the economic crisis are greatly diminished.

He Qinglian argues that inequality, like corruption, increased through the 1980s and expanded dramatically after 1992. Between 1992 and 1995, when the size of China's economy was growing at unprecedented rates, the number of what the government calls "poverty counties" was also rising. Between 1987 and 1994, average personal income fell in the provinces of Anhui, Guizhou, Ningxia, and Xinjiang. (By 1994 the disparity between rich and poor was already greater in China than in the United States. In that year the richest 20 percent of the US population owned 44.3 percent of the country's wealth, whereas in China the richest fifth owned 50.2 percent of the wealth; the poorest fifth in the US owned 4.6 percent of the wealth, in China 4.3 percent.)[11] Urban residents (not counting the 120 million rural migrants) are about one fifth of China's population, produce about two fifths of the wealth, and consume three fifths of it. Rural people (including the migrants, and including residents of small towns) make up four fifths, produce three fifths, and consume two fifths.

Some have argued that in any transition from a planned to a market economy, corruption and inequality are necessary, or perhaps even useful. He Qinglian acknowledges that when a society and economy are stultified by political terror, as China's were during the late Mao years, the unofficial trading of favors can indeed have a part in loosening up the system. But she argues that this stage has long passed in China, and that the effects of the corruption of the 1980s and 1990s have badly hurt the economy. She calculates that in recent years about 130 million yuan in public property has been diverted annually to private use. But she also calculates that only about 30 million of this sum actually reaches the economy as private capital. The other 100 million is spent on bribes, entertainment, and favors that are necessary to divert the money and to cover it up. Corruption thus hardly leads to efficiency.

The argument that inequality is beneficial in a period of transition had the personal blessing of Deng Xiaoping right from the beginning of the reform period. Deng argued that overall wealth will grow in a situation of inequality and that the resulting income will trickle down. He Qinglian accepts neither view. If it is true that accumulating capital is necessary in order to get private enterprise going, it is also plain, she shows, that the structure of privilege in China brought about cronyism more than efficiency. And she refutes the "trickle down" theory with the overwhelming evidence of growing inequality.

When reform began, many Chinese intellectuals hoped that economic growth would erode the authority of the Communist Party and lead to diversification of power under the rule of law.

Twenty years later, in He's account, the Party indeed has lost some of its political power, but has lost it not to the citizens but to a new robber-baron class that now allies itself with the Party in opposing the rule of law.

Chinese readers have received He Qinglian's book with enthusiasm. When its Beijing edition was published in January 1998, the entire first printing of 100,000 copies sold out in less than two weeks. After that, five different pirated editions put 330,000 more copies into circulation. This extraordinary response can hardly be attributed to the book's prose, which is laden with statistics and technical terms. It comes rather from the author's untiring demonstration of a repressed truth: that the strategy of the Deng years—fast economic change and no political change—was a huge and terrible mistake. The symptoms of the mistake surface in the economy, but the root problem is political.

About a quarter of He's book addresses the effects of rampant money-making on social morality. She finds, first, an "immense public indignation at social unfairness," as the mocking popular sayings (*shunkouliu*) that circulate widely in China make clear. One adopts the viewpoint of an elderly state worker:

> I worked my whole life for the Party
> And had nothing at the time I retired;
> Now they tell me to live off my kids,
> But my kids one by one have been fired.

He Qinglian observes that "the complaints of most people about inequality are not against inequality *per se* but about the sordid methods by which wealth is achieved." When ordinary people hear stories about greed at the top, they come to feel that it is pointless, and even a bit stupid, for the ordinary citizen to stick to moral behavior. If anything "trickles down," in her view, it is cynicism and the abandonment of responsibility. Many of the shoddy goods that circulate in China come from state enterprises. If the government can cheat farmers with bad seeds or fake fertilizers, who is to blame ordinary people for injecting red coloring into watermelons or mixing water into ground meat? Another popular saying, archly entitled "A Short History of Comradely Sentiment," runs:

In the 50s we helped people.
In the 60s we criticized people.
In the 70s we deceived people.
In the 80s everybody hired everybody else.
In the 90s we "slaughter" whoever we see.

The word "slaughter" (*zai*), which corresponds in both sense and tone to "rip off" in American English, is now widely used. Few people in the outside world appreciate how pervasive the attitude and practice of *zai* have become in China. Probably in no other society today has economic good faith been compromised to the extent it has in China. Contracts are not kept; debts are ignored, whether between individuals or between state enterprises; individuals, families, and sometimes whole towns have gotten rich on deceitful schemes. He Qinglian sees the overall situation as unprecedented. "The championing of money as a value," she writes, "has never before reached the point of holding all moral rules in such contempt." She finds the collapse of ethics—not growth of the economy—to be the most dramatic change in China during the Deng Xiaoping era. The challenge facing China is not just "survival" (which the Chinese government lists as the most basic human right) but "how to avoid living in an utterly valueless condition." She does not hold out much hope.

He Qinglian's book has much to say about China's underworld economy—including drug trafficking, smuggling, sale of human beings, counterfeiting, prostitution, and pornography—and on the ways in which it has merged with the legitimate economy. In parts of the countryside, underworld leaders have either assumed political power or made alliances with Communist officials "to form a force that treats farmers almost like slaves." He Qinglian concludes that:

> the emergence of the "government-underworld alliance" shows that progress toward a civil society ruled by law is no more likely an outcome for our country than is descent into a "mafia model."

She leaves no doubt that, among many in the Communist elite, the zest for economic reform had little to do with abstract ideals about civil society and everything to do with enriching themselves and assuring that their socially privileged positions would be transferred smoothly from one economic system to another. The Communist Party has varied immensely over its seventy-seven years: from a guerrilla movement in the hills of Shaanxi to a cadre of bureaucratic managers; from "resist Japan" to "resist America" to "oppose the Soviets"; and from slogans like "fight selfishness" (late 1960s) to ones like "getting rich is glorious" (early 1980s). But essentially the same elite has remained dominant. This remarkable group, like a seal on a rolling ball, may not be graceful but it stays on top.

He Qinglian was born in Hunan Province in 1956. She was part of a generation of Chinese youth who were shaped by Mao's Cultural Revolution. In 1966, He's school, like all others in China, was closed down so that students could "make revolution." When she was twelve she was shaken by the sight of human corpses floating in a local stream. At seventeen, after she went to work at a railroad construction site in the remote hills of West Hunan, she found a circle of friends whose social idealism became all the stronger as they became disillusioned with Mao. Most books were banned during the Cultural Revolution, but an unusual number of books circulated informally; she and her friends became devotees of works of the Russian literary and social critic Vissarion Belinsky (1811–1848), who commented that Russia must draw on the intellectual resources of Europe. In an afterword to her book, He writes that she owes to her friends in those years "my basic outlook on life as well as a sense of moral responsibility that has stayed with me ever since." Wei Jingsheng, Xu Wenli, Zheng Yi, and many others in this generation also illustrate the paradox that Mao Zedong's misguided moral crusade had beneficial consequences for China that Mao never imagined.[12]

With the changes following Mao's death, He studied history at Hunan Normal University in Changsha beginning in 1978, and in 1985 began graduate work in economics at Fudan University. In 1988 she went to Shenzhen, the boom town just north of Hong Kong, to work as a newspaper reporter. She was irritated to see newspaper advertisements such as "Our company urgently seeks high level staff. . . . Preference will go to those with good connections in government," and soon began collecting material for her book.

In passing, she makes telling comments on the state of academic economics as practiced in China today. She finds that the field is dominated either by "toady writing" that provides academic backing for the favorite ideas of politicians or by "techniques for dragon slaying"—a Chinese cliché for technically brilliant skills that have little practical use. She refers here to the field of "pure" economics, primarily an import from the West, that tends to ignore the ways in which politics and morality impinge upon economic questions. In a preface to He's book, Zhu Xueqin, a professor of history at Shanghai University, writes:

> In China, ever since the arrival of the planned economy in the 1950s, every cell of economic life has in fact been saturated with politics. Such a condition does not change just because "reform" is announced. What can it mean to study "pure" economic questions in such a context? . . . To talk about reform while ignoring the political content of Chinese economic structures is to weave a set of emperor's new clothes.

After finishing her manuscript in August 1996, He Qinglian sent it to nine publishers in different parts of China. Editors were impressed but none would accept the risk of publishing her book. Eventually she settled for publication in Hong Kong, knowing that circulation into China would be limited. After the book was published there, she found an ally in Liu Ji, vice president of the Chinese Academy of Social Sciences in Beijing, who read the book, discussed it with He Qinglian for five hours, and backed its publication in Beijing. It appeared in January 1998 from China Today Publishers in nearly complete form, although some of He's more provocative language—and two prefaces (including the one by Zhu Xueqin, quoted above)—were deleted. The title was revised from *China's Pitfall* to the more euphemistic *A Pitfall of Modernization*.

Publication in China led to book reviews and interviews with He in the Chinese press, and she used her new celebrity to press her ideas further. In a recent article she notes that 1998 is the hundredth anniversary of the 1898 reforms that were aimed at saving the moribund Qing dynasty. She identifies five major problems that held China back in 1898—population size, agricultural stagnation, inequality, corruption, and low standards in education—and argues that all five are at least as severe now.[13]

Her emphasis on this anniversary was not arbitrary. Anniversaries are taken seriously in China, and "anniversary momentum" is now gathering there. Next year will be the eightieth year since the "Chinese enlightenment" of May Fourth, the fiftieth year since the founding of the People's Republic, the twentieth of the "reform era," and the tenth since the Beijing massacre. Chinese people tend to see in such anniversaries an opportunity to "take stock." The fiftieth year of the People's Republic, for example, will lead to comparisons between the Communists and the Nationalists whom they displaced. The corruption of the Nationalists was ugly in the late 1940s, but many say it is far worse now. Problems of inequality, vice, and crime, which the revolution swept away in the 1950s, have returned. A popular saying goes:

> For forty-some years, ever more perspiration,
> And we just circle back to before Liberation;
> And speaking again of that big revolution,
> Who, after all, was it for?

Each year since June 4, 1989, the police have taken steps to repress memorials of the Tiananmen massacre; next year the tenth anniversary will raise the stakes for both sides. Recently the government dealt with the hundredth anniversary of Peking University—a perennial source of democratic thought in China—by smothering open discussion under elaborate official ceremonies, which included a presidential visit to the campus and rigidly organized dances by uniformed children in Tiananmen Square.

Under the rule of a government as wary as China's, how can conspicuously critical work such as He Qinglian's be published at all? It helped that she had the backing of an important official like Liu Ji, and it helped as well that for the last twenty years economists have had more freedom to express themselves than others because the government views them as essential to the country's modernization. It is significant, moreover, that He's book was published in early 1998, when the government was more tolerant of critical commentary than it had been in the preceding year. In December 1997, Premier Li Peng, one of the more authoritarian of China's leaders, had praised the popular television show *Focus,* which sometimes exposes official wrongdoing, especially in the provinces. In March, Li Peng also called for "criticism of problems and corruption in the Party" while Xiao Yang, chief of China's Supreme Court, ordered an inquiry into corruption in the justice system. Such events, together with a relaxation of restrictions in book publishing, seem to amount to a coordinated policy.

This spring there was considerable speculation in the Chinese-language press in Hong Kong and Taiwan that the show of liberalization was designed to bamboozle Clinton, who was preparing to visit China in late June. But this explanation cannot account for Li Peng's approval of an audacious television show or the appearance of a book like He Qinglian's.

It seems more likely that the leadership felt it needed to calm popular unrest. With layoffs accelerating and the perception spreading that the rich are corruptly getting richer, the top leaders feel pressure to dissociate themselves from such trends. Since the Mao years, control of private speech has loosened to a point where the Party leaders can no longer suppress widespread informal complaints. The thousands of sardonic popular sayings that pass along the oral grapevine make this plain. When Li Peng praises *Focus,* he probably does so because he recognizes that he and others in the ruling group are better off when they seem to be siding, at least to some extent, with the critics.

There may be more to the question of why the authorities allowed publication of He's book. Liu Ji, the official who sponsored it, is known to have some sympathy for He Qinglian's humanist values, but he is also a member of President Jiang Zemin's brain trust. It is hard to imagine him sponsoring a controversial book unless he thought that doing so would serve Jiang's political interests.

He's book can be useful to Jiang in the same way that "scar literature," which exposed the painful history of the late-Mao years, was useful to Deng Xiaoping twenty years ago. In 1978 Deng wanted to inherit Mao's mantle even as he distanced himself from the "catastrophe" of Mao's Cultural Revolution. Scar literature was useful to him because it denounced the "Gang of Four," who stood for Mao's rule, without naming Mao himself. It thus helped to turn popular resentment of Maoism into popular support for Deng.

Jiang Zemin now inherits from Deng a Chinese economy that, along with rapid growth, has produced terrible problems and rising popular resentment. Jiang does not want to take personal responsibility for the mess, and in this he has a point. Deng Xiaoping, in his own words, was the "chief architect" of reform. Anyone who reads He's book will understand that the problems of the reform period were deeply entrenched by the time Jiang took over. But even if Jiang Zemin succeeds in dissociating himself from the problems created by Deng, it does not follow that Jiang will lead China (as Deng did) in a fundamentally new direction. Jiang Zemin's program for China remains largely a mystery. Indeed he may not have one.

If Jiang is unsure about where China is headed, he is not alone. The political thinking of Chinese intellectuals is more bewildered than it has been for a long time. Ten years ago there were two fairly clear camps in Chinese political thought: the conservatives, or "old leftists," who defended the Maoist establishment, and the reformers or liberals who favored change—the camp that included most intellectuals. Today there is a third camp, one that is by nature conservative but that seeks to preserve not Mao's China but Deng's, arguing that the troubles discussed in He Qinglian's book are the growing pains of a basically healthy process, which must be pursued. Many others dissent from this view, but disagree about what to do instead.

In order to get her book published at all, He Qinglian had to soften some of her criticisms of the Deng-era reforms. She could not name names, but still issued a daring challenge:

> If the preponderance of new wealth we see today was gained illegally or through means that are inconsistent with fairness and justice, then we should launch a moral inquiry and an analytical crusade.

Her book itself begins this "crusade." Beneath its surface, packed as it is with facts, numbers, and technical terms, the reader senses a deep anger. She raises fundamental questions about twenty years of reform: "China," she writes, "is headed toward joint rule by the government and a mafia." She asks: "When you have development that is built on the premise that people will pursue their interests at the cost of the . . . property and lives of others, is it really worth it?"

Even if one answers "yes," He Qinglian argues, such a system will eventually destroy itself. "The systemic corruption in which pursuit of private interest undermines society's legal system and public morality will inevitably kill [China's] reform before it matures." Today, eleven months after the appearance of He's book, events in China are confirming her prediction. In March 1998 China's top leaders announced emergency measures to address the current crisis: a plan to transform state enterprises and to pay their debts within three years; a plan to cut government employees by 50 percent, also within three years; and plans to reform the financial system, to rid it of corruption, and so on. In June, however, reliable sources in direct contact with the top leadership revealed that these plans were meeting stiff, and perhaps fatal, opposition. They had been proposed too late, the sources said. Had they been carried out in the early 1990s, there might have been hope for success.

What happened in China in the 1990s is thus becoming clear. Reform was aborted when Deng Xiaoping strangled China's democratic forces in 1989 and when—as He Qinglian shows in detail—he decided in 1992 to buy stability for his regime by pursuing a rapid economic growth whose price was sharply increased corruption, financial deception, and the erosion of the moral basis of society.

NOTES

1. In *The New York Review*, Perry Link is listed as a co-author. In fact, Liu Binyan was the analyst for the piece, Link the composer of the language. Here we are listing Liu as author and Link as translator, which in broad terms is an equally true description.

2. Adjusted for inflation, personal income during the 1980s rose 329 percent in cities and 355 percent in the countryside. For 1990–1995, it rose 226 percent in cities and 196 percent in the countryside. (Cheng Xiaonong, "Fanrong cong he er lai? Zhongguo jingji xianzhuang he qushi de fenxi," *Dangdai Zhongguo Yanjiu,* No. 54 (1996), p. 59.)

3. November 28, 1992, "China Survey" supplement, p. 3.

4. May 17, 1993, p. 4.

5. Chinese government statistics for the first quarter of 1998 show an overall annual increase of only 0.5 percent over the same quarter last year in rural areas (*Shijie ribao* [New York], July 15, 1998). In cities, for 1997 as a whole, about 40 percent of residents saw a clear decline in personal income. The downturn was sharpest in the smallest cities (*Pinguo ribao* [Hong Kong], April 1, 1998).

6. The far-reaching implications of the crisis of China's state enterprises are well analyzed in Edward S. Steinfeld, *Forging Reform in China: The Fate of State-Owned Industry* (Cambridge University Press, 1998).

7. There are a few carefully controlled exceptions for new industry, such as aircraft, where "joint enterprises" with foreign companies are allowed.

8. Modern international banks try to observe a bad debt ratio of under 3 percent, compared to China's 20 percent (or much more). They also maintain "capital adequacy ratios" ensuring that at least 6 percent of the capital they hold is their own, so that bad debt can be covered by a safe margin. The capital adequacy ratio of China's state banks is about 3 percent. See Peter Chan and Mark O'Neill, "Asia Woes Spur Beijing to Act," *South China Morning Post,* May 14, 1998.

9. *Zhongguo gaige bao* [China Reform News], February 18, 1998. He Qinglian also notes the irony that artificially high housing prices hamper the government's policy that "commercial housing" should be a key to bringing the economy out of its current decline.

10. See André Dua and Daniel C. Esty, *Sustaining the Asia Pacific Miracle: Environmental Protection and Economic Integration* (Washington, D.C.: Institute for International Economics, 1997); He Bochuan, *Shan'aoshang de Zhongguo* [China on the Brink] (Guiyang: Guizhou renmin chubanshe, 1992); and Vaclav Smil, *China's Environmental Crisis* (M.E. Sharpe, 1993).

11. He Qinglian uses the "Gini coefficient," a standard measure of income disparity, to place China within a world setting. A coefficient of 0.3 or less indicates substantial equality; 0.3 to 0.4 indicates acceptable

normality; and 0.4 or higher is considered too large. 0.6 or higher is predictive of social unrest. In one 1994 survey, China measured 0.45; in another, 0.59.

12. See Laifong Leung, *Morning Sun: Interviews with Chinese Writers of the Lost Generation* (M.E. Sharpe, 1994).

13. "Yige jingji xuejia yanzhong de wuxu bainian" [The Hundred Years Since 1898 as Seen by an Economist], *Nanfang Zhoumo* [Southern Weekend], April 17, 1998.

Contributors

Richard W. Bodman teaches Chinese and Asian Studies at St. Olaf College in Northfield, Minnesota. Together with Pin P. Wan, he translated *Heshang* by Su Xiaokang and Wang Luxiang as *Deathsong of the River.*

Michael S. Duke teaches Chinese and Comparative Literature at the University of British Columbia Department of Asian Studies. He is author of many books and articles, including *Blooming and Contending: Chinese Literature in the Post-Mao Era* and *The Iron House: A Memoir of the Chinese Democracy Movement and the Tiananmen Massacre.*

James V. Feinerman is Associate Dean for International and Graduate Programs and James M. Morita Professor of Asian Legal Studies at Georgetown University Law Center. He earned a Ph.D. in East Asian Languages and Literature at Yale University and a J.D. from the Harvard Law School, where he specialized in East Asian Legal Studies. He began working on a translation of "People or Monsters?" while studying at Peking University during 1979–80.

Perry Link teaches Chinese language and literature at Princeton University. His thirteen books include *Evening Chats in Beijing; Banyang suibi* (Notes of a semi-foreigner); *The Uses of Literature: Life in the Socialist Chinese Literary System;* and (co-edited) *The Tiananmen Papers* and *Popular China.*

John S. Rohsenow is Professor of Linguistics and director of the Chinese language program at the University of Illinois at Chicago. He has taught and done research in Taiwan and at Hangzhou University, Nanjing University, and the Chinese Academy of Social Sciences in Beijing. He is author of *A Chinese-English Dictionary of Enigmatic Folk Similes (Xiehouyu)* and *The ABC Dictionary of Chinese Proverbs,* as well as numerous articles on Chinese language and linguistics.

Madelyn Ross is China Coordinator at George Mason University. She has worked at the US-China Business Council and the US-China Policy Foundation, and has served as editor of *The China Business Review* and the *Washington Journal of Modern China.* She has a B.A. in East Asian Studies from Princeton University and an M.A. in International Affairs from Columbia University. She studied and taught English at Fudan University in Shanghai during 1979–80.

Kyna Rubin has worked for many years as a freelance writer and editor, and first went to China (Fudan University) in 1979 on a National Academy of Sciences study grant. Her translation of Wang Ruowang's *Hunger Trilogy* appeared in 1991. She is a long-time contributor to *International Educator* magazine.

Liu Binyan (1925–2005) was born in Heilongjiang, China, and left school after ninth grade for lack of tuition money. He continued to read, taught himself Russian, joined the Communist Party underground in 1943, and eventually emerged as twentieth-century China's most distinguished investigative journalist. He was expelled from the Communist Party in 1957, re-admitted in 1979, and re-expelled in 1987. He lived in exile in the United States from 1988 until his death. His books include *People or Monsters? And Other Stories and Reportage from China after Mao* (Indiana University Press, 1983); *"Tell the World": What Happened in China and Why; A Higher Kind of Loyalty: A Memoir by China's Foremost Journalist;* and *China's Crisis, China's Hope: Essays from an Intellectual in Exile.*